The Epistles of Paul the Apostle
to the Thessalonians

The Epistles of Paul the Apostle to the Thessalonians

by
Oliver B. Greene

The Gospel Hour, Inc., Oliver B. Greene, Director
P. O. Box 2024, Greenville, South Carolina

First printing, July 1965—10,000 copies
Second printing, June 1967—10,000 copies
Third printing, November 1969—15,000 copies
Fourth printing, March 1970—15,000 copies
Fifth printing, February 1972—15,000 copies

$5.00

Library of Congress Catalog Card Number: 64-13522

THE EPISTLES OF PAUL THE APOSTLE TO THE THESSALONIANS

INTRODUCTION

Most of the ancient cities in which Paul ministered and established churches have, in the course of the ages, perished or sunk into insignificance. The cities of Rome and Thessalonica remain.

In Paul's day Thessalonica, a very important seaport of Macedonia, lay at the head of the Bay of Thermaicus, also known as the Gulf of Thessalonica. The city was on the great Egnatian Way and was known primarily for its commerce. Ships came to that port from throughout Asia Minor, as well as from other countries. The city was located southwest of Philippi, a short distance northeast of Berea.

Thessalonica was inhabited by Greeks, Romans and Jews. Idolatry was prevalent on every hand. There were many gods, but the outstanding god was Jupiter. In Paul's day thousands of Jews lived in the city, and there was a Jewish synagogue there.

We know little of the moral situation in Thessalonica, but there is strong reason to believe that it was very ungodly, because idolatry always produces gross immorality, especially among females.

This town, which in modern times has been called Saloniki, is now officially known as Thessaloniki and continues to occupy a place of importance. According to the International Standard Bible Encyclopaedia, "Thessalonica in 1204 became the center of a Latin kingdom under Boniface, marquis of Monferrat, and for over two centuries it passed from hand to hand, now ruled by Latins, now by Greeks, until in 1430 it fell before sultan

i

Amurath II. After that time it remained in the possession of the Turks, and it was, indeed, the chief European city of their dominions, with the exception of Constantinople, until it was recaptured by the Greeks in the Balkan war of 1912. Its population includes some 32,000 Turks; 47,000 Jews (mostly the descendants of refugees from Spain) and 16,000 Greeks and other Europeans. The city is rich in examples of Byzantine ecclesiastical architecture and art, and possesses, in addition to a large number of mosques, twelve churches and twenty-five synagogues."

Thessalonica has always owed its importance to its geographical position. It is a very picturesque city, guarded on two sides by extremely high ridges or mountains. Paul visited Macedonia a second time on his way from Ephesus to Greece, during his third missionary journey (Acts 20:1,2), and it is believed that he spent considerable time at Thessalonica on this occasion. In Acts 20:4 we learn that two Thessalonians traveled with him to Jerusalem when he departed: "And there accompanied him into Asia Sopater of Berea; and of the Thessalonians, Aristarchus and Secundus; and Gaius of Derbe, and Timotheus; and of Asia, Tychicus, and Trophimus."

Aristarchus remained with Paul for a long while, and is honorably mentioned by him in Colossians 4:10. (Paul was in prison in Rome at that time and refers to Aristarchus as "my fellow prisoner.") It was from Macedonia that Paul addressed his second epistle to the Corinthians (II Cor. 2:13; 7:5; 8:1). Writing to the Philippians in A. D. 63 from his cell in the Roman prison, he said: "But I trust in the Lord that I also myself shall come shortly. Yet I supposed it necessary to send to you Epaphroditus, my brother, and companion in labour, and fellow soldier, but your messenger, and he that ministered to my wants" (Phil. 2:24,25). Later, when Paul was released from prison, he did visit Macedonia (I Tim. 1:3).

The last reference to Thessalonica to be found in the New Testament is in II Timothy 4:10: "For Demas hath forsaken me, having loved this present world, and is departed unto Thessalonica." Could it be that Demas had his eyes on riches? Was he a fortune hunter? If so, we can understand why he went to Thessalonica, because it was certainly a rich and promising city for anyone desiring to make money.

It was Paul's second great missionary journey that carried him to Thessalonica, where he preached the Gospel and brought about the church of the Thessalonians, 52 or 53 A. D. Paul traveled very slowly across Asia Minor from the southeast to the northwest, being detained in Galatia for considerable time because of sickness; but this delay gave him the glorious opportunity to preach the cross to the people. He preached Jesus crucified, buried, risen, coming again—according to the Scriptures. Important churches were born because of this time of Gospel ministry. Read Acts 16:6; 18:23; Gal. 4:13–15.

Paul was God's minister—called of God, ordained of God, and sent by God to declare the Gospel to the Gentiles. Twice his plans were frustrated during this particular journey. It seems that his chief intention was to evangelize the Roman province of Asia (Acts 16:6), where he afterward spent three full, fruitful years preaching the Gospel (Acts 20:31). This region, with its capital city of Ephesus, was for Paul's mission probably the most important district between the cities of Jerusalem and Rome; however, at that particular time he was "prevented by the Holy Spirit." A little later he attempted to go into the province of Bithynia, but again "the Spirit suffered them not" (Acts 16:7).

So Paul and his faithful companions, Silas and

Timothy, found themselves in the city of Troas. Luke also joined them there, and it was at this time that God made known to Paul his future directions: "And a vision appeared to Paul in the night; There stood a man of Macedonia, and prayed him, saying, Come over into Macedonia, and help us" (Acts 16:9). In Macedonia the Gospel was received by a people prepared for the Lord and much eternal good was accomplished. Paul longed to see his people saved; he cried out, "My heart's desire and prayer to God for Israel is, that they might be saved" (Rom. 10:1). In Romans 9:1–3 Paul declared that he would be willing to be accursed from Christ himself if it would save his people, his kinsmen in the flesh. God called him to the Gentiles, but at every opportunity he attempted to slip away and preach the Gospel to the Jews.

The Gospel was first preached in Thessalonica by Paul and his co-worker Silas. They visited there after they were released from prison in Philippi. They passed through other cities on the journey, but went directly to Thessalonica—probably because there were many Jews there. Paul always visited the Jewish synagogue when he was in a town where there was one, and preached to the Jews the Gospel of the grace of God. There was a Jewish synagogue in Thessalonica, and he entered into the synagogue and for three Sabbath days reasoned with his own people regarding the Messiah. He had a deep, burning love for his own people, and he endeavored to convince the Jews that according to the Scriptures it was necessary that Messiah be put to death, that He should rise from the dead, and that all of the prophecies pointing to Him were fulfilled in Jesus of Nazareth (Acts 17:1–3).

Paul preached sincerely and fervently to the Jews in Thessalonica—and some few believed; but the greater number of his converts were "devout Greeks" (Acts 17:4).

There were a considerable number of ladies saved also as Paul preached the Gospel of the death, burial and resurrection. It was from these Thessalonian converts that the church there was organized, and probably from the very beginning the church was blessed with a goodly number of converts.

Historians do not agree as to just how long Paul and Silas remained in Thessalonica during their first visit. We know that they preached in the synagogue for three Sabbaths; and if they remained there for no more than three Sabbaths, their visit would have been about three weeks. They could have remained in the city longer; it could be that they left the synagogue and preached in some other place. The duration of their visit there is not the important thing, however. The thing that *is* outstanding is the fact of the power of the Gospel. Even though he preached only three Sabbath days in the synagogue, a tremendous church was organized; and the Gospel still has that power today.

In Acts 17:5 it seems that Paul and Silas, at least for a time, made their home with Jason, and that large numbers of people came to hear their preaching. In I Thessalonians 2:9, Paul tells us that when he was among them, he "labored night and day" because he would not be chargeable unto any of them, and he preached unto them the Gospel of God. This seems to suggest that Paul was there much longer than three Sabbaths, and it also appears that the believers at Philippi sent supplies to him during his stay in Thessalonica: Philippians 4:16: "For even in Thessalonica ye sent once and again unto my necessity." There is a good possibility that Paul and Silas ministered several weeks—perhaps months— in that city.

The devil is always on the job, and in Paul's day he seemed to work overtime. Paul and Silas were finally driven from Thessalonica by opposing Jews. A mob was organized by the Jews, the house of Jason was attacked, and "certain brethren" were dragged before the authorities and accused of receiving those "who have turned the world upside down." They were therefore accused of being guilty of treason against the Roman empire (Acts 17:5–7).

So gigantic was this tumult, and such was the danger to Paul and Silas if they should remain in the city, that some of the members of the church judged their beloved preacher and his helper should be sent to a place of safety; and they were slipped out by night to the neighboring city of Berea. Everywhere Paul went, they had a revival or a riot. Somebody was either saved or jailed every time he invaded a city with the bombshells of the Gospel.

In Berea the Gospel was received with glad hearts, and Paul preached without opposition for some time, until the Jews who had caused so much trouble in Thessalonica heard that he was in Berea and came over to excite the people against him. (Read Acts 17:13.) Paul was again forced to flee to a place of safety and was transported to Athens, while Silas and Timothy remained in Berea preaching the Gospel. It appears that Timothy had accompanied Paul and that he and Dr. Luke had been with him at Philippi and also at Thessalonica; however, he is not mentioned as being present with them until Paul arrived in Berea.

When Paul went to the city of Athens, he gave commandment to those who were responsible for him, that Silas and Timothy should come to him as soon as possible. While he waited for them at Athens, he preached his memorable sermon on Mars' hill, which we find recorded in Acts 17:22 ff.

Paul's actual arrival at Athens, together with Timothy

and Silas, is not recorded in this chapter; but that Timothy joined him there appears certain from I Thessalonians 3:1–2: "Wherefore when we could no longer forbear, we thought it good to be left at Athens alone; and sent Timotheus, our brother, and minister of God, and our Christ, to establish you, and to comfort you concerning your faith." Therefore, Timothy was probably with Paul at Athens for a short time. Paul sent him back to Thessalonica, and before his return Paul himself had gone to Corinth, Timothy following later (Acts 18:5).

Most Bible scholars agree that I Thessalonians was written in 52 A. D. The second epistle was probably written the same year. The church at Thessalonica was made up of Jews—to whom Paul preached first. (Paul believed "to the Jew first, and also to the Greek." Therefore he always delivered the message first to his own people when at all possible.) A few Jews believed, but the massed rejected his message (Acts 17:4).

There was a second group in the church (Greeks), who had been proselyted into the Jewish faith and who had been attending the synagogue in Thessalonica (Acts 17:4). Paul refers to these believers as "devout Greeks"; that is, they were religious Greeks who had renounced idol worship and were attending the Jewish synagogue . . . *religious but lost!* They were probably the group called by the Jews *proselytes of the gate.* These Greeks who were admitted to the synagogue were also admitted to many of the privileges of the Jewish religion.

There was a third group referred to as *women*, and these ladies were members of the elite—the elevated rank of the community (Acts 17:4). A great host of idol worshippers were converted, and they, too, made up the first members of the church at Thessalonica. In chapter 1:9 of I Thessalonians we read: "For they themselves shew of us what manner of entering in we had unto you, and how ye turned to God from idols to serve the living and true God."

The church was made up of Jews, Greeks, outstanding ladies, and those who were converted from rank idolatry. These different groups harmoniously embraced the message of the Gospel—the death, burial, resurrection and coming again of the Lord Jesus. They forgot all their former differences and dwelt in peace, unity and love one for another. Note I Thessalonians 2:13.

Paul was in Corinth at this time and could not visit his children in the Lord in the church in Thessalonica. He loved them dearly, and they loved him with a deep, faithful love. The unusual characteristics of the church in Thessalonica and the circumstances existing in the city prompted two epistles to that church. Please read Acts 17—the entire chapter.

The members of the church in Thessalonica had willingly, cordially and fully embraced the Gospel delivered by Paul. They were warm, close friends of his and greatly desired to receive his teaching and spiritual instruction. But since he could not visit them, these earnest longings of the heart of the Thessalonians prompted him to write the words he would have loved to speak to them in person. Read I Thessalonians 2:17, and then compare I Thessalonians 1:5–6; 2:8, 9, 13, 19 and 20. In Paul's heart there was a strong love for the believers in Thessalonica—the kind of love a nurse has for children committed to her keeping (I Thess. 2:7,11). Hence the writing of the two epistles.

Not only did the Jews, Greeks, elite women and idol worshippers accept the Gospel Paul delivered, but they desired to spread it to other communities (I Thess. 1:8). Paul knew about this, and it thrilled his heart so much he longed to commend them for their deep love and zeal for those who were without the true Gospel and true salvation. Therefore, Paul wrote to encourage them to a greater love and a greater zeal in the missionary endeavors that had been born in their hearts through the power of the Gospel he preached.

The believers at Thessalonica had first received the Gospel during times and scenes of much strife (I Thess. 2:2). They were persecuted and opposed by Jews and by their own countrymen (I Thess. 2:14). It seems that the Thessalonian believers were called upon to suffer peculiar trials and tribulations. Some of the outstanding citizens of Thessalonica were led astray by teachers of error. They had lost to the errorists some who were dear to their hearts. (Read II Thess. 2:3–5 and 3:13.) Paul desired to comfort and console them in their hour of sorrow.

The believers at Thessalonica were brokenhearted because of the passing of some of their dear loved ones. It seems that some of them had gotten the understanding that Jesus would come even before any of them departed this life. There was a misunderstanding concerning the Rapture and the Revelation of the Lord Jesus; therefore, Paul wrote the second Epistle to clear up the difference between the catching away of the saints and the revelation of the Lord WITH His saints. They had been under the impression that Jesus would come to change them and catch them up into the air before any of them departed this life.

It seems also that an error concerning the resurrection was prevalent among the Thessalonian believers. They seemed to think that those who were alive when Jesus comes would have great advantages over believers who had died, and that living believers would be allowed to behold the glory and participate in the glorious appearing and the splendor of the personal reign of Jesus here on earth, whereas those in the graves would miss this glorious kingdom and reign. Paul taught no such doctrine; Satan was the instigator of such belief among the Christians there. To correct these views seems to have been one of the main reasons for both Epistles to the Thessalonians.

Paul declares that at the coming of the Lord Jesus in the Rapture, all who are living or dead will participate in His glory. The dead in Christ will be raised first, then we who are alive will be changed, and together we will be caught up to meet the Lord in the clouds in the air (I Thess. 4:13–18). You may rest assured that the devil will warp and twist the truth in the mind of a believer if it is possible to do so. If the devil cannot damn you, the next best thing for him to do is to rob you of your spiritual birthright—and it is the spiritual birthright of every believer to experience abundant life and full joy (John 10:10; I John 1:4).

The enemies of Paul apparently had spread the falsehood among the believers at Thessalonica that he had left them at the time they really needed a leader, and had left no one in charge to instruct them. Those enemies endeavored to lead the Christians there to believe that what Paul preached was untrue—a man-made gospel. They wanted the believers to think that Paul was an impostor and a religious rabble-rouser; but to meet this charge, Paul declared that, as they knew, he preached the same Gospel in Thessalonica that he preached in Philippi, even though he was persecuted severely in Philippi because of his preaching. Persecution did not stop him; he came to the city of Thessalonica and preached the *same Gospel*, receiving the *same opposition* (I Thess. 2:2).

Paul declared that his preaching had been without fraud and without guile, that he had given them positive proof of his sincerity (I Thess. 2:3–5). He had proved

x

to them that he was not seeking the glory of men, nor was he seeking money. He labored with his own hands and preached the same message to both the elite and to the fallen man in the gutter. He had not come to Thessalonica for a selfish reason, because he gained nothing but persecution by coming there; and had he not departed thence he no doubt would have been martyred for the preaching of the Gospel of the grace of God.

In I Thessalonians 2:17–18 he assured them that he had attempted to return and visit them, but Satan had prevented his returning; and since he could not return in person, he parted with his favorite friend Timothy and sent him to visit the church in his place (I Thess. 3:1,2).

As was common in all churches in Paul's day, the people who made up the churches were converted from heathenism, idolatry and gross sins of lust. Knowing the danger of falling back into such sins, Paul warned the believers to be on guard at all times against idolatry and the vices and lusts to which they were exposed (I Thess. 4:1–7). According to I Thessalonians 5:12–14 it seems that there was a very small nucleus in the church who were hostile toward their church leaders, and who, under the pretense of edifying others, were guilty of causing disorder. Paul wrote to correct this gross sin in the church.

Paul's love for the Thessalonian Christians was deep. His heart was warm toward them, and the warmth of his heart and the depth of his love is evident throughout the epistles. Expressions of tenderness, as well as stern words of duty, are prevalent. It was his heartfelt desire that his children in the faith should grow into full stature of the perfect man in Christ. His heart's desire and prayer to God *for his own people (the Jew)* was that they be saved. His heart's desire and prayer

for the believers in the churches he established was that
they press toward the mark of the high calling of God
in Christ Jesus. He wanted his babes in Christ to grow,
he wanted the children to become men, and he wanted
the men to become *good soldiers*. He desired that the
believers live and conduct themselves in such a manner
that they could enjoy their spiritual birthright.

The two Thessalonian epistles were written from a
heart filled with praise for the love, devotion and faithfulness of the Thessalonian Christians. But the epistles
were also warnings concerning those who would lead
them astray and inject error into the teaching presented
in the assembly there.

CONTENTS

FIRST THESSALONIANS

SECOND THESSALONIANS

The First Epistle of Paul
the Apostle
to the Thessalonians

I THESSALONIANS -- CHAPTER ONE

1. Paul, and Silvanus, and Timotheus, unto the church of the Thessalonians which is in God the Father and in the Lord Jesus Christ: Grace be unto you, and peace, from God our Father, and the Lord Jesus Christ.

2. We give thanks to God always for you all, making mention of you in our prayers;

3. Remembering without ceasing your work of faith, and labour of love, and patience of hope in our Lord Jesus Christ, in the sight of God and our Father;

4. Knowing, brethren beloved, your election of God.

5. For our gospel came not unto you in word only, but also in power, and in the Holy Ghost, and in much assurance; as ye know what manner of men we were among you for your sake.

6. And ye became followers of us, and of the Lord, having received the word in much affliction, with joy of the Holy Ghost:

7. So that ye were ensamples to all that believe in Macedonia and Achaia.

8. For from you sounded out the word of the Lord not only in Macedonia and Achaia, but also in every place your faith to God-ward is spread abroad; so that we need not to speak any thing.

9. For they themselves shew of us what manner of entering in we had unto you, and how ye turned to God from idols to serve the living and true God;

10. And to wait for his Son from heaven, whom he raised from the dead, even Jesus, which delivered us from the wrath to come.

I Thessalonians is the earliest of Paul's letters to the churches, and we should therefore note the form of his introduction; for, although his greetings were enlarged as time went on and the Holy Spirit dictated other epistles to him, he never departed from that form. The greetings in his other epistles were lengthened, having to do with varied circumstances in different areas and in the churches to which the letters were directed.

In Paul's day the ordinary address of a letter ran thus: The person writing the letter used his own name

17

first, and then the name of the person to whom he was writing . . . "X to Z, greetings." The greetings were in Latin, Greek or Hebrew. The ancient greeting in Latin was a sincere wish of health; in Greek, such greeting signified joy; while in the Hebrew language it signified "peace to thee."

Paul's salutation to the churches combined the Hebrew and Greek (Jewish and Gentile) forms of courtesy, for in these epistles he was greeting all peoples who were believers—and all believers are one in Christ. Paul wished for them *health* in body, *joy* in spirit and *peace* in their hearts. He wished grace and peace to abide upon and within all believers in the churches he established. The grace of God that brings salvation also produces peace and brings joy unspeakable and full of glory; therefore, Paul addressed the Thessalonians thus: "*Grace be unto you, and peace, from God our Father, and the Lord Jesus Christ.*"

The grace of God is the sum total of all the blessings so freely and willingly bestowed upon believers by Almighty God through His beloved Son. Jesus was grace (John 1:14), and peace is the sum total of all spiritual blessings received by man and experienced by believers in the Lord Jesus Christ. *Peace is grace in its fullest fruit*—it is the fullest realization of the fruits and benefits of grace.

Nothing on this earth is more precious than peace. Jesus said, "Peace I leave with you, my peace I give unto you." Peace cannot be purchased, merited nor attained except by God's grace. Peace is more than the cessation of hostility and disorder between the sinner and Jehovah God: it denotes health and harmony of nature and spirit between God and man . . . it is inward tranquility and well being. Peace with God knows no inward fear or dread, and such peace goes much deeper than the average believer has ever realized. The peace of God produces complete tranquility of heart.

Grace is God's unmerited favor to the undeserving, hell-deserving sinner, and cannot be merited, earned nor obtained except through faith in God. Grace also becomes an inward possession of the believer the moment he exercises faith in the finished work of the Lord Jesus, manifesting itself as the *spirit and habit* of his life. Titus 2:11–15 tells us that the grace of God brings salvation— and then becomes our teacher, teaching us what we should do and what we should refrain from doing. The supreme exhibition of God's grace was demonstrated in the crucifixion death of His only begotten Son, the Lord Jesus Christ.

Jesus on the cross for sinful, hell-deserving mankind was an exhibition of *God's greatest* and *man's worst*. Apart from the cross there can be no peace, because the great instrument of peace IS THE DEATH OF JESUS on the cross. May God help you and me to see the solemn Bible fact that Jesus BY GOD'S GRACE TASTED DEATH FOR EVERY MAN (Heb. 2:9). It was Jesus, the Son of God's love, dying on the cross in agony and shame that words cannot describe, who, as He died, was making peace "through the blood of His cross" (Col. 1:20; Eph. 2:14–18).

Paul's watchword is GRACE—and that is the Gospel he preached, whether to Jew or Gentile, bond or free, rich or poor. Without grace there is no salvation, no redemption; but with grace in one's heart, peace automatically follows. Wherever this great apostle preached, he was determined to know nothing save Jesus Christ and Him crucified. Paul's. conversion and his call were, above all else, a revelation of divine grace (I Cor. 15: 9,10). He said, "By the grace of God, I am what I am." Please read Ephesians 2:7; 3:2–8; and I Timothy 1:12–15.

19

In verse 1 of our present study Paul introduces himself without the title of Apostle, without any personal designation. (This is also true in his epistle to the Philippians and in his letter to his friend, Philemon.) In these epistles Paul had neither desire nor need to stand on his dignity as an apostle. In dealing with the Thessalonians, the Philippians and with Philemon, he is as gentle as a nurse with her children. (See I Thessalonians 2:6–8.) He desires to present himself as a dear friend with a deep desire to encourage, comfort and help those to whom he is writing.

Verse 1: "Paul, and Silvanus, and Timotheus, unto the church of the Thessalonians which is in God the Father and in the Lord Jesus Christ: Grace be unto you, and peace, from God our Father, and the Lord Jesus Christ."

The opening words of this verse are "Paul, and Silvanus (Silas), and Timotheus (Timothy)." Silas and Timothy had been Paul's companions when he preached the Gospel in Thessalonica and established the church there. Paul always gave the names of his associates when writing to the churches, naming any of his helpers who were known by believers in those various churches. He no doubt did this partly by way of courtesy; but also, by naming those who were loved by the churches he promoted mutual understanding and sympathy. Paul was never jealous or envious of his co-workers.

Silvanus is the same Silas mentioned in Acts, chapters 15 through 18. Read also II Thessalonians 1:1, II Corinthians 1:19 and I Peter 5:12. Paul and Silas, though Jews, were both Roman citizens (Acts 16:37); and Silas was a leading member of the church in Jerusalem. He was also a prophet, an inspired man (Acts 15:22,23). He worked with Paul and shared the honor of delivering the Gospel, as well as sharing Paul's sufferings for the sake of the Gospel in Europe. The name of Silas worthily stands at the beginning of these epistles, the earliest of Paul's writings. Although the association of these two men of God ended with Paul's second missionary journey, Silas is without a doubt the "Silvanus" mentioned in I Peter 5:12 and also with Mark in other passages.

Timotheus (mentioned also in chapter 3:1–2) is Timothy, who also shares in the first and second Corinthian epistles, in the epistle to the Philippians, in Colossians and in both Thessalonian letters. Near the end of Paul's journey, just before he sealed his testimony with his blood, he wrote two inspired letters to this beloved young companion, his son in the Gospel.

Timothy joined Paul's company in the course of his second missionary journey (Acts 16:1–3) and remained close to him to the end of Paul's earthly sojourn. At the time of the establishing of the Thessalonian church, Timothy was no doubt very young, for Paul refers to him as a young man in I Timothy 4:12 and II Timothy 2:22, and this was at least twelve years after the epistle to the believers at Thessalonica. In the book of Acts, Timothy is in the background, with Silas as Paul's outstanding helper and Timothy as their youthful assistant, just as John Mark was assistant to Paul and Barnabas in an earlier period of Paul's ministry (Acts 13:5).

These three ministers—Paul, Silas and young Timothy—set forth the truth that the Church is one in Christ, whether Jew or Gentile. The first church was made up of mixed society: Paul and Silas were Jews, yet they were Roman citizens with Roman names, while Timothy was a Greek, the son of a Jewish mother and a Greek father (Acts 16:1–3). Everywhere the Apostle Paul ministered he declared that we are all one in Christ—one Lord, one faith, one baptism, one body made up of many members all baptized into one body by one Spirit, all having been made to drink into that one Spirit. The middle wall (partition) was broken down by Jesus; therefore, in the Church there is no more Jew or Gentile, rich or poor, bond or free. Paul preached to the slavemasters that born again slaves and slavemasters belong to the same body, the New Testament Church, of which Jesus is the head.

The letter is directed "unto the church of the Thessalonians which is in God the Father and in the Lord Jesus Christ." This singular form of address used by Paul in I and II Thessalonians is never again used by him. What he is saying literally is simply this: "To the assembly of Thessalonians, gathered in the twofold name, confessing God as Father and Jesus Christ as Lord."

John warns us in his second epistle that if anyone confesses NOT that Jesus is come in flesh, that one has not God; we are not to invite such a person into our house, neither bid him God speed; for if we do offer such a one our hospitality, we are partaker of his evil deeds! If we confess the Father, we confess the Son; and if we confess the Son we have both Father AND Son; but if we deny that Jesus is come in the flesh *we possess neither Father nor Son.*

There are two things I would like to point out in this description of the believers at Thessalonica: First—the local qualification, *"the church of the Thessalonians."* The nearest Paul came to using this phrase again is in Galatians 1:2, ". . . church of Galatia," which points out the *district*—not the people.

In writing to the Corinthians, Paul addresses his letters, "unto the church of God which is at Corinth." To the Ephesians he writes, "to the saints which are at Ephesus." Please remember that the church in Thessalonica is one of the very first, and therefore this epistle is one of the oldest books of the New Testament. The change from *"church of the Thessalonians"* to the term *"church in Corinth"* is noteworthy; it indicates an enlargement of the conception of the Church during the four years between the establishment of those two assemblies. This clearly shows that the Church in Paul's day was no longer just a local group in a given city; but whether in Corinth, Ephesus, Colosse, Rome or Jerusalem, *it was one and the same Church.* In I Thessalonians 2:14 Paul refers to "churches of God which in Judaea are in Christ Jesus." Regardless of how many local churches may be on earth today, all true believers belong to the ONE invisible Church of which Jesus Christ is the head and the foundation (Eph. 5:25–33; I Cor. 3:11–15).

The second point I would like to point out in this description is *the assembly* (church) ". . . in God the Father and in the Lord Jesus Christ." The word CHURCH in the New Testament comes from the Greek word *ecclesia*, and means "assembly." It also has a meaning referring to any legal meeting of citizens, any group "called out" by the leaders or rulers of the day. Therefore, Paul is very careful as the Holy Ghost directs, to make the distinction that this group, "called out" to assemble in Thessalonica, is not just a called out assembly as such, but is an assembly IN GOD THE FATHER AND IN THE LORD JESUS CHRIST. Thus the assembly in Thessalonica is distinguished from pagan or legal assemblies which could also be called *ecclesia*. The assembly of Christians in Thessalonica confessed one God—the Father and the Lord Jesus Christ. This introduction in verse one distinguished *the church* at Thessalonica from Jewish and pagan assemblies. The confession of the church ("one Father, one Lord") sets it apart from all other assemblies (I Cor. 8:5,6).

The believers at Thessalonica had been baptized into the local church in the name of Father, Son, and Holy Ghost. They believed in one God manifest in three persons. They knew God as Father, and they were His children. They believed in one God—*Jehovah God*, sovereign and supreme—*but they also confessed His Son* who came in the flesh. (If any man confess NOT that Jesus is come in the flesh, that man is *antichrist*, not Christian.)

To the Romans, Paul said, "That if thou shalt confess with thy mouth the Lord Jesus, and shalt believe in thine heart that God hath raised Him from the dead, thou shalt be saved. For with the heart man believeth unto righteousness; and with the mouth confession is made unto salvation" (Rom. 10:9,10). It is imperative to confess that Jesus Christ is come in flesh, and that He has accomplished what the Law could not accomplish because of the weakness of the flesh (Rom. 8:1–3). God has not changed His mind about the Law—the Law is holy; but Jesus fulfilled every jot and tittle of it (Matt. 5:17,18). Therefore, "Christ is the end of the Law for righteousness to everyone that believeth" (Rom. 10:4).

Verse 1 continues, "Grace be unto you, and peace, from God our Father, and the Lord Jesus Christ."

The grace through which we are saved (Eph. 2:8) is God's unmerited gift to hell-deserving sinners (Heb. 2:9), and that grace is in the Lord Jesus Christ (John 1:14). All the blessings of the New Testament Church originate in HIM. Those who are true believers and have been baptized into the body of Christ (I Cor. 12:12,13) have the promise of all spiritual blessings in the Lord Jesus Christ, apart from whom there is no salvation, no victory, no reward and no spiritual blessing.

Verse 2: "We give thanks to God always for you

all, making mention of you in our prayers."

Galatians is the only epistle in which Paul does not give thanks and praise in the very outset. In all his writings except the letter to the believers at Galatia, his first words are those of thanksgiving and praise to God for the spiritual fruit of God's grace, found in the lives and stewardship of his children in the Lord in the churches; but in the Galatian epistle, after the salutation of verses 1 through 4, Paul immediately begins a stern warning concerning the teachers of error and the preachers of spiritual poison, declaring that anyone—regardless of who they are or from whence they come—should be accursed if they preach any gospel other than the Gospel of God's grace (Gal. 1:6–9).

In I Thessalonians 5:18 Paul admonished, *"In every thing give thanks"*; but in the case of the church at Galatia Paul *could not* give thanks, because those dear people were listening to (and, in a sense, were obeying) error of the Judaizers and legalizers who were attempting to mix law and grace. Paul was jealous for Jesus, for His cross and for the grace of God that brings salvation and teaches us to live spiritual lives, instructing us to look for God's Son from heaven in the glorious appearing described in I Thessalonians 4:13–18.

In verse 2 the expression, "We give thanks to God always for you all, making mention of you in our prayers," is the warmest and tenderest language possible. Paul had a very warm spot in his heart for his spiritual children in Thessalonica. There are good grounds for his unhesitatingly showering this praise and thanksgiving upon the believers there, because they had demonstrated earnest, devoted, Christian living in their daily activities (verse 3). In turning to God from idols, stedfastly *serving* the true and living God, they had proved their conversion to be genuine; and because of this devoted service the Gospel had spread to other communities (verses 7 and 8). In every community throughout that country the believers at Thessalonica were known to have completely forsaken idolatry to become bondslaves of the true and living God. They were waiting for and desiring the return of Jesus from heaven (verses 9 and 10).

Paul opens verse 2 with the pronoun "we," thus including himself, Silas and Timothy. The statement, "WE give thanks to God ALWAYS for you ALL," is used only one other time by Paul. (See Philippians 1:4.) Certainly in the churches in Galatia, Corinth and Rome things were not ALWAYS in a spiritual status for which Paul could be thankful, because some of the members were far from being what they should have been in the service of the Lord (I Cor. 3:1–3).

According to II Thessalonians 1:3, there was charity one toward another in this assembly: ". . . and the charity of every one of you all toward each other aboundeth." Certainly it is very unusual to find a church where all members of the local assembly love each other. Through hook or crook the devil plants jealousy, envy and strife in the hearts of many church members—yea, even true believers are sometimes guilty of such vices; but the Thessalonian believers loved each other, and there seems to have been no jealousy among the people there.

". . . *Making mention of you in our prayers.*" What Paul is saying is simply this: "When Silas, Timothy and I engage in prayer, we never forget the true, beloved saints in Thessalonica. We make mention of you in our prayers—ALL of you, *always.*" Note I Thessalonians 5:17 and 18. I am sure one of the besetting sins of most Christians today is lack of prayer—especially one for another. Certainly all believers face the same devil, the same temptations, the same heartaches. In I Corinthians 10:13 we are told, "There hath no temptation taken you but such as is common to man (all men, all believers, all persons); but God is faithful, who will not suffer you to be tempted above that ye are able; but will with the temptation also make a way to escape, that ye may be able to bear it."

We need to pray one for another, we need to bear one another's burdens and share one another's sorrows; but this is a cold, selfish age in which we live, and very few believers have either time or desire to pray for fellow believers. Thank God *there are exceptions,* however, and today there are some dedicated believers who are just as given to intercessory prayer—and prayer without ceasing—as were the Christians in Thessalonica.

Verse 3: "Remembering without ceasing your work of faith, and labour of love, and patience of hope in our Lord Jesus Christ, in the sight of God and our Father."

The believers in this church had made such a deep impression upon Paul with their stewardship, love, devotion, evangelistic fervor and missionary endeavor in spreading the Gospel to other communities that as he stood in the presence of the omnipresent God who witnessed all of his thoughts, he prayed unceasingly for the believers at Thessalonica.

Paul uses the term, "in the sight of God and our Father." Similar terms are used many times in his writings. He was keenly conscious of the fact that God Almighty knows every thought and every motive. In I Thessalonians 3:9 he cries out, "For what thanks can we render to God again for you, for all the joy wherewith we joy for your sakes *before our God*!"

Paul frequently appeals to God as his witness—the witness of his feelings, his thoughts and his behavior. (Read I Thessalonians 2:4, 5 and 10.) Writing to the believers at Rome, he said, "God is my witness . . . how unceasingly I make mention of you always in my prayers" (Rom. 1:9). Again in Philippians 1:8 he said, "God is my record (witness), how greatly I long after you all . . . ." When we read these words from the heart and lips of the Apostle Paul, we think of Elijah as he cried out, "AS THE LORD LIVETH, BEFORE WHOM I STAND!" (I Kings 17:1).

Paul says, "in the sight of (before) God and our Father," for it is in God's character of "Father" that Paul approaches Him in prayer. (Read I Thessalonians 3:11 and II Thessalonians 2:16.) You will recall that the disciples asked, "Lord, teach us to pray," and Jesus replied, "After this manner pray ye: OUR FATHER which art in heaven . . . ." It was "in God" as FATHER (verse 1) that the Thessalonians became members of the Church of the living God. The blessings they had received for which Paul was so grateful, had come because of God's grace (Heb. 2:9) in permitting Jesus to taste death for every man and thereby become the head of the New Testament Church (Eph. 5:26). In Romans 5:11 Paul said, "We joy in God."

"Remembering without ceasing your work of faith, and labour of love, and patience of hope . . . ." Paul remembered how active and faithful those believers were, how devoted they were to each other. Faith, hope and love are the essence, heart and soul of practical Christianity: "And now abideth faith, hope, charity, these three; but the greatest of these is charity" (I Cor. 13:13). Faith, hope and love express themselves in work and patience. Read the account of the church at Ephesus as recorded in Revelation 2:2–3.

There was remarkable vigor, unusual and untiring labor, extraordinary moral courage and activity in the lives of the believers in the Thessalonian church. Paul rejoiced in this fact even more than he rejoiced in the

28

eloquence and knowledge of the church in Corinth (I Cor. 1:5). The outstanding, most distinguishing feature of the church at Thessalonica was the demonstration by believers of warm hearts and practical energy in service in their daily living. They were not lazy nor slothful; their hearts were filled with love, and their bodies were dedicated, living sacrifices to God. They proved this dedication by their unusual energy and zeal in service.

The "work of faith" mentioned here includes the two expressions that immediately follow: "labour of love" and "patience of hope in our Lord Jesus Christ." The work of faith embraces the entire practical issue of the life of a true believer. The *work* of faith denotes that which faith effects . . . its outcome and result as shown in the life of the believer. In Bible language, the work of faith is "the fruit of the Spirit" (Gal. 5:22) and "fruit of the light" (Eph. 5:8,9). Paul uses this same expression in II Thessalonians 1:11: ". . . and the work of faith with power." He did not preach a sentimental faith . . . he believed in a *working faith*.

In Galatians and Romans we find true faith contrasted with works—"the works of the law." The teachers of error had been setting forth the doctrine that men could not be saved by grace alone; that grace was supplemented by the Law of Moses or the rituals of Judaism—and Paul stood firmly against such teaching. You will find the heart of Paul's doctrine concerning salvation as totally and entirely apart from works, if you will carefully study Romans 4:1–4; 9:32; Galatians 2:16; 3:10–14. This heresy (grace plus law, or grace plus rituals) had not yet invaded the church at Thessalonica.

There is no conflict between Paul and James. Paul declared, "For by grace are ye saved through faith; and that not of yourselves: it is the gift of God: not of works, lest any man should boast" (Eph. 2:8,9). But he also agreed with James that faith without works is dead (James 2:17).   Paul taught that true faith is the operative principle of the Christian life—a working power in the life of the believer. In Galatians 5:6 he called it *"faith which worketh by love."*

In the Thessalonian church the "work of faith" was manifest in two forms: First, *the toil of love*; second, *the endurance of hope*.   In II Thessalonians 1:3–4 Paul said, "We are bound to thank God always for you, brethren, as it is meet, because that your faith groweth exceedingly, and the charity of every one of you all toward each other aboundeth; so that we ourselves glory in you in the churches of God for your patience and faith in all your persecutions and tribulations that ye endure."

Here we see that faith is joined *hand in hand with love* on the one side, and *hand in hand with patience* on the other.   The Thessalonian Christians love each other fervently in the church, and with patience they endure persecution, trials and tribulation as they witness to those who are without. These are the two chief branches of the tree of Christian stewardship—loving service IN the church to the brethren, and fearless, untiring testimony for Christ before the world as having to do with unbelievers OUTSIDE the church, with Christian endurance, suffering—and even being forsaken by family and friends.   In our present study, consider carefully chapters 4:9–10 and 5:13, and then compare chapters 2:13–14 and 3:2–4.

Paul refers to "the good fight of faith" (I Tim. 6:12). Paul did not preach a sentimental, soft, "sissy" Gospel—he was every inch a man.   Before his experience on the Damascus road he had been alert and untiring—a good soldier for Judaism; and he was just as fervent and untiring in his dedication to the warfare of Christianity. Paul preached love—but he also preached hardness, endurance and suffering for the sake of the cross. *True love is willing to suffer for the one loved.*

In the Greek language there is a distinction between the words "work" and "labor." *Work* points to the thing done, as a matter of achievement, while *labor* points to pains spent in doing it, as a matter of exertion. Paul uses the latter when he speaks of his *manual* labor, as in I Thessalonians 2:9 and II Thessalonians 3:8. With his many infirmities Paul's labors must often have been a heavy task. He also speaks of his labors *as a minister of the Lord Jesus Christ*, as in I Thessalonians 3:5 and II Corinthians 10:15. In I Corinthians 3:8 we read, "Every man shall receive his own reward according to his own labour." To the believer, *work* may be a joy, easy and delightful; but *labor* is toilsome and can sometimes become wearisome to the flesh. You may rest assured that no selfish, self-centered person will endure labor for the good of another; labor is the test of true love.

". . . *Patience of hope* . . . ." The Greek word used here implies active and continuous endurance. It is not the resignation of the passive sufferer; it is the endurance and fortitude demonstrated by a stout-hearted soldier, a soldier who marches on in hope to victory. He does not become weary in the long days of marching conflict, for he looks *beyond the conflict* to glorious victory. Christian hope inspires the soldier of the cross to look beyond this vale of tears to the glorious day unending with our Saviour!

One outstanding Bible scholar has said, "Hope is the balm and lifeblood of the soul." Jesus demonstrated this hope: ". . . Jesus, the author and finisher of our faith; who for the joy that was set before Him endured the cross, despising the shame, and is set down at the right hand of the throne of God" (Heb. 12:2). Our Lord did not enjoy the cross nor its shame . . . He ENDURED

31

it; He saw the joy on the other side of Calvary!

The believers in the church at Thessalonica were imitators of the Lord (I Thess. 1:6). They followed the example of patience set by the Lord Jesus (II Thess. 3:5). It was not an easy road for them; they were tried, tested, and from the very beginning they endured fierce persecution (I Thess. 1:6; 3:2–6). Because of their patience and endurance, Paul gloried in the Thessalonian church and Christ was glorified in them (II Thess. 1:4–12). Such courage and endurance could not be overlooked by the enemies of the Gospel, but, on the contrary, gave powerful, unquestionable testimony to the power of the Gospel and the hope of salvation (I Thess. 1:7,8). True hope in the heart of a believer inspires and produces Christian patience. In Romans 5:3 and 4 we read, "Knowing that tribulation worketh patience; and patience, experience; and experience, hope." The hope of the believers in Thessalonica was *"in our Lord Jesus Christ."*

Let me point out here that OUR LORD JESUS CHRIST, in His final return to this earth, is frequently and with much emphasis represented in both epistles as the main object of the hope of the believers at Thessalonica (I Thess. 1:10; 2:12–19; 3:13; 4:14; 5:11; II Thess. 1:7–10; 2:1–8). The second coming of the Lord Jesus and the final judgment of the wicked was Paul's main theme in his preaching there. The doctrine of the Rapture and the final judgment of the wicked had gripped the hearts and minds of the Thessalonian believers, for these dear people believed every word of their beloved preacher Paul. They did not question the coming of the Lord Jesus, and in speaking to them concerning the Lord's return to this earth, Paul said, "But of the times and seasons, brethren, ye have no need that I write unto you. For yourselves know perfectly that the day of the Lord so cometh as a thief in the night" (I Thess. 5:1,2). According to these words, Paul had drilled into their hearts the doctrine of Christ's second coming, declaring that He would come as a thief in the night; and he had preached that truth to them so consistently that they knew it perfectly. The keynote in the two epistles to the Thessalonians is "HOPE," while the keynote of the epistle to the believers at Philippi is "JOY."

Verse 4: "Knowing, brethren beloved, your election of God."

The Greek language here reads, "Knowing, brethren, beloved of God, your election." II Thessalonians 2:13 uses the term "brethren beloved of the Lord." Paul always thinks and speaks of those in the churches where the epistles are directed as "brethren"—and truly we ARE all brothers in Christ. (The Fatherhood of God and the brotherhood of man is not in the Bible; but all BELIEVERS are brothers, regardless of nationality or whatsoever.)

Knowing that God the Father loves His children and has chosen them for His own, Paul gives assurance and confidence as he prays for the believers in the church that is being severely tested and tried. He does not doubt that they will stand the test, and he prays with joy and thanksgiving. II Thessalonians 2:13: "We are bound to give thanks alway to God for you, brethren beloved of the Lord, because God hath from the beginning chosen you." Compare Ephesians 1:3–5: "Blessed be God . . . who hath blessed us with all spiritual blessings . . . according as He hath chosen us in (Christ)." The Greek word used here for "beloved" signifies a love which was born and lived in the eternity behind us. The meaning is not that God loved at that particular moment, but that He loved even before He laid the foundation of this world! The Greek word suggests love that existed in the eternities behind us, *now realized in the hearts of the Thessalonians because of their faith in Jesus.*

33

John describes this love thus: "Behold what manner of love the Father hath bestowed upon us, that we should be called the sons of God" (I John 3:1a). The love that makes us sons of God, heirs of God and joint heirs with Christ, is a love *bestowed upon us* when we *believe*—yet a love that has *existed* from all eternity: "GOD is love!" (I John 4:8). "In the beginning—GOD . . ." (John 1:1). The love that makes us sons of God *was in the beginning*, but becomes ours when we embrace Christianity by faith in the finished work of the Lord Jesus Christ. The sovereignty of God, Bible election, Bible predestination and the foreknowledge of God have nothing to do with the free will of man. Jesus said to His own people, "And ye will not come to me that ye might have life." Yet He loved them so tenderly that He sat outside Jerusalem on the Mount of Olives and wept bitter tears: "O, Jerusalem, Jerusalem! How often would I have gathered thy children together, even as a hen gathereth her chickens under her wings—and ye would not!" Please read carefully Matthew 23:37–39 and John 5:40.

If you go to hell when you die it will not be God's will . . . it will be because of your own stubborn will; it will be for the same reason the unbelieving Jews burn in hell today. They rejected Christ and shouted, "Give us Barabbas! We will not have this Man to reign over us!" The Jews who shouted those angry words are now in hell simply because they would not come to Christ that they might have life. If you spend eternity in hell, dear reader, it will be because YOU will not come to Jesus that you might have life.

For the first time in Paul's epistles we have the word "election," which expresses one of the most important doctrines in the New Testament—and in this day and hour this doctrine needs careful study. The word used in the New Testament originated in the Old Testament, having to do with the nation Israel as God's "PE-CULIAR POSSESSION." Israel is referred to in the Old Testament as "the people whom He chose for His inheritance." Please read Psalm 33:12; Deuteronomy 14:2; Isaiah 43:1-7.

True Bible election implies two things:

1. *Selection out of others*—(that is, from nations or peoples)—a people for His very own. God is the one who provides the power to prepare these peoples spiritually to be presented to Him, spotless and without wrinkle; and those who come to God cannot come unless drawn by the Holy Spirit (John 6:44).

2. These peoples, drawn by the Holy Ghost to God, thus embracing the finished work of Christ by hearing the Word and obeying the Spirit, are *appropriated by God* for His very own to love and protect, and for His very own in spiritual service.

The Gospel was preached to the people in Thessalonica, and all had the same opportunity to hear it; but no doubt a vast number—especially of the Jews—rejected Paul's message. They would not come to Christ that they might have life, but "As many as received Him, to them gave He power to become the sons of God, even to them that believe on His name." Therefore, those who heard the message of the God-appointed, God-ordained Apostle, those who received the death, burial and resurrection of the Christ, became members of *the true election* . . . they became part of THE ISRAEL OF GOD (Gal. 6:16). Those who rejected the death, burial and resurrection of the Lord Jesus were those "which have no hope"; they were the "others" mentioned in I Thessalonians 5:6.

Paul knew that as a people, Israel had rejected Jesus. He knew that when Pilate asked, "Whom shall I release unto you?" they had shouted, "Barabbas!!" He was therefore compelled to face the fact that the nation which was the apple of Jehovah's eye, the chosen of God in the Old Testament, had rejected the Messiah whom Paul met on the Damascus road. In the light of that knowledge, there must be a distinction made between national Israel and the true election—the spiritual kernel of the chosen people of God, who were the real objects of God's eternal favor. It is in honor of this distinction that Paul cries out in Romans 11:7: "What then? Israel hath NOT obtained that which he seeketh for; but *the election hath obtained it*, and the rest were blinded." Therefore, in this present dispensation we have the true election of God through the crucified, buried and risen Christ. All Gentiles who believe in His finished work are identified: ". . . Wild olive branches grafted into the good olive tree" (Rom. 11:17—24). Thus we see the national give place to spiritual election—"the Israel of God."

Paul's message to Jew and Gentile alike was "by grace, through faith, ALL become ONE in Christ," and he applies this doctrine without discrimination. In I Peter 2:9 we read, "But ye (*who believe in Christ*) are a chosen generation, a royal priesthood, a peculiar people." In this dispensation of grace, God's true election no longer applies to a specific nation or body of men as such, but concerns INDIVIDUALS. Regardless of race or social standing, each believer in Christ is the personal object of God's loving choice known in Paul's epistles as "the election of grace" (Rom. 11:5).

In II Thessalonians 2:13 we have a clear statement as to why God, in His loving kindness, tender mercy and saving grace, chooses men: GOD CHOSE YOU UNTO SALVATION. That means God has chosen all who believe in His Son Jesus Christ, to final deliverance from sin, death and all evil; each believer is destined to be conformed to the image of God's dear Son. This will take place when Jesus returns in the Rapture, and because of the great love bestowed upon us we will then receive a body just like His glorious resurrection body!

Notice the wording of I Thessalonians 1:10: "And to wait for His Son from heaven, whom He raised from the dead, even Jesus, which delivered us from the wrath to come." That last statement plainly tells us, *"which delivered us from the wrath to come."* (Not "GOING to deliver us" at some future date, but we are ALREADY delivered.) Final deliverance from death, hell and the grave, from the corruption of the flesh, is included in the salvation grace brings.

In I Thessalonians 2:12 we read, "God . . . called you unto His kingdom and glory," and in I Thessalonians 5:9 and 10: "God hath not appointed us to wrath, but to obtain salvation by our Lord Jesus Christ who died for us, that, whether we wake or sleep, we should live together with Him." Believers are not in jeopardy as having to do with their eternal destiny; all true believers are predestined to be conformed to the image of God's beloved Son. The God who loved us so much that He chose us did not choose and save us for the purpose of surrendering us to the evil one.

In Ephesians 1:4 Paul clearly states that God chose us to be holy and without blame before Him in love," and in Romans 8:28–34 we read: "And we know that all things work together for good to them that love God, to them who are the called according to His purpose. For whom He did foreknow, He also did predestinate to be conformed to the image of His Son, that He might be the firstborn among many brethren. Moreover whom He He did predestinate, them He also called: and whom He called, them He also justified: and whom He justified,

37

them He also glorified. What shall we then say to these things? If God be for us, who can be against us? He that spared not His own Son, but delivered Him up for us all, how shall He not with Him also freely give us all things? WHO SHALL LAY ANYTHING TO THE CHARGE OF GOD'S ELECT? It is God that justifieth. Who is he that condemneth? It is Christ that died, yea rather, that is risen again, who is even at the right hand of God, who also maketh intercession for us."

Every believer can rest assured that all things work together for good to them that love God, and that all believers are predestined to be conformed to the image of God's Son; therefore, *if God be for us, who can be against us*? God spared not His own Son that we might have this grace that brings salvation; He delivered up His Son that we might be saved. In the face of such love, who shall be able to lay anything to the charge of God's elect? It is God who justifies—and the only way a holy God can be just—and yet justify the ungodly—is in Christ. God was in Christ reconciling the world unto Himself. Jesus took upon Himself the likeness of sinful man, and in that body of flesh He conquered the world, the flesh and the devil. Thus, "What the Law could not do in that it was weak through the flesh," God did in His Son IN the flesh (Rom. 8:1-3).

Now God can be holy, just and righteous—and yet justify the ungodly when the ungodly believe on the Lord Jesus Christ and trust in His death, burial and resurrection. *Who is he that condemneth*? It is Christ who died, Christ who is risen, Christ who sits at the right hand of God, and Christ who makes intercession for all believers. There is one God, and one Mediator between God and men—the MAN, CHRIST JESUS (I Tim. 2:5). Jesus loved me enough to shed His blood for me, He loved me enough to call me through the Holy Spirit, He loved me enough to "born" me into God's family through the power of the Gospel (I Pet. 1:23 and Rom. 1:16); and Jesus now sits at the right hand of God the Father to make intercession for me! If it is Jesus who condemns—and no one BUT Jesus can condemn me—then why should I fear the outcome of my Christian experience? Christ is the author and the finisher of our faith. "This is the record, that God has given to us eternal life, and this life is in His Son. He that hath the Son hath life; and he that hath not the Son of God hath not life" (I John 5: 11,12). Please read I John 5:1–13. Every born again believer is predestined to be conformed to the image of God's dear Son.

I Peter 1:18–23 is a passage easily understood. These verses tell us that before God Almighty ever laid the foundation of this earth—before one grain of sand was created, before Adam was formed from the dust of the ground, before Eve was taken from his side in the form of a rib—God thought, planned, blueprinted, perfected and finished salvation for all who will believe and trust in Him. We are redeemed with the precious blood of Jesus, not with any corruptible thing. Our faith and hope are in God; we purify ourselves by believing in God; we are born again through the incorruptible seed—the Word. Salvation is of the Lord—yea, salvation is Christ in YOU (Col. 1:27). Some believers could enjoy their spiritual birthright if they would face the solemn Bible fact that *salvation* is not "religion," it is not "going to church," it is not baptism nor living a good life. *Salvation is divine nature within the heart, in the Person of the Holy Ghost.*

As an organism of which Jesus Christ is the head, the New Testament Church was chosen and elected by God in the beginning; and the election of the BODY has nothing to do with the conversion of the individuals who make up the body. In Acts 2:47 (shortly after Pentecost) we read, "And the Lord added to the church daily such as were being saved." The Scripture does not say the Lord added to the church daily such individuals as were *elected* to be saved—and rejected other individuals who were NOT elected to be saved. Salvation from sin is a personal matter of personal faith in the Lord Jesus.

Bible election has nothing to do with the salvation of the individual. *We who believe* were chosen by God in the beginning, but that does not determine our salvation. Our salvation is determined by whether or not we receive or reject the Lord Jesus: "He that believeth on Him is not condemned; but he that believeth not is condemned already, because he hath not believed in the name of the only begotten Son of God" (John 3:18). Souls who burn in hell do not do so because they were *elected* to burn in hell, nor do those who go to heaven go there because they are loved with a deeper love than the sinners who burn in hell. God so loved the WORLD—and it is not His will that ANY should perish. Jesus is the propitiation for OUR sins—and for the sins of the whole wide world!

I believe in the sovereignty of God. God knows the end in the beginning; but that has nothing to do with the freedom of will for the individual. God created Adam, put him in the Garden of Eden and gave him the right to choose. The prophet of old said, "Choose you this day whom ye will serve" (Joshua 24:15). *God's choice of us* certainly preceded *our choice of Him* as having to do with salvation; but His choosing us does not alter the fact that we must, as individuals, believe on the Lord Jesus Christ in order to be saved. The Church of the living God is one body, made up of many members (I Cor. 12:12–31); and these individual members accept the Lord as their Saviour after hearing His Word (John 5:24; Romans 10:17; John 3:3,5; I Peter 1:23).

The body was chosen, elected and predestined before the foundation of the world, but the individuals who make up the body must trust the Lord of their own free will.   God is love, and love never forces or dictates. *Love leads.*   Love is the good shepherd; and a good shepherd leads the sheep, he does not drive them.

Speaking to the Philippians Paul said, ". . . Work out your own salvation with fear and trembling.   For it is God which worketh in you . . ." (Phil. 2:12b, 13a). After we are saved by God's grace, we are workers together with God.   We are "created in Christ Jesus unto good works, which God hath before ordained that we should walk in them" (Eph. 2:10).

I honestly and wholeheartedly confess before God that the consistency of the free will of all men with God's sovereignty certainly is an insolvable mystery. I believe in the sovereignty of God, but I also believe John 3:16 and many other verses like it.   I cannot understand nor explain the sovereignty of God, neither can I fathom His great love; yet I know God loves me, that He is sovereign and that He knows all things.   I also know that men are saved by trusting Jesus of their own free will and accord, after hearing the wonderful story of God's love—the message of salvation provided by the grace of God in Christ Jesus.

Possibly Paul was not sure of the final salvation of every person in the church at Thessalonica, for he writes, "For this cause, when I could no longer forbear, I sent to know your faith, *lest by some means the tempter have tempted you, and our labour be in vain*" (I Thess. 3:5). He says practically the same thing to the Galatians: "I am afraid of you, lest I have bestowed upon you labour in vain" (Gal. 4:11).

These statements do not mean that the people to

whom Paul refers were genuinely born again—saved by grace—and that they would lose grace and redemption; but rather *that they had stopped short of the full message of redemption* through faith in the death, burial and resurrection of the Lamb of God. Paul did not mean that every individual in the local assembly was part of the elect when he said, "knowing your election," but he was referring to the church in general.

True believers are to ". . . walk worthy of God, who hath called you unto His kingdom and glory" (I Thess. 2:12). "But let us, who are of the day, be sober, putting on the breastplate of faith and love; and for an helmet, the hope of salvation" (I Thess. 5:8). And finally, "FAITHFUL IS HE THAT CALLETH YOU, WHO ALSO WILL DO IT" (I Thess. 5:24).

God had directed Paul to Thessalonica and had honored the Gospel in power and much assurance. The people had received it with an open heart, and in spite of the severe persecutions inflicted upon them by Satan and the enemies of the Gospel, they had gone forward and spread the good news throughout that part of the country. Paul knew the Holy Ghost had sent him there, and he had much joy concerning the work accomplished through the Gospel in Thessalonica.

Verse 5: "For our gospel came not unto you in word only, but also in power, and in the Holy Ghost, and in much assurance; as ye know what manner of men we were among you for your sake."

Paul and Silas were keenly conscious of the power of the Holy Ghost as they delivered their message in the city of Thessalonica. Since they were assured of the power of the Holy Ghost upon their ministry they knew that their preaching would not be in vain. It was clear to Paul and Silas that God "had much people in this city."

"Our Gospel" is God's good news that He so loved sinners that He gave His only begotten Son, willingly and freely, to pay the sin-debt; and this good news is proclaimed by God's servants. (Read Romans 1:1–17.) Therefore, while the Gospel is GOD'S Gospel, it is also OUR Gospel. God's message is the message preached by every true minister of God.

The message Paul delivered in Thessalonica was a peculiar message—not peculiar in that it was strange, but Paul had unusual power and his message came in the power of the Holy Ghost. Before Jesus ascended back to heaven He said, ". . . THE SPIRIT OF TRUTH . . . SHALL TESTIFY OF ME: AND YE ALSO SHALL BEAR WITNESS . . ." (John 15:26,27).

The disciples were sad when Jesus told them that He must go away. They did not understand what He meant when He said, "If I go not away, the Comforter will not come. But if I depart, I will send Him unto you; and when He comes, He will testify of ME." The Spirit did not come into the world to testify of Himself, nor to bestow supernatural power upon man in order that man might glory in his own ability. The more completely an individual is controlled by the Holy Spirit, the more that individual will magnify Jesus and the less he will speak of himself and his ability. The Holy Ghost always magnifies the Son of God.

Jesus instructed the disciples to tarry in Jerusalem until they be endued with power from on high. Just before His ascension He said, "Ye shall receive power when the Holy Spirit is come upon you . . ." (Acts 1:8). In I Corinthians 2:4 Paul said, "My speech and my preaching was not with enticing words of man's wisdom, but in demonstration of the Spirit and of power." The devil does not care how much we preach, how often we preach, how long nor how fervent our message may be, so long as it is not the pure Word of God, bathed in and permeated by the Holy Spirit. It is not by might, not by power, but "BY MY SPIRIT, saith the Lord of hosts," and no man can come to God except the Spirit draw him. The Spirit is in the world to reprove men of sin, of righteousness, and of judgment; and unless the Holy Spirit empowers a message, that message will be as sounding brass or tinkling cymbal.

The Gospel Paul preached in Thessalonica was preached "in the Holy Ghost, and in much assurance." The Greek word here translated in its fullest means "full assurance of the understanding." The same statement is found in Colossians 2:2 and 3: "That their hearts might be comforted, being knit together in love, and unto all riches of the FULL ASSURANCE OF UNDERSTANDING, to the acknowledgement of the mystery of God, and of the Father, and of Christ; in whom are hid all the treasures of wisdom and knowledge." Paul uses the same statement in Hebrews 6:11−12: "And we desire that every one of you do shew the same diligence to the full assurance of hope unto the end: That ye be not slothful, but followers of them who through faith and patience inherit the promises." Hebrews 10:22 tells us, "Let us draw near with a true heart in full assurance of faith, having our hearts sprinkled from an evil conscience, and our bodies washed with pure water."

In our present verse, "fullness" is ascribed to the Gospel as Paul, under divine leadership, had presented it to the hearers at Thessalonica. The message came to them *in the power of the Holy Ghost and in much assurance*, signifying that the Gospel had its full effect upon them.

In writing to Timothy, Paul said, "Notwithstanding the Lord stood with me, and strengthened me; *that by me the preaching might be fully known*, and that all the

Gentiles might hear: and I was delivered out of the mouth of the lion" (II Tim. 4:17). Bear in mind the fact that Paul was called, ordained and commissioned by God to preach the Gospel to the Gentiles, and all hell could not stop him until he had fulfilled that calling.

The Gospel contains the power to lift men from the miry clay of sin, the power to "born" them into the family of God and make them *sons* of God. The hearer *hears the Gospel*, the Holy Spirit bears the truth home to the heart, *convicts* through the power of the Gospel, *draws men* through that same power and *"borns"* them into the family of God (John 5:24; I Peter 1:23). Apart from the Word of God there is no salvation.

Verse 5 closes with these words: "Ye know what manner of men we were among you for your sake." What Paul is really saying here is, "Even as you know, we showed ourselves toward you." Paul wants these fellow Christians to remember that he and his co-workers preached the Gospel to them, which Gospel they believed and received. Thus, because of their faith in the message and their wholehearted reception of the Gospel, Paul labored, suffered and gave his best to them, motivated by love and a fervent desire to see the church go forward. He knew in his heart that God had sent him there and that many people in that city would be saved through the the Gospel. Paul wanted the idol-worshipping Thessalonians to be saved "to God's own kingdom and glory" (I Thess. 2:12), and he declared, "I endure all things for the elect's sakes (II Timothy 2:10a).

Behind the purpose of Paul and his co-laborers was the purpose of God—that of bringing sons into the New Testament Church, the body of Christ. Therefore Paul labored, endured affliction and persecution—not for fame and vainglory, but *"to His own kingdom and glory."* He literally lived to please God! Whether eating, drinking, or whatsoever he did, it was done to God's glory—and if eating meat offended a weaker brother, Paul refused to eat meat. (Read Romans 14:15 and I Corinthians 8:13.) Apart from Jesus Christ, I think no human ever lived so close to the heart of God as did the Apostle Paul.

Verse 6: "And ye became followers of us, and of the Lord, having received the word in much affliction, with joy of the Holy Ghost."

The Greek here literally is *"imitators of us."* In I Thessalonians 2:14 Paul says, "For ye, brethren, became followers of the churches of God which in Judaea are in Christ Jesus: for ye also have suffered like things of your own countrymen, even as they have of the Jews."

You will find a corresponding statement in II Thessalonians 3:9. In the true sense of the word, one who is an imitator not only embraces the teaching of the one imitated, but also copies his example. In the case of the Thessalonians, this imitation consisted in the joyful and untiring endurance of suffering for the sake of the Gospel. (Read I Thessalonians 2:2, 14, 15.) Not only did they imitate Paul in suffering; they also imitated his zeal, his vigor and his untiring labor.

By imitating Paul, the believers at Thessalonica were walking in the steps of the Lord Jesus, for "Though He were a Son, yet learned He obedience by the things which He suffered" (Heb. 5:8). Jesus Himself received (from the heavenly Father) the Word "in much affliction," and Himself "with joy of the Holy Ghost" ministered the words given to Him BY the heavenly Father. In John 17:8a Jesus said, "I have given unto them the words which thou gavest me." In John 16:33 Jesus told His disciples, "In the world ye shall have tribulation: but be of good cheer; I have overcome the world." He did not promise them a flowery bed of ease nor a ministry without persecution; but He DID promise grace sufficient for all occasions and circumstances. Read John 17:8 and John 15:20.

Writing to the believers at Colosse, Paul said, "Filling up what is left behind of the afflictions of Christ" (Col. 1:24). That is, Paul was willing to take up the sufferings of Christ where He left off when He finished His earthly ministry. Jesus came not to be ministered unto, but to minister—and to give His life a ransom for many. He who knew no sin bore our sins in much suffering on the cross. We are to follow His example.

It must have been encouraging and inspiring to the believers at Thessalonica when they read the words of their beloved Apostle: "Ye became followers of us and of the Lord. You are walking in the very steps of Jesus." To walk in HIS steps makes toil and labor welcome. To walk in His steps makes reproach and shame a glorious privilege.

Paul had a clean heart, a clear conscience—and spiritual boldness that only the Holy Ghost can give. This is evidenced by the fact that he invited his children in the Lord to follow in his steps even as HE followed in the steps of the Lord Jesus. *"Be ye followers of me, even as I also am of Christ"* (I Cor. 11:1).

Verse 6 closes thus: ". . . having received the Word in much affliction, with joy of the Holy Ghost."

This "much affliction" (tribulation) is described in Acts 17:5–9, and in his epistles Paul frequently refers to this great affliction. Severe persecution marked the path the Thessalonians were called to follow as they walked with Christ. Following in His steps in persecution and great affliction gave them opportunity to prove the genuineness of their faith. If we suffer with Him, we shall reign with Him; if we deny Him, He will deny us.

In Philippians 1:29 Paul wrote, "For unto you it is given in the behalf of Christ, not only to believe on Him, but also to suffer for His sake." Joy always attends suffering for the truth's sake on the part of a believer. There is neither glory nor joy in suffering for the sake of ignorance; but if we suffer for the sake of truth, we are to rejoice and be exceedingly glad. Paul was an example of true suffering; he did not become discouraged by suffering or persecution. In II Corinthians 6:10 he said, ". . . Sorrowful, yet alway rejoicing!" When we rejoice in persecution and great affliction for the sake of the Gospel and a true Christian testimony, we know that such joy comes from the Holy Spirit and is a positive sign of true conversion. A true believer is the only person who can rejoice in sorrow and smile through a veil of tears.

The Holy Spirit enabled Paul to preach with power, and the same Holy Spirit enabled the Thessalonians to receive his message and believe with joy, even though they suffered great affliction and much persecution. In verses 5 and 6 of this chapter Paul introduces the Holy Spirit without hesitation, knowing that the Thessalonians knew the true teaching concerning Father, Son and Holy Spirit; and in the first six verses of this—the first of Paul's epistles—we have the clear and unmistakable doctrine of the Trinity:

In verse 1: ". . . The church of the Thessalonians which is in God the Father and in the Lord Jesus Christ."

In verse 5: The Gospel came, "not unto you in word only, but also in power, and in the Holy Ghost."

In verse 6: The believers at Thessalonica became followers of Paul, Silas and Timothy, and in following (imitating) their example, they were walking in the steps of the Lord, having received the Word in much affliction,

48

"with joy of the Holy Ghost."

Verse 7: "So that ye were ensamples to all that believe in Macedonia and Achaia."

"Ensamples" is the old English word for "example, pattern, or type." Paul uses the same word in Titus 2:7 and Hebrews 8:5. He applies the expression to himself in II Thessalonians 3:9, again in Philippians 3:17 and in I Timothy 4:12.

In verse 7, the expression "all that believe" refers to those who believe in God (in Christ), and it is frequently used by Paul when referring to Christians (I Thess. 2:10–13; II Thess. 1:10). He refers to the believers in Galatia as "they that are of faith" (Gal. 3:7–9). In Romans he says, ". . . him which believeth in Jesus" (Rom. 3:26). Faith is the very heart and essence of all that makes a man a true Christian. God's grace saves us, but that grace becomes ours by faith. To the Hebrews Paul said, "Without faith it is impossible to please (God): for he that cometh to God must believe that He is, and that He is a rewarder of them that diligently seek Him" (Heb. 11:6).

The believers at Thessalonica were so dedicated and consecrated to Christianity that their example of Christian living had affected all the believers in Macedonia, Achaia, and throughout that part of the known world. At the time of the writing of the Epistle, Paul was in Corinth—the capital of Achaia, a Roman province—and he had witnessed the effect of the believers in Thessalonica on the church in that particular district. Timothy and Silas had just returned from a missionary trip to the northern province—touching various towns in Macedonia—and had firsthand information concerning the influence of the believers in Thessalonica on the people there (I Thess. 3:6; Acts 18:5).

The Apostle Paul patterned his life after Christ; the

believers followed in his footsteps, thus following in the footsteps of their Lord; the neighboring Christians then patterned *their* lives after the pattern set by Paul and the Thessalonian believers. In this manner these devout, conscientious Christians had set the example for many believers throughout that part of the world.

Verse 8: "For from you sounded out the word of the Lord not only in Macedonia and Achaia, but also in every place your faith to God-ward is spread abroad; so that we need not to speak any thing."

The Greek language in verse 8 suggests a clear, ringing note, *as of a trumpet*. It has the meaning—not of a blast and then silence, but rather of a prolonging effect—a continuation of the sound. By way of the believers in Thessalonica the Gospel had "sounded out" (or resounded). The statement "the word of the Lord" is an Old Testament expression designating God's Word and God's will revealed to men. Paul uses the expression in the Thessalonian epistles only. (Note I Thessalonians 5:18 and II Thessalonians 3:1.) In his other epistles, Paul refers to "the word of God" or "the word of Christ." He is very careful to make it known that it was not his word nor the word of man—"not as the word of men, but as it is in truth, the word of God" (I Thess. 2:13).

Peter also makes known the authorship of the Word: "The word which God sent unto the children of Israel, preaching peace by Jesus Christ: (He is Lord of all:)" (Acts 10:36). In verse 8 we have proof of the earnestness and sincerity with which the Thessalonians had received the Gospel as delivered by Paul. They received it, they believed it, and they preached it far and wide—nor did they attempt to alter the message by adding to or taking from the grace of God preached by their beloved Paul.

Violent persecution was directed against them; but

regardless of persecution, the enemy failed to shake their faith in the message delivered to them. On the contrary, such violent persecution drove them to a much more fervent declaration of the Gospel—not only in Macedonia and Achaia, "but also in every place your faith to Godward is spread abroad."

What Paul is saying in the first part of verse 8 is simply that from the believers in Thessalonica *"hath sounded out" the true message of salvation* by grace through faith in the finished work of the Lord Jesus Christ. Conversion of the Thessalonians made a great sensation in that day in their part of the world; it had even reached far beyond the boundaries of Greece.

A short time before this, Aquilla had come from Rome to the city of Corinth (Acts 18:2), and he no doubt brought word from Rome that news of the church at Thessalonica had reached that city. In Acts 17:6 and 7 the charge of treason against Caesar is recorded, and this had probably been reported in the city of Rome.

Verse 8 closes with the statement, "So that we need not to speak any thing." The saying here is simply this: "There is no need for us to tell the story of your glorious conversion, your full surrender and dedication to the ministry of the Gospel of grace, for we hear of it on all sides. Everywhere we go, people are talking about the conversion of the Thessalonians, and of how you have bravely, untiringly and unhesitatingly sounded out your testimony for Christ concerning His finished work and redemption by faith in His shed blood. Therefore, there is no need for us to say anything; the news has already spread like wildfire!"

Verse 9: "For they themselves shew of us what manner of entering in we had unto you, and how ye turned to God from idols to serve the living and the true God."

51

In this verse, *"they"* refers to those in Macedonia, Achaia, and "in every place." Everywhere Paul went, instead of people waiting to be told about the church at Thessalonica, they immediately told HIM about the report that had already reached them. Reports concerning the believers at Thessalonica strengthened the testimony of Paul, Silas and Timothy—because such reports not only told of the Thessalonians, but also of the power with which Paul had delivered the message in that great city of idolatry, and the effect that message had had upon the people there.

"What manner of entering in we had unto you" does not refer to the reception given Paul and his co-workers by the Thessalonians, but rather to the way in which they (the Thessalonians) presented themselves whole-heartedly to their ministry in the city. Reports being sounded out through the countryside told of the fearless faith of the Thessalonians—and also of the wonderful success with which Paul and Silas had preached the Gospel to them.

When Paul entered into the city—preaching Jesus Christ crucified, buried, risen again—the idolaters "turned to God from idols." When a sinner becomes a Christian, the first step is repentance toward God—and *repentance* is turning *face-about*, not turning *around*, which would mean that the unbeliever would still be traveling in the same direction. When a sinner hears the Gospel, is convicted by the Gospel and is drawn by the Holy Spirit to turn face-about, he automatically turns FROM idols when he turns TO God.

The church at Thessalonica was made up primarily of Gentiles who had been heathen (I Thess. 2:14; Acts 17:4,5); however, there were a few Jews among them. There was also a great multitude of proselytes who had seemingly already turned *from idolatry*, but had not yet turned *to the living God.* It is not enough to turn from idols, for *turning FROM* does not save anyone. We must turn TO the living God—by faith in His beloved Son.

The term "faith toward God" used here by Paul means faith in the whole Bible, from start to finish—faith in the message of God's holy Word in which, from beginning to end, God asserts Himself as THE LIVING AND TRUE GOD. There are thousands of forms of idolatry—but there is only ONE GOD. There were many idols in the city of Thessalonica, and the believers who made up that church completely turned away from all forms of idolatry when they turned by faith to the living and true Jehovah God (who so loved the world that He gave His only begotten Son that through faith in Him we might be saved).

The Greek word for *idol* means "an appearance or image." Paul defines idolatry in two passages (I Cor. 8:4; 10:19,20) as being half lies and half deviltry. In Paul's day there was much gross idolatry, and in Romans 1:18—32 he gives a solemn warning against it, setting forth its terrible consequences.

Verse 9 closes with the statement, ". . . to serve the living and true God." *True* is used here to signify *truth of fact.* That is, these Christians had turned from all other gods to serve the *ONE true God.* He is very God; He is the great "I AM"—the "I AM" who spoke to Moses, and the "I AM" who spoke to the officers when they came to arrest the Christ in the garden. When Jesus said, "Whom seek ye?" they answered, "Jesus of Nazareth." Then Jesus simply said, "I AM . . ." and they fell to the ground (John 18:6). Jehovah is very God, true God, the ONLY true God. "And this is life eternal, that they might know thee the only true God . . ." (John 17:3a). "THIS IS THE TRUE GOD, AND ETERNAL LIFE" (I John 5:20).

Having heard the Gospel of the grace of God, the idolaters in Thessalonica turned from idols—but they did not stop there; they turned TO GOD to serve Him. The Greek language used here sets forth the truth that the service rendered to God by the Thessalonians was that of a bondslave to his master, indicating that they were His property, that they were no longer their own, having been purchased with the tremendous price of the blood of Jesus. Therefore, they were yielded to the true God, and at His absolute disposal.

Paul often refers to himself as Christ's bondman, and in Titus 1:1 he speaks of himself as *God's* bondman. In Galatians 4:8 he speaks of those who "knew not God" as being in bondage to false gods. In Romans 1:15–22 he shows that when one becomes a Christian, that one exchanges the bondage of sin for bondage unto righteousness, the believer being in bondage to God under grace. When one becomes a true believer he is no longer his own; he belongs to Christ.

The relationship of a Christian to God is a twofold combination. We are sons of God in respect to affection and privilege: God loves us as His dear children, and being sons of God we enjoy the privilege of sons as having to do with the Father; but we are also bondslaves of God *as having to do with our duty and submission to Him*, since He purchased us at such a tremendous price. We love God because He first loved us—and it is not difficult to serve one whom you love.

Let me sum up the testimony of the believers at Thessalonica—such testimony as was sounded out through the whole countryside:

Paul preached the Gospel—"in the power of the Holy Ghost and with much assurance." The Thessalonians heard the Gospel, received it—and automatically turned to the true God from their dead idols *to become His servants (bondslaves).* Until the day they heard the Gospel of the grace of God they were bondslaves to idols, continually serving them, worshipping in their shrines and sacrificing to them; but now—having heard of the salvation that is in Christ Jesus and having turned to the true God, they render untiring service to Him as fervently as they had formerly served their idols.

They further proved their testimony by the truth set forth in verse 10:

Verse 10: "And to wait for His Son from heaven, whom He raised from the dead, even Jesus, which delivered us from the wrath to come."

The literal Greek reads, "From the *heavens*." In II Corinthians 12:2, Paul speaks of being caught up into the third heaven, and in Hebrews 4:14 he says, "Jesus . . . who (in ascending) hath passed through the heavens." In the Hebrew language *heaven* is a plural word, implying successive regions and stages between earth and the present chamber of the most high God. Jesus said to the disciples, "In my Father's house are many mansions . . . *I go to prepare a place for YOU*" (John 14:1–6). When Jesus spoke these words to the disciples, the Father's house at that time was made up of many mansions; Jesus declared that He would *prepare* a place for the Church—and that place is the Pearly White City described in Revelation 21.

The fact that believers are said "to wait for His Son from heaven" separates the New Testament Church from the Jewish synagogue (Judaism). The Church is not a continuation of Judaism, and has no right to the promises of God to Israel. The Church is not looking for a kingdom on earth, but is waiting and longing for the Bridegroom from heaven, and will reign with Christ over the millennial earth.

The Thessalonians had embraced faith in Jesus as the Christ of God (Acts 17:3); they had accepted Christ as the Son of the one true God and King of His kingdom among men—the kingdom and glory of God to which He is calling believers from all races (I Thess. 2:12). When the Gentile bride is taken out of all peoples the Lord Jesus will return and build again the tabernacle of David. He will sit on the throne of David, and the knowledge of the Lord will cover the earth as the waters now cover the sea. There will be peace on earth, good will toward men; but this can happen only when Jesus returns for His Church, and that is the event for which the believers at Thessalonica are waiting. Study Acts 15:13–18, and you will find a clear blueprint of God's program for this age and His program to immediately follow the day of grace.

I Corinthians 15:1–5 clearly outlines Paul's message to whomsoever He preached: the death, burial, resurrection and ascension of the man Christ Jesus—and in the latter part of the same chapter, His coming again at the last trump, "in the twinkling of an eye." Jesus returned to heaven that He might receive His kingdom and return. (Read Luke 19:12 and Acts 3:21.) *He will return* to judge and reward the faithful servants of God, giving to each his due reward for faithful stewardship; and to render vengeance and judgment upon the oppressors and persecutors of the saints (II Thess. 1:5–10).

This was the theme of the message delivered by Paul and Silas at Thessalonica. The believers in that church looked for the return of the Lord Jesus in His second coming. That firm belief was a chief part of their religion and their hope. They were in truth "like unto men who wait for their lord, when he will return from the wedding" (Luke 12:36).

The Bible definition of true Christianity is *one who*

has trusted the Lord Jesus Christ by faith, depending totally and entirely upon His shed blood for the remission of sins; and since sins are forgiven, divine nature is possessed in the inner man. A true believer is one who is serving and waiting, but we are not to be star-gazers; *we are commanded to occupy until He comes!*

The believers at Thessalonica were "waiting for His Son from heaven, whom He raised from the dead." The resurrection of Jesus Christ is proof positive that He IS God's only begotten Son, ". . . declared to be the Son of God with power, according to the spirit of holiness, by the resurrection from the dead" (Rom. 1:4).

The resurrection of the Lord Jesus from the dead assures His future kingdom that He will be king and the righteous Judge, "whereof (God) hath given assurance unto all men, in that He hath raised Him from the dead" (Acts 17:31). The resurrection of the Lord Jesus from the dead was the seal of the message of the Apostle Paul. (Study carefully I Corinthians 15:3–14; I Peter 1:3–5; Acts 2:32–36; Acts 3:13–21.) Jesus said, "Destroy this temple and in three days I will raise it up." Three days after He was buried He arose from the dead; He was exalted as God's Son—alive forevermore; and this Saviour, Lord of all things in heaven and in earth (Eph. 1:20–22), who tasted death for all men, who conquered him who had the fear of death, *this same Jesus*, in this same position and character, *will return*. He promised— and He cannot lie (Heb. 6:18; Titus 1:2). He will return with His Father's glory and with His holy angels, to render unto every man according to his deeds (Matt. 16:27; Mark 8:38).

Jesus came the first time born of a virgin, with His eye singled on Calvary; He came to pay the sin-debt and give His life a ransom to purchase redemption at the tremendous price of His blood (I Peter 1:18–23). All hell could not stop Him until He said, "It is finished" (John 19:30). He came the first time on a mission and He completed that mission; but He promised, "If I go, I will come again!" (John 14:1,2). He is coming—and our salvation will never be one hundred percent complete until we have a body just like His glorified body. We will get that body when Jesus comes (I John 3:1–3).

". . . Being now justified by His blood, *we shall be saved from wrath* through Him. For if, when we were enemies, we were reconciled to God by the death of His Son, much more, being reconciled, *we shall be saved by His life*" (Rom. 5:9,10).

"For I reckon that the sufferings of this present time are not worthy to be compared with the glory which shall be revealed in us. For the earnest expectation of the creature waiteth for the manifestation of the sons of God. For the creature was made subject to vanity, not willingly, but by reason of him who hath subjected the same in hope. Because the creature itself also shall be delivered from the bondage of corruption into the glorious liberty of the children of God. For we know that the whole creation groaneth and travaileth in pain together until now. And not only they, but ourselves also, which have the firstfruits of the Spirit, even we ourselves groan within ourselves, waiting for the adoption, to wit, the redemption of our body. For we are saved by hope: but hope that is seen is not hope: for what a man seeth, why doth he yet hope for? But if we hope for that we see not, then do we with patience wait for it" (Rom. 8:18–25).

We will not receive our glorified bodies until Jesus comes in the Rapture and the first resurrection. To be absent from the body is to be present with the Lord in a conscious state with some form of spiritual body—but we will not receive our glorified bodies until He comes for us in the Rapture.

Jesus died on the cross, shed His blood to deliver us from the penalty of sin; and when we accept Him as our personal Saviour we are delivered from that *penalty*. Day by day, through His grace and power, we are also kept and delivered from the POWER of sin (I Cor. 10:13; Heb. 13:5,6). Finally, when Jesus comes in the Rapture we will be delivered from *the very PRESENCE* of sin (I Thess. 4:13–18; I John 3:1,2). We are justified by His blood, reconciled to God through His death, and we shall be saved from God's wrath when Jesus comes to make up His jewels . . . when He catches the true Church up in the clouds in the air to meet Him, where we will sit down at the marriage supper.

Believers are not children of wrath. We are not appointed unto wrath, but to obtain full, complete and final salvation—soul, spirit and body. God is angry with the wicked every day. God decreed, "The soul that sinneth, it shall surely die," and *God has not changed His mind about sin*. His anger against sin has not abated, but is like a giant wave of the sea, rising continually until it reaches its full height, then breaking in upon the beaches of humanity, upon those who have hated God's Christ and rejected His blood in remission of their sins (II Thess. 2:11, 12; Rom. 1:18–28).

In Colossians 2:10 Paul guarantees, "Ye are complete in Him." The Gospel Paul preached guaranteed full, free and *complete* salvation. The death, burial, resurrection and return of Jesus was his message; the cross was the center, soul and the heart of his preaching. Apart from the blood there is no redemption of the soul and no final deliverance for the body. God the Father blesses us with all spiritual blessings, but only in the finished work of the Son of His love.

I THESSALONIANS — CHAPTER TWO

1. For yourselves, brethren, know our entrance in unto you, that it was not in vain:

2. But even after that we had suffered before, and were shamefully entreated, as ye know, at Philippi, we were bold in our God to speak unto you the gospel of God with much contention.

3. For our exhortation was not of deceit, nor of uncleanness, nor in guile:

4. But as we were allowed of God to be put in trust with the gospel, even so we speak; not as pleasing men, but God, which trieth our hearts.

5. For neither at any time used we flattering words, as ye know, nor a cloke of covetousness; God is witness:

6. Nor of men sought we glory, neither of you, nor yet of others, when we might have been burdensome, as the apostles of Christ.

7. But we were gentle among you, even as a nurse cherisheth her children:

8. So being affectionately desirous of you, we were willing to have imparted unto you, not the gospel of God only, but also our own souls, because ye were dear unto us.

9. For ye remember, brethren, our labour and travail: for labouring night and day, because we would not be chargeable unto any of you, we preached unto you the gospel of God.

10. Ye are witnesses, and God also, how holily and justly and unblameably we behaved ourselves among you that believe:

11. As ye know how we exhorted and comforted and charged every one of you, as a father doth his children,

12. That ye would walk worthy of God, who hath called you unto his kingdom and glory.

13. For this cause also thank we God without ceasing, because, when ye received the word of God which ye heard of us, ye received it not as the word of men, but as it is in truth, the word of God, which effectually worketh also in you that believe.

14. For ye, brethren, became followers of the churches of God which in Judaea are in Christ Jesus: for ye also have suffered like things of your own countrymen, even as they have of the Jews:

15. Who both killed the Lord Jesus, and their own prophets, and have persecuted us; and they please not God, and are contrary to all men:

16. Forbidding us to speak to the Gentiles that they might be saved, to fill up their sins alway: for the wrath is come upon them to the uttermost.

17. But we, brethren, being taken from you for a short time in presence, not in heart, endeavoured the more abundantly to see your face with great desire.

18. Wherefore we would have come unto you, even I Paul, once and again; but Satan hindered us.

19. For what is our hope, or joy, or crown of rejoicing? Are not even ye in the presence of our Lord Jesus Christ at his coming?

20. For ye are our glory and joy.

The ministry of Paul, Silas and Timothy in Thessalonica had been genuine and successful. The boldness with which these ministers delivered their message, and the boldness with which the believers demonstrated their faith in Christ as preached by Paul and his co-workers, proved that their labor was not in vain. The believers in the church at Thessalonica can be described in four words: *Courage, purity, love* and *fidelity*. They had unusual courage; they lived lives of unusual purity; they demonstrated extraordinary love and fidelity.

Verse 1: "For yourselves, brethren, know our entrance in unto you, that it was not in vain."

The term "*entrance in*" is the same term as the "entering in" used in chapter 1:9; and the "*for*" in this verse is parallel to the same word found in chapter 1:9. That is, "What '*they themselves*' (other peoples, strangers, throughout the countryside) report concerning your faith, love and stewardship is confirmed by what YOU yourselves know." The Gospel had successfully entered into Thessalonica and had overcome the forces of evil in the lives of many idolaters and others. Everything said from chapter 1:4 through chapter 2:1 is divine proof that God had chosen the Thessalonians to become a part of His Church; even though they were Gentiles they were not excluded; even though they were idolaters, sinners of a baser sort, God had chosen them unto salvation.

Concerning "our entrance unto you"—that is, "the message of the Gospel we brought unto you"—the believers at Thessalonica knew better than anyone else on earth that that message had *not* been in vain, for it had completely transformed their lives and had brought about *a settled result*—which is the meaning of the Greek language here. Not only did the message Paul delivered produce a striking and powerful impression at the time of delivery, but since receiving the message they had proved by their lives that they had truly been born of the Spirit into the family of God. The fruit they were producing was proof positive because it was permanent fruit.

"Vain" in verse 1 literally means *empty*, or *void of miracle-working power*; and if the tempter had destroyed the faith of the Thessalonians, then Paul's preaching *would have been empty* and their faith would have been vain. Paul declared to the Corinthians that if Christ be not raised from the dead, then his preaching was vain and their faith was also vain (I Cor. 15:14); but Christ WAS raised from the dead, and Paul said he saw Him last of all "as one born out of due season." Paul knew the reality of the resurrection in his own life, and he preached it with such power that those who heard him could not doubt the sincerity of the message. His message was not empty and powerless; but rather, his preaching was in the demonstration of the power of the Holy Spirit.

This verse might be rendered, "For you know of yourselves, brethren, that our coming amongst you has not proved vain." To me, this is clear, positive, unmistakable teaching of personal assurance. Any person who is not sure beyond a shadow of doubt that he is born again has been given a counterfeit by the devil. The power of the Gospel of the resurrection in the life of an individual produces assurance that cannot be denied by the individual nor by those with whom he has to do.

Verse 2: "But even after that we had suffered before, and were shamefully entreated, as ye know, at Philippi, we were bold in our God to speak unto you the Gospel of God with much contention."

The Greek reads, "Having suffered before and been shamefully entreated," or "Though we had already suffered and were shamefully treated at Philippi." What Paul is saying is this: "In spite of the treatment we received in other places for preaching the message of the cross, the burial and the resurrection of Jesus; in spite of it all, we preached it unto you at Thessalonica also." "Spitefully entreated" or "shamefully entreated" is one word in the Greek, meaning *outraged*. It implies insult and injury combined. It goes so far as to imply injury that would be classified as a legal crime against the one injured.

When Paul and Silas were arrested, beaten and thrown into the dungeon at Philippi, they prayed at midnight—and God answered by opening all doors in the prison and loosing all the bands from all the prisoners. The Philippian jailer was saved, received Paul and Silas into his home and fed them at midnight after this tremendous demonstration in the power of the Gospel. The magistrates then requested that Paul and Silas leave the city; but Paul said, "They have beaten us publicly—uncondemned, being Romans . . . let them come themselves and fetch us out" (Acts 16:37). Paul felt this insult very keenly because he was a freeborn Roman citizen.

In verse 2 of our present chapter Paul said, "*As ye know*," signifying that the believers at Thessalonica were aware of the treatment he and Silas had received at Philippi. (Thessalonica was only three days' journey from Philippi, and even in that day news traveled rapidly, no doubt reaching Thessalonica long before Paul arrived there.)

We will never know the impact this news had upon the hearts of the idolaters in Thessalonica, even before this unusual minister reached their shores. It could be that some of the Thessalonians thought that Paul would preach with fear and trembling, but Paul declares, *"We were bold in our God* to speak unto you the Gospel of God with much contention!"* Paul feared no power or person save the God who saved him, called him and ordained him. God pity a preacher who professes to be called of God, but approaches the pulpit with fear and trembling because of men!

". . . To speak unto you the Gospel of God with much contention." The conflict Paul and Silas encountered at Philippi followed them to Thessalonica in another form. Satan did not stand idly by and let these spiritual giants move into his territory to deliver the powerful message that transformed the lives of the fortune teller, the elite lady Lydia, and the Philippian jailer. Paul's first missionary journeys in that part of Europe were difficult times; the struggle was great between the powers of evil and the power of God. The Gospel found footing in many cities—but only after much conflict. Paul was not a bully, he was not extraordinarily bold within himself; he said, "We were bold *in our God.*" God's minister always wins when his boldness is in God, for God will never let His servant down; but if we are bold in the flesh, anything can happen. Romans 8:28 and 31 are ours to claim.

Jesus said to His disciples, "It is not YE that speak, but the Spirit of your Father that speaketh in you . . . FEAR THEM NOT THEREFORE" (Matt. 10:16–32).

Paul preached the Gospel of God. God gave him the message, and the God who called him and gave him the message also gave him boldness with which to proclaim it. The fact that Paul *knew* God had called him, ordained him, sent him, and had given him the message is the secret of his boldness and spiritual heroism.

Verse 3: "For our exhortation was not of deceit, nor of uncleanness, nor in guile."

What Paul is saying in this verse is simply this: "We—Paul, Silas and Timothy—preached the Gospel fearlessly at Thessalonica because our ministry was free from all that is false, impure and in error. We delivered the pure truth in every detail of our teaching, and that fact is the secret of our fearlessness and boldness." Men who *know* the truth, who *hold and declare* the truth, are brave men in any walk of life—and especially so in the spiritual realm.

The word *"exhortation"* in verse 3 hardly conveys Paul's full meaning . . . "our *appeal"* is perhaps better. "The appeal to the Thessalonians," said Paul, "is not of error. What we are preaching is not the product of dissension or illusion, for THE GOSPEL OF GOD is truly THE WORD OF THE TRUTH OF THE GOSPEL (Col. 1:5), because I personally received it and know the power thereof in my own life" (I Thess. 2:2). Paul could never have been made to doubt what he experienced, both on the Damascus road and when Ananias came to him at the bidding of the heavenly Father. He never once doubted the light from heaven that met him on the road to Damascus, nor the voice he heard saying—first, "This is Jesus whom thou persecutest," and later, "Depart, for I will send thee far hence unto the Gentiles" (Acts 22:21).

This experience and these instructions caused Paul to say, "I KNOW WHOM I HAVE BELIEVED!" (II Tim.

1:12). Paul experienced assurance of heart and preached it wherever he went. He was sure that the message he had from God was genuine, and he was conscious of the *purity of his motives* in preaching the Gospel—not for the sake of filthy lucre "nor in uncleanness." Vainglory and self-seeking on the part of a minister makes his testimony corrupt (I Thess. 2:5). Paul was not guilty of such.

In I Peter 1:22 we read, ". . . Ye have purified your souls in obeying the truth." Truth and purity go together; they promote and guard each other. Paul speaks in II Thessalonians 2:10 of the "deceivableness of unrighteousness." In I Timothy 6:5 he speaks of "men of corrupt minds, and destitute of the truth, supposing that gain is godliness." Paul's motive was pure and therefore he could face God and the people to whom he preached with a clear conscience and a bold heart.

The last part of verse 3 has to do with Paul's *method*. As his motive was pure, so was his method: ". . . *nor in guile*." Here he is saying the same thing he said in II Corinthians 4:2: ". . . Not walking in craftiness, nor handling the word of God deceitfully; but by manifestation of the truth commending ourselves to every man's conscience in the sight of God."

God's servant dare not use any weapon except the sword of the Spirit, which is the Word of God—the truth (Rom. 8:32; John 14:6). No doubt Paul's enemies in Thessalonica accused him of guile. In Corinth his enemies accused him of being crafty: ". . . Being crafty (as they say) I caught you with guile" (II Cor. 12:16).

Verse 3 can be summed up as follows: Paul declared that his doctrine was true, not mixed with error; his motives were pure, not selfish or self-centered. Whether he ate or drank—or whatsoever he did—it was all to God's glory and not his own. His conduct in all things at all times was straightforward; he had nothing to hide.

Verse 4: "But as we were allowed of God to be put in trust with the Gospel, even so we speak; not as pleasing men, but God, which trieth our hearts."

The Greek language here means, "As we have been approved by God to be entrusted." The word *"allow"* in older English bears the stronger sense of *accept*, but even so, falls short of the meaning of Paul. This same Greek word is used in I Thessalonians 5:21, where Paul says, "Prove all things; hold fast that which is good." The same word is used again in I Corinthians 3:13: ". . . The fire shall try (prove) every man's work of what sort it is." The Greek word includes proving and *approving* on trial—or testing. Paul had been put to the test; God counted him worthy—and entrusted unto him the message of salvation by grace through faith in the finished work of Jesus in His death, burial and resurrection.

Study I Timothy 1:12 and you will readily see that Paul had been tested *for* his work, tested *by* his work, *God had approved him* as a minister of Christ, and he was worthy of His trust. "To be put in trust with the Gospel" is the highest honor that could be placed upon any man; it also carries the highest conceivable responsibility that could rest upon any human being. A minister who has been called of God to preach the Gospel should be very careful to exclude every impure motive and deceitful practice concerning his ministry of the Gospel. Concerning Paul's trust and the Gospel, study carefully I Timothy 1:12–17 and Acts 9:15 and 16. "He is a chosen vessel unto Me . . . ." Therefore Paul says, "So we speak," with a deep sense of the solemn trust God placed in him.

"Not as pleasing men, but God, which trieth our hearts." Paul was concerned, not with pleasing the people to whom he preached, but pleasing God, who had

called, ordained and sent him to preach—God, who tries the hearts, proves the hearts and rewards in righteousness.

The statement, *"God, which trieth our hearts,"* is an Old Testament expression declaring a standing, undeniable attribute of Jehovah God. Read Psalm 17:3, Jeremiah 11:20—and Acts 1:24, which says, "Thou, Lord, which knowest the hearts of all men . . . ." In the Bible the heart is not only the seat of feelings and emotions; it is also *the inner man.* The heart denotes the real self— the center (the meeting point) of all thoughts, feelings and issues of life. Men judge us from outward appearances, but God looks on the heart.

Paul knew God was continually watching and listening—knowing his every thought, his every move; and this fact caused dishonesty, guile and selfishness to be completely erased from his mind, heart and practices (I Cor. 4:1–5; II Cor. 5:9–12). "He that judgeth me is the Lord" (I Cor. 4:4). God called Paul, gave him a message and the boldness with which to preach it. God would be his judge, so why should he fear any man? Why should he be selfish or dishonest in any way? He was a servant of God—not of man!

It was Paul who said, "My God shall supply all your need." It was Paul who said, "God will never leave us nor forsake us, that we may boldly say, The Lord is my helper, and I shall not fear what man may do unto me." Paul and Silas preached the Gospel God had entrusted to them; God gave them strength and courage to preach the message with boldness. Therefore, the utmost desire of their hearts was God's approval. They must give an account to HIM and not to man. Men such as the magistrates in Philippi who arrested and beat them without a cause, hoping to silence them, did not alter their boldness nor their message.

The magistrates and authorities in the city of Jerusalem charged Peter and John "not to speak at all nor teach in the name of Jesus. But Peter and John answered and said unto them, Whether it be right in the sight of God to hearken unto you more than unto God, judge ye" (Acts 4:18,19). Men with this conviction, knowing the sovereignty and power of God, knowing that they are delivering God's message, give Christianity its rightful place among all religions. Christianity is the cap stone of the pyramid of all religions. There is only one pure religion that will stand the test of righteous judgment, and that religion is *Christianity*. The only way to become a Christian is by receiving the Christ—crucified, buried, risen and coming again. Such conviction as was held in the hearts of Paul, Silas, Timothy, John and others gives men the boldness to become martyrs for the message of the cross.

Ministers who seek only to please men are enemies of the men whom they please. The dirtiest thief this side of hell is a preacher who compromises the Gospel and allows people to go to hell under his preaching—when, *if he would preach the whole truth*, that truth would set men free! Paul "pleased all men in all things . . . for the profit of many, that they may be saved" (I Cor. 10:33; Rom. 15:2). When we please men in any way that displeases God, it is to man's destruction. Paul said, "If (under such circumstances) I pleased men, I should not be the servant of Christ" (Gal. 1:10).

To be a slave to public opinion is not to be the servant of God, whether it be in ignorance or whatsoever. If we are the servants of God we are His bondservants (or slaves); we are His, to do His will. God pity some ministers when they stand before Him to give an account of their stewardship in preaching the Gospel. A minister called of God, sincere in heart and loyal to God, will never fear the audience before which which he stands.

Verse 5: "For neither at any time used we flattering words, as ye know, nor a cloke of covetousness; God is witness."

Paul never used flattering words. He could have; he was one of the best educated men of his day; but he never used enticing words of man's wisdom, never flattered the people to whom he preached. The Thessalonians KNEW that Paul preached in words easily understood, in straightforward language with no frills on his words. He preached with boldness and in terms that could be understood by his hearers.

Note that in verse 5 he called *the believers* at Thessalonica to witness that he did not preach in flattering language; but when declaring that he did not wear a cloke of covetousness, *he calls GOD to the witness stand.* Paul uses this term on other occasions: "God is my witness, whom I serve with my spirit in the Gospel of His Son . . ." (Rom. 1:9). Notice also Romans 2:15 and 9:1.

In verse 4 of our present study Paul refers to God as the one "which trieth our hearts." Since God tries the hearts, then God knew *Paul's* heart; and Paul calls Him to witness that his preaching was not tainted with covetousness. The Greek word here signifies greed of any nature, but primarily for money or for the sake of filthy lucre. Covetousness is a passion and denotes selfishness—or the act of being self-centered . . . selfishness to the point where one would defraud (I Thess. 4:6). Certainly covetousness in the heart of a minister of God would lead him into uncleanness from many standpoints.

Verse 5 gives double evidence that Paul's zeal for God was pure—first *outward* (from his lips), and then *inward* (from his heart). God knew Paul's heart, and Paul was willing for God to testify in defense of the motives of his heart and lips. The Psalmist refers to one having "a flattering lip and a double heart" (Psalm 12:2).

Verse 6: "Nor of men sought we glory, neither of you, nor yet of others, when we might have been burdensome, as the apostles of Christ."

This is a continuation of the thought in verse 5. Paul is saying, "We were not seeking glory of men when we came to Thessalonica; neither sought we glory from you after we arrived, nor from others." While on earth, speaking to His own people Jesus said, "How can ye believe, which receive honour one of another, and seek not the honour that cometh from God only?" (John 5:44).

It is true that they who preach the Gospel shall live by the Gospel (I Cor. 9:14); but Paul refused to be a burden to the people in Thessalonica. These people had been heathen (idol worshippers), and had Paul come into their community demonstrating the spirit that they owed him a living, I doubt if his message would have been received; certainly it would have been received much less fervently. But he proved to them by his conduct that he was not seeking praise nor material gain from them.

While Paul was in Thessalonica he did receive help from Philippi on at least two known occasions, which he gratefully remembered and referred to in his epistle to that church (Phil. 4:15,16). Later, in the city of Corinth, he permitted contributions to be sent to him from Macedonia (II Cor. 11:9). But in the outset of his ministry to the Gentiles he refused to be a burden. He labored untiringly with his hands to provide food and raiment for himself; and he preached the Gospel freely, willingly, unselfishly, without covetousness. In so doing he proved to these people that his message was truth in reality.

God forbid that I judge or that I hurt anyone—but today I am afraid some ministers demonstrate the attitude that the world owes them a living—not only a living, but that it be presented to them on a silver platter in an air-conditioned parsonage! Paul was very careful—today we might accuse him of being a bit fanatical—in that he refused to be a burden to anyone; and he was extremely careful lest his attitude and practices of life bring reproach on the Gospel. May God help us as ministers to pattern our ministries after this great man of God.

Verse 7: "But we were gentle among you, even as a nurse cherisheth her children."

The deep meaning of this verse is that Paul demonstrated the love, gentleness and devotion of a mother toward her child—for here the term "nurse" goes further than a hired nurse or custodian of a child; it is a picture of a babe on a mother's breast. Paul is pouring from his heart the same feeling shown by Jesus when He wept over the holy city: "O Jerusalem, Jerusalem, thou that killest the prophets, and stonest them which are sent unto thee, how often would I have gathered thy children together, even as a hen gathereth her chickens under her wings . . ." (Matt. 3:37).

Paul did not mean that he mixed and mingled with the believers in Thessalonica in a baby-like way, speaking baby talk . . . *not at all*! He is setting forth here the love, devotion and tenderness of a mother *toward* her baby. Paul was just that tender, kind and loving toward his spiritual children . . . children whom he had "begotten through the Gospel."

Verse 8: "So being affectionately desirous of you, we were willing to have imparted unto you, not the Gospel of God only, but also our own souls, because ye were dear unto us."

The one Greek word used for the three English words *"being affectionately desirous,"* has a rare depth of meaning; it implies the fondness of a mother's love yearning over her baby. It signifies such deep affection as is known on this earth only by a mother. Paul so loved the believers at Thessalonica that he would have been pleased to impart to them *his very life* had it been possible.

In Romans 9:1–3 Paul said that he would be willing to be accursed from Christ if it would save his brothers in the flesh. Paul, Silas and Timothy were not only willing to bestow themselves on the Thessalonians—but they actually DID bestow their very lives upon them, even as a mother nourishes her baby from her own life. Paul sacrificed all personal desires, all personal interests and aims for the sake of the believers in Thessalonica. He said, "What things were gain to me, those I counted loss for Christ" (Phil. 3:7). Paul was dedicated to the cause of the Gospel—soul, spirit and body. He was willing to hazard his life on behalf of the believers; he was willing to go the limit (apart from compromising the Gospel) to win men to God and help those whom he had won. He could say from his heart, "Yea, and if I be offered upon the sacrifice and service of your faith, I JOY, AND REJOICE WITH YOU ALL" (Phil. 2:17).

To the thankless, worldly-minded, divided Corinthians Paul said, "And I will very gladly spend and be spent for you; though the more abundantly I love you, the less I be loved" (II Cor. 12:15). That is the only way a true minister can impart the Gospel of God; he must give his own heart and soul with the Gospel he proclaims! To impart the Gospel in the right spirit is to follow the example set by our God, "who spared not His own Son, but delivered Him up for us all" (Rom. 8:32); and the spirit of the Son, our Christ and Saviour, who gave Himself for us (Gal. 1:4; 2:20). It was Jesus who set the example for all Gospel ministers; *He "poured out His soul unto death"* (Isaiah 53:12).

Verse 8 closes with "because ye were dear unto us."

This is the same Greek word used for "beloved," often applied to Christ in the Gospels by God the Father—as when He said, *"My beloved Son."* It is also the same word used in Ephesians 1:6: *"accepted in the beloved."* The believers at Thessalonica had won such a place of affection in the heart of Paul as has been known by few mortals—even in the ministry. They were lovable people, dear to his heart; he loved them with such love as a mother shows toward her newborn babe.

Verse 9: "For ye remember, brethren, our labour and travail: for labouring night and day, because we would not be chargeable unto any of you, we preached unto you the Gospel of God."

In chapter 1:3 Paul speaks of his thankfulness for the work of faith and labor of love rendered by the Thessalonian believers. They were walking in his steps as he had set the example before them, walking in the steps of the Lord Jesus. Paul had demonstrated a life of faith and pure love, and they followed his example.

Paul adds "travail" to "labour" in this Scripture. Note also II Thessalonians 3:8 and 9. In both places he is referring to manual labor. Paul had labored and toiled in their midst to provide his own bread and livelihood. He was a tentmaker by trade (Acts 18:3); for in Paul's day all Jewish fathers—even the most wealthy—taught their sons some trade, as a precaution against poverty and idleness. Jews love their children with exceeding devotion, and seemingly the sons are loved even more than the daughters. It is to the advantage of those sons that they be taught some trade; and Paul was a tentmaker.

In Paul's day tents were made from cloth of goat's hair, and this was very hard work—far different from tent-making today. Our tents are made of canvas stitched on electric machines; but Paul sewed the goat's-hair cloth by hand, and it was an irksome, difficult task, with no elaborate rate of pay. I do not doubt that Paul's hands were calloused and rough from such labor (Acts 20:23), but through it he earned for himself the necessities of life and avoided being a burden to the infant churches he founded and to whom he ministered during the days of his earthly sojourn. Thus he delivered himself from much mean criticism since he did provide his own livelihood and took nothing from the young churches. Later he did receive gifts from the Philippians, but I am sure he knew that church and its members well enough to know that if he did not accept their gifts he would hurt them by his refusal. Study carefully I Corinthians 9:1–19; II Corinthians 11:7–12; Philippians 4:10–20 and Acts 20:33–35.

In this verse Paul uses the plural pronouns "our" and "we," thus denoting that Silas and Timothy are included. It does not seem that these two ministers were tentmakers, but they undoubtedly had some other means of support. In Acts 20:34 Paul speaks of "these hands," referring to his hands as ministering "to my necessities and to them that were with me." Therefore it seems that Paul probably supported not only himself through his tentmaking, but that he might also have contributed to the livelihood of Silas and Timothy.

". . . *Labouring night and day*" would indicate that Paul probably preached and taught through the daylight hours, and then far into the night plied his trade as a tentmaker.

". . . *Because we would not be chargeable unto any of you.*" What Paul is saying here is simply this: "I did not want to be a burden to any of you; therefore, in daylight hours I preached to you and taught you concerning things of the Spirit. And then, lest I burden you or lest you feel that I had come to you for material gain, I

75

provided my own livelihood by laboring with my own hands during the night hours."

Paul did not provide his own livelihood through a heart of envy nor with the attitude of "I will show you!" No, no! He supported himself because he bore such deep love for these Christians and wanted to influence them all the way in the Spirit, teaching them in the Gospel and allowing nothing to hinder their spiritual growth. Paul was quite different from some of the ministers described in Ezekiel 34:3 as false shepherds who "eat the fat and clothe them with the wool, but feed not the flock."

It is probable that most of the believers in the Thessalonian church were very poor. In the church at Philippi we know Lydia was a merchant who dealt in purple and fine linen—materials worn in that day by only kings and the elite. This would indicate that Lydia was a woman of means, and probably there were others in the church there who had material means or, as we would say today, who were "well fixed." Therefore the believers at Philippi could afford to send "once and again" to Paul's necessity (Phil. 4:15,16).

The church in Thessalonica met in the home of Jason, but we are not told whether or not he *owned* his home. It could have been a house belonging to a slaveowner or landlord. It also could be that Jason had money enough to own his home, and that that is the reason he invited the church to meet there (Acts 17:5–9). We know that there were many women in the church at Thessalonica; and although there were many others, no doubt, in the local assembly, it was—from all indications—a poor church. So Paul did here as he later did at Corinth: "Making the Gospel without expense (charge)" (I Cor. 9:18). Paul preached the Gospel of God—he heralded the good news that Jesus died for the sins of the whole world—without charge and without price.

In verse 2 of this chapter Paul mentions "the Gospel of God." Then in verse 4 he says, *"We were allowed of God to be put in trust with the Gospel."* In verse 8 he says, "We were willing to have imparted unto you, not the Gospel of God only, but also our own souls," thus referring to *the Gospel of God* three times in one chapter. In verse 2 he suggests the greatness of the ministry God had entrusted to him; in verse 9 when he refers to "the Gospel of God," he is reminding the believers at Thessalonica of the greatness of the Gospel bestowed upon them—the Gospel they had received that had turned them to God from idols, to serve the true and living God and to wait for His Son from heaven. Paul had a singular message: The Gospel that God so loved sinners that He gave His only begotten Son, permitting Jesus to die. He was buried and raised "according to the Scriptures," that we might be saved through the Gospel which is the power of God unto salvation to everyone that believeth—first to the Jew, then to the Gentile (Rom. 1:16).

Verse 10: "Ye are witnesses, and God also, how holily and justly and unblameably we behaved ourselves among you that believe."

If you will carefully note the wording of Paul's statements concerning himself as a believer, he never demonstrates self-righteousness nor a holier-than-thou spirit. Note that in verse 10 he says, "YE are witnesses," and then he assures them that *God also* is his witness. Not only did the *Christians* watch his daily living among them, but *GOD* also witnessed every move he made. In the same chapter, in verse 5, he refers to the witness of man (man looks on the outward appearance), but he also mentions the witness of God (who looks on the heart). So twice in this chapter Paul calls the believers at Thessalonica and the sovereign God of heaven to witness concerning his conduct in that city.

God have mercy on those of us today who are ministers of the Gospel, if we do not live above reproach—blameless lives, setting an example of holiness before those to whom we minister! Paul says to the church, "You are witnesses to the life of holiness and righteousness we lived before you, how that we lived and behaved unblameably (not *sinless*, but *without blame*). You observed our blameless living day by day."

"Without holiness no man shall see God" (Heb. 12:14). The holiness referred to here must come from God through the blood applied to the heart of the believer. No one can, by his own labor or right living, produce holiness that will allow entrance into the presence of a holy God; such holiness comes only through the shed blood of Jesus. Christ is made unto us wisdom, righteousness, sanctification and redemption—and *without Jesus* we will never stand in the presence of God to hear Him say, "Well done."

The Greek Lexicon says, "The word 'holy' in verse 10 is not the ordinary New Testament word for holy—*hagios*; i.e., *saint*. This sainthood is not an attainment; it is a state in which God in grace calls men." That is grace imparted, and denotes the relationship to God. But the word used here for "holy" is *hosios*, and the lexicon gives this definition as "pure from evil conduct, and in I Thessalonians 2:10 is used of the conduct of the apostle and his fellow missionaries."

Holiness (*the holy man*) has regard to sanctities; but the *righteous man* has to do with the duties of life. Duty as having to do with God and righteousness is sacred. Piety is duty! The two cover the entire field of Christian conduct as having to do with the believer while journeying here on earth. I Thessalonians 3:13: "To the end He may stablish your hearts unblameable in holiness before God, even our Father, at the coming of our Lord

Jesus Christ with all His saints." I Thessalonians 5:23: "And the very God of peace sanctify you wholly; and I pray God your whole spirit and soul and body be preserved blameless unto the coming of our Lord Jesus Christ." One who is blameless has the seal of approval from both God and man.

Verse 11: "As ye know how we exhorted and comforted and charged every one of you, as a father doth his children."

In verse 7 Paul compared himself to a nurse-mother—tender, gentle, loving, kind, affectionate, long-suffering; but now he refers to himself as dealing with the Thessalonians as a father deals with his children—thus signifying strength, counsel, fidelity and manly manners. In I Corinthians 4:14—21 he gives a different message of admonition, writing to his sons in the Lord—not to shame them, but rather to warn them. Read those verses carefully.

While Paul's message to the believers at Thessalonica was a message of consolation, it was also a message of admonition. The believers in the church there were suffering persecutions and temptations, and Paul desired to send them the message they most needed— a message that would encourage them and lead them on into deeper experiences in their spiritual life.

The statement "every one of you" in the Greek reads, "*each single one*," denoting Paul's deep love for each individual. Read II Thessalonians 1:3 and Acts 20:20. My prayer today is, "O, God, give us more pastors with the kind of love for the church that Paul had for the churches God used him to establish!"

Verse 12: "That ye would walk worthy of God, who hath called you into His kingdom and glory."

"*Walk*" is a very common Hebrew term or figure that

denotes conduct of daily living. Paul delivered God's message to the Thessalonians concerning *the walk of a true believer.* In our same chapter, verses 2 and 9, Paul reminds the believers of his *own* persecution and suffering for the Gospel, and admonishes them to follow him even as he followed in the footsteps of Jesus. He reminds them that since they turned to the living God from their dead idols, they must now walk *worthy* of the true and living God. They must not stand in the way of sinners nor sit in the seat of the scornful; and if eating meat offends a weaker brother, then they should abstain from meats. In other words, whether they eat or drink, or whatsoever they do—they should do it all to the glory of God. To *walk worthy of God* should be the deep desire of every believer, for thus is fulfilled the noblest possible ideal of the Christian life . . . a life so high that it would appear visionary and impracticable, if it were not for what follows:

"Walk worthy of God, *who hath called you unto His kingdom and glory.*" This is a call that continues until its purpose is accomplished (Phil. 1:6). Such is the confidence of "you that believe," and this conviction gives the believer the will and courage to aspire to the loftiest moral attainments. "Faithful is He that calleth you, who also will do it" (I Thess. 5:24). God's call could not be purposeless or powerless.

The announcement of the kingdom of God was a leading feature of Paul's preaching in Thessalonica. Read II Thessalonians 1:5. Paul also referred to the kingdom as "the kingdom of the Son" (Col. 1:13); then, "of Christ and God" (Eph. 5:5).

Matthew's Gospel refers to a kingdom on earth—"the kingdom of heaven." Similar terms are found in Daniel 2:44,45; 7:13,14 and in Micah 4:7. These prophets prophesied concerning the coming kingdom and the throne of

David (Luke 1:32). Study carefully the seventh chapter of II Samuel and also Psalm 2. There will be a kingdom on earth; Jesus will sit on the throne of David; the knowledge of the Lord will cover the earth as the waters now cover the sea, and there will be peace on earth, good will toward men (Isaiah 9:6,7; Luke 1).

In the eternal ages God will display the exceeding riches of His grace in us, the New Testament Church (Eph. 2:6,7). Paul is admonishing the believers at Thessalonica (and also you and me) that since the voice of God has called us into His glorious kingdom, we certainly should walk worthy of the God who called us and saved us.

The Bible proof of true conversion is clearly and unmistakably demonstrated in the lives of the Thessalonians. They heard the Gospel; they turned to God— thus automatically turning from idols to serve Him and to wait for His Son from heaven. ". . . The grace of God that bringeth salvation hath appeared to all men, teaching us that, denying ungodliness and worldly lusts, we should live soberly, righteously, and godly, in this present world; looking for that blessed hope, and the glorious appearing of the great God and our Saviour Jesus Christ" (Titus 2:11—13).

Verse 13: "For this cause also thank we God without ceasing, because, when ye received the word of God which ye heard of us, ye received it not as the word of men, but as it is in truth, the word of God, which effectually worketh also in you that believe."

At this time in the Apostle's Gentile mission he was being severely persecuted by unbelieving Jews. Study Acts, chapters 16, 17 and 18, and you will see that Paul suffered bitterly and unmercifully because of his ministry to the Gentiles. Paul's manner of reference to the Jews in verses 15 and 16 of our present chapter indicates that he feels they are doomed as a nation. In Romans, chapters 9, 10 and 11, he speaks of "Israel after the flesh," declaring that God had not forgotten them, but had cut them off as a nation—and the Gentile wild olive branch has been grafted in. He also sounds a solemn warning to the Gentiles that, if God spared not the natural branches, woe be unto the wild branches! However, in I Thessalonians 2:14 Paul pleads for unity between Jewish and Gentile believers. He preached that Jew or Gentile, bond or free, *all are one in the Lord Jesus.*

In spite of the bitter persecution from the Jews, Paul again commends the believers at Thessalonica and thanks God for their wholehearted reception of the Gospel of the grace of God. The fact that they faithfully endured the terrible persecution of the Jews, and in the face of such tribulation had locked arms with other Judaean churches, was positive proof that their faith was genuine. Paul then denounces the Jews in unmistakable terms because they opposed the Gospel, and warns them that their punishment is sure.

In verse 13 he declares that he and his co-workers continually thank God that the Thessalonian Christians received the Word—not as the word of man . . . not as the words of Paul, Silas and Timothy—but as the Word of the sovereign God. Paul had positive proof that they HAD received his message as God's very Word, because that Word was operating in them. He knew that no power on earth could have transformed these idolaters into the lovely Christians they had become, which transformation shone forth day by day in every aspect of life.

The *work of faith and labour of love* Paul so admired in the believers at Thessalonica (chapter 1:3) was the work of the Word of God in their hearts. That Word had taken root in their hearts, and their every move, word and deed had been affected by it. The Word brought forth love, faith, energy and blameless living. Luke 8:11 tells us that "THE SEED" of Christian fruit and Christian stewardship is "THE WORD OF GOD."

The Word of God is also the *power of God* unto salvation when we believe it (Rom. 1:16; John 5:24); but when we *reject* the Word of God, then that Word will stand to judge us (John 12:48). We will never know this side of eternity the importance of God's holy Word. No wonder the devil is trying to destroy and discredit the Word today!

Believers produce fruit. *"Faith without works is dead."* Life *produces* . . . it is impossible to keep life FROM producing; it may be thirty, it may be sixty, it may be a hundredfold—but where there is life, there is production. The Word of God brings life, and the Word working in the believer produces fruit. Paul *saw that fruit* in the believers at Thessalonica.

Verse 14: "For ye, brethren, became followers of the churches of God which in Judaea are in Christ Jesus: for ye also have suffered like things of your own countrymen, even as they have of the Jews."

Here the word *"followers"* should have been translated *"imitators."* Just as in chapter 1:6 they were imitators of Paul and of his Lord, the Thessalonians were also imitating the churches in Judaea, and willingly endured suffering for the Word's sake. This reference to the home churches creates a link between far-off Thessalonica and Judaea. The Thessalonians were not alone in their troubles; they were fighting the same battle as were the Judaean churches and the first disciples of our Lord.

". . . *Which in Judaea are in Christ Jesus.*" Judaea marks the locale, but *in Christ Jesus* marks the spiritual

83

place of these churches. The Thessalonian converts were also in Christ Jesus; they were members of the true Church, His body. They were in union and communion with the true Church; they were incorporated into the Church of which Jesus is the head (Eph. 5:25–30).

These Christians were suffering at the hands of their own countrymen (Acts 17:5–9). Paul tells them that the same was true in the early churches in Judaea— that indeed, due to feelings precisely similar to those aroused in their city against themselves, the Lord Jesus and the prophets of old were persecuted and killed by *their* own countrymen. This proved that the Thessalonian church was a true church, because it was suffering the same bitter opposition from Satan that the prophets, Jesus and the Judaean churches had suffered. Jesus had said, "A man's foes shall be they of his own household." Paul spoke the words of verse 14 to the Thessalonians to comfort them in their hour of bitter suffering for the sake of the Gospel.

It must indeed have grieved the heart of the Apostle Paul to refer to the Jews, his own brothers in the flesh, as he did in the last part of verse 14, and then to again be constrained to set forth their horrible crime against the Lord Jesus:

Verse 15: "Who both killed the Lord Jesus, and their own prophets, and have persecuted us; and they please not God, and are contrary to all men."

The Lord Jesus, while here on earth, represented His own death as the last of the murders of the ancient prophets. Study carefully Luke 11:47–52; 13:31–33; 20:9–16. Stephen, the first deacon—full of faith and full of the Holy Ghost—preached a sermon that stirred to anger the hearts of the ungodly haters of the Gospel, and they stoned him. (At that time, Paul was Saul of

Tarsus, and the murderers of Stephen laid their coats at his feet as he consented unto the death of God's first deacon.) But Paul heard Stephen when he said, "Which of the prophets have not your fathers persecuted? and they have slain them which shewed before of the coming of the Just One; of whom ye have been now the betrayers and murderers" (Acts 7:52).

Paul now says "Amen!" to what Jesus said, and "Amen!" to what Stephen said; and by so doing he is saying that his own people murdered Jesus. What he is literally saying is that *the Jews killed their Lord, even Jesus*—and this sets the deed in an appalling light. They killed *the Lord*, who bore a title that belongs to God. I Corinthians 2:8 tells us, ". . . Which none of the princes of this world knew: *for had they known it, they would not have crucified the Lord of glory*!" The Lord whom they crucified was Jesus, their Saviour: "Neither is there salvation in any other: for there is none other name under heaven given among men, whereby we must be saved" (Acts 4:12). They crucified the One of whom it is said, "God hath made that same Jesus, whom ye have crucified, both Lord and Christ" (Acts 2:36). Read also Luke 20:9–18; Mark 12:1–11. The husbandmen said, "This is the heir. Come, let us kill Him."

They killed their prophets, they killed their Lord and Saviour, "and," Paul continues, "they have persecuted US." The literal Greek suggests, "*They drove us out.*" They did the same thing to Paul that they did to Jesus. Luke 11:49: "Therefore also said the wisdom of God, I will send them prophets and apostles, and some of them they shall slay and persecute." Matthew 23:34 also tells us that the apostles were driven out and forced to flee from city to city to avoid being murdered by the same angry Jewish haters of the Lord Jesus. Read also Acts 9:28–30; 12:1–9; and the entire chapters of Acts

21, 22 and 23. These Scriptures describe the persecution which the apostles endured for the sake of the Gospel. Jesus said, "If they hated me, they will hate you"—*and they did*! The hostile Jews followed Paul and Silas all the way from Philippi to the city of Corinth; and had it not been for the Roman governor Gallio (Acts 18:12–17), Paul would not have been allowed to remain in Corinth, for he, too, was "in perils from mine own countrymen." Read II Corinthians 11:26.

"*. . . And they please not God . . . .*" The Jews were not pleasing Jehovah in their actions against the prophets, against the Lord Jesus and against the apostles, which fact was not due to these acts alone, but to their whole conduct. In the days of Isaiah Jehovah said, concerning rebellious Israel, "These are a smoke in my nose, a fire that burneth all the day" (Isa. 65:5). Jeremiah 32:30 tells us that the people of Israel did that which was evil continually in the sight of God.

"*. . . And are contrary to men . . . .*" They were at war with both men and God. The sense of God's displeasure often shows itself in sourness and ill temper toward one's fellowman. Unbelief and cynicism go together. The rancor of the Jews at this time was notorious. Paul is thinking, however, not of the Jewish hatred in general, but of the opposition of his people to the rest of the world on that one point that concerned him so deeply—*the salvation of men through Christ.*

Verse 16: "Forbidding us to speak to the Gentiles that they might be saved, to fill up their sins alway: for the wrath is come upon them to the uttermost."

Paul is saying here that if the Jews had their way, every Gentile on earth would burn in hell. Certainly the statement in verse 16 stamped the Jews as enemies of the entire human race. They were furious because unclean

86

Gentile dogs claimed a share in their Messiah. They hated Paul enough to murder him—and would have done so had not God taken care of him. Paul said, "I suffer these things for the Gospel's sake." They hated him because he declared that God was the God of the Jews—and of the Gentiles also; that there was neither Jew nor Greek, rich nor poor, bond nor free in God's sight. All are ONE in the New Testament Church.

In their anger against him they would have torn him to bits or burned him at the stake had God not protected him. A minister called of God, ordained of God and sent by God with God's message—faithfully proclaiming that message—*is indestructible until God is through with him*! The devil cannot kill him, nor can all the demons in hell stop him.

In Acts 22:21–23 Paul was giving his defense testimony in the temple, and during the course of that testimony said, "And (God) said unto me, Depart, for I will send thee far hence unto the Gentiles." When Paul said this, the Jews broke out in a demented, uncontrollable rage, "*lifted up their voices and said, Away with such a fellow from the earth; for it is not fit that he should live!*"

It seems that the Jews at Thessalonica were extremely mean and fanatical (Acts 17:5–13). Paul wanted the Thessalonians to be sure that he stood on the side of the Gospel . . . that he stood with true believers and against his fanatical fellow-countrymen, even though he carried such a burden for them that he was willing to be accursed of God, if by so doing he could save his brethren after the flesh (Rom. 9:1–3).

". . . *To fill up their sins alway* . . . ." After the crucifixion of the Lord Jesus Christ, God granted a space in which the Jews could have repented; but they did not. In Hebrews 3:9–17 it is certainly suggested or intimated that after the death of Jesus, God gave the Jews a space in which they could have turned to Christ. Study these verses very carefully.

Had the Jews accepted the message of reconciliation delivered by the apostles, their judgment would have been averted (Acts 3:19). The measure God allowed Israel was not yet full; but the Jews refused the message of Jesus, cried out for Barabbas and declared they wanted Jesus crucified. "Let His blood be upon us and upon our children!" Then after God raised Him from the dead, *they rejected the message of the resurrection.* They also refused to hear Paul. Every day the cup of indignation was slowly filling—and finally God set the Jews aside as a nation. Jesus said to them, "Fill ye up then the measure of your fathers" (Matt. 23:32). Certainly the Jews did this. "Fill ye up then the measure of your fathers (sins)" signifies ripeness for judgment, the cup of wrath being filled to the brim. The statement is also used in Genesis 15:16 concerning the Amorites in the days of Abraham.

". . . *For the wrath is come upon them to the uttermost.*" Stephen said, "As did your fathers, so do ye!" (Acts 7:51). In the days of Jeremiah the Lord God said concerning Israel, "Yet will I not make a full end" (Jer. 4:27). God made this statement many times concerning Israel; but now the fate of the Jew as a nation is fixed and sealed. When they finally and flatly refused the Gospel of the death, burial and resurrection of Jesus, God made a full end of the old covenant and of national Israel as His elect people. The nation is set aside; the fig tree has been cut down to the ground; however, the roots remain—and in Romans 11 we are clearly taught that one day God will turn again to His chosen people.

Lest someone misunderstand me, let me explain that all the Jews who have died in unbelief since the crucifixion of Jesus—those who did not accept Him as Saviour through His shed blood—are in hell; but there is a time coming when "a nation will be born in a day" (Isaiah 66:8). The Jews who are alive when Jesus comes will see the scars in His hands and will ask, "Where did you get these scars?" He will answer, "I received them in the house of my friends." They will know Him, they will fall at His feet to worship and accept Him as their Messiah. Yes, there is a glorious kingdom awaiting the seed of faithful Abraham.

In the year 70 A. D. the Holy City of Jerusalem fell; not one stone was left upon another. The city was completely levelled in the most dreadful and destructive siege known to history—secular or sacred. Jesus predicted in Mark 13:1—2 and in Luke 19:41—44 that the temple would be destroyed, with not one stone left upon another—and that prophecy was literally fulfilled when Titus the Roman overran the city. (He is said to have butchered five million Jews in one day; think of it!) Since that day, the Jewish people have wandered without a home, without an altar and without a flag—until 1948, when the new state of Israel was born and recognized by the governments of earth. When the state of Israel came into being, that was the greatest fulfillment of prophecy since the angels announced the birth of Jesus in Bethlehem of Judaea!

Today the Jews are returning to their land—in unbelief, of course—but the stage is being set for the appearing of the false messiah. Jesus said, "I am come in my Father's name, and ye receive me not; if another shall come in his own name, him ye will receive" (John 5:43). This refers to the Antichrist, who will reign during the seven years between the Rapture (when Jesus comes FOR His saints) and the Revelation (when He comes WITH His saints). The first three and one-half years of this period will be a time of peace. The Antichrist will make a covenant with Israel, he will allow them to rebuild their temple and offer sacrifices; and then after three and one-half years he will break the covenant, and all hell will break out on earth! There will be such destruction and slaughter as has never been, and Jesus tells us that "except those days be shortened, there should no flesh be saved" (Matt. 24:22).

Verse 17: "But we, brethren, being taken from you for a short time in presence, not in heart, endeavoured the more abundantly to see your face with great desire."

When Paul was forced to leave Thessalonica, he intended to be gone only a short while; therefore he could truly say that his heart was there even though he was absent in body. Acts 17:10 teaches us that the Thessalonian brethren were the ones who sent Paul and Silas away by night into Berea to prevent their being killed by the Jews. The beloved ministers were unwilling to go, but the believers sent them away for their own safety; and since they had been reluctant to leave, they had a deep desire to return.

In I Thessalonians 3:10 Paul declares that he and Silas prayed night and day *exceedingly*, that they might see the faces of the believers at Thessalonica. Paul had a deep spiritual interest in his sons and daughters in the Gospel, and he also had a tender human love for them and longed to be with them in body. He was continually with them in prayer and in spirit, but he longed to see their faces.

Verse 18: "Wherefore we would have come unto you, even I Paul, once and again; but Satan hindered us."

What Paul is saying in this verse is simply this: "We had our minds set upon returning unto you—we had no idea we would be away this long. We had resolved to come to you immediately, but Satan and the forces of spiritual enemies of the Gospel hindered us." Paul speaks primarily of himself when he says, *"Even I, Paul."* Timothy DID return (chapter 3:1–3). Silas had been left behind in the city of Macedonia (Acts 17:14; 18:5). Paul wanted his children in the Lord to know that it was not by his will nor his desire that he stayed away; he had wanted to return every moment since he left.

In Romans 1:13 Paul declares that many times he purposed to come to *Rome*, but was hindered by the enemy. Paul was a great apostle—but that did not save him from disappointment and heartbreaks, nor did it exempt him from the onslaughts of the devil. The deeper meaning of "Satan hindered us" is, "I strove eagerly to find a way to return. As for ME, I made up my mind more than once to return to you dear believers whom I love; but I was blocked by Satan."

There is no need to speculate as to what kind of hindrance Satan used here. No doubt it embraced Jewish hatred and malice against Paul, and through hook or crook they prevented his return to Thessalonica. The devil is a murderer, a deceiver and a slanderer; if he cannot damn an individual he will do everything he can to hinder that individual as he travels life's journey to heaven after becoming a believer. Satan is the accuser of the brethren; he is the enemy of every child of God. The Old Testament presents him as the adversary (which name in Hebrew means "the leader of evil spirits"). Satan is the enemy of God and man. He is called the devil, which means "the slanderer, the evil one" (II Thess. 3:3). He is called "the tempter" in I Thessalonians 3:5—our present epistle.

The New Testament presents Satan as a personality—not as an evil spirit or a figure of speech—but as a real person (II Thess. 2:9; Rev. 12:9). It was Paul who said,

"Let him that thinketh he standeth take heed lest he fall" (I Cor. 10:12)—but thank God for the next verse: "There hath no temptation taken you but such as is common to man: but God is faithful, who will not suffer you to be tempted above that ye are able; but will with the temptation also make a way of escape, that ye may be able to bear it!" I John 4:4 adds, "Greater is He that is in you, than he that is in the world."

Verses 19 and 20: "For what is our hope, or joy, or crown of rejoicing? Are not even ye in the presence of our Lord Jesus Christ at His coming? For ye are our glory and joy."

The word used here for "crown" does not mean a king's diadem, but *the crown of glory*. This crown is the wreath of the victor in a game (I Cor. 9:24,25). Paul calls the believers at Philippi his *joy and crown*: "Holding forth the word of life; that I may rejoice in the day of Christ, that I have not run in vain, neither laboured in vain. . . . Therefore, my brethren dearly beloved and longed for, my joy and crown, so stand fast in the Lord, my dearly beloved" (Phil. 2:16; 4:1). What Paul is saying in these verses to the Philippians is, "Who will furnish our crown at Christ's glorious coming? Who, *indeed*? YOU!"

Paul loved the believers in Thessalonica for what they were and for their testimony to other peoples throughout that entire area; but he loved them most of all FOR WHAT THEY WILL BE in that glorious unveiling of the sons of God: "For the earnest expectation of the creature waiteth for the manifestation of the sons of God" (Rom. 8:19). Jude 24 tells us that all believers will be presented "faultless before the presence of His glory with exceeding joy."

In that glorious day Paul will see the fruits of his

labors and be exceedingly glad. The prayer of the Apostle Paul concerning all those to whom he ministered was that he might present every man perfect in Christ. Read I Thessalonians 3:13; 5:23,24; Colossians 1:28,29.

Notice carefully Paul's statement concerning the return of the Lord Jesus. He will return in glory—and He will also return as the righteous Judge. This is the same Lord Jesus whom Paul declared the Jews killed with wicked hands (verse 15 in our present chapter).

In Revelation 5:6 John saw in the midst of the throne, a *Lamb*—as though He had been slain. Jesus said to His enemies (those who judged Him and condemned Him to die on the cross), "Hereafter shall ye see the Son of Man sitting on the right hand of power, and coming in the clouds of heaven" (Matt. 26:64). He is the divine Judge, the conqueror of the world, the flesh and the devil, death, hell and the grave, sin and temptation. Read John 5:27 and Acts 17:31.

Verse 19 closes with the words, ". . . *at His coming.*" The Greek here signifies "His arrival." Jesus is coming back to this earth again in body (Acts 1:10,11; John 14:1–3). There is no doctrine in all of the Word of God that is any clearer than that of the return of the Lord Jesus. You will find His own words concerning His second coming in Matthew 24 and 25, Mark 13 and Luke 12:35–59. Also in Luke 17:20–37; 19:11–27; John 5: 27–29; 14:1–3; 16:22——and many, many others.

Paul uses this solemn expression seven times in the two Thessalonian letters. He also uses it in I Corinthians 15:23. In these three letters we learn just about all Paul gives concerning the second coming—the Rapture, when Jesus comes for His bride, the New Testament Church. In Matthew 24:36–44 Jesus taught His disciples concerning the Rapture. It is also referred to in the Epistle of James; Peter speaks of it, and so does John the Beloved.

Regardless of what men say, preach or teach—Jesus Christ one day will descend from heaven with a shout, with the voice of the archangel and the trumpet of God. The dead in Christ will be raised, believers who are alive will be changed in a moment, in the twinkling of an eye, and we will all be caught up together to meet the Lord in the clouds in the air; and so shall we ever be with the Lord. We will study this when we reach chapter 4.

Chapter 2 closes with the statement, *"For ye are our glory and joy."* Paul emphasizes both "YE" (referring to believers) and "ARE" (referring to that particular moment). His delight was not only a matter of hope when the Rapture occurs and believers are rewarded; but he also delighted in the believers at Thessalonica *at that very moment.* Notice chapters 1:2–4 and 3:9 in our present epistle, and II Thessalonians 1:4. The believers in the church at Thessalonica were Paul's glory; *glory is praise and honor from others.* They were also his joy; *joy is one's own delight!*

Paul had no fear in heaping glory and honor upon the church at Thessalonica; he knew they were genuine. They had proven their experience to be real; therefore he gloried in them, praised them and honored them to the highest. Down deep in his heart he had joy that was unspeakable and full of glory. He had delight that words could not express; so he simply said, "For ye are our glory and joy!"

I THESSALONIANS –– CHAPTER THREE

1. Wherefore when we could no longer forbear, we thought it good to be left at Athens alone;

2. And sent Timotheus, our brother, and minister of God, and our fellowlabourer in the gospel of Christ, to establish you, and to comfort you concerning your faith:

3. That no man should be moved by these afflictions: for yourselves know that we are appointed thereunto.

4. For verily, when we were with you, we told you before that we should suffer tribulation; even as it came to pass, and ye know.

5. For this cause, when I could no longer forbear, I sent to know your faith, lest by some means the tempter have tempted you, and our labour be in vain.

6. But now when Timotheus came from you unto us, and brought us good tidings of your faith and charity, and that ye have good remembrance of us always, desiring greatly to see us, as we also to see you:

7. Therefore, brethren, we were comforted over you in all our affliction and distress by your faith:

8. For now we live, if ye stand fast in the Lord.

9. For what thanks can we render to God again for you, for all the joy wherewith we joy for your sakes before our God;

10. Night and day praying exceedingly that we might see your face, and might perfect that which is lacking in your faith?

11. Now God himself and our Father, and our Lord Jesus Christ, direct our way unto you.

12. And the Lord make you to increase and abound in love one toward another, and toward all men, even as we do toward you:

13. To the end he may stablish your hearts unblameable in holiness before God, even our Father, at the coming of our Lord Jesus Christ with all his saints.

Verse 1: "Wherefore when we could no longer forbear, we thought it good to be left at Athens alone."

In this chapter the opening word, "wherefore," points back to what we have learned in verses 17 through 20 in the preceding chapter. "Wherefore when we could no longer forbear . . . ." That is, Paul yearned to see the believers at Thessalonica until he could bear that yearning no longer. He loved them so deeply and fervently that the long separation and repeated disappointments were more than he could endure. Therefore, he decided it was best that he be left alone at Athens, even in his loneliness, and that young Timothy be sent to the church in Thessalonica.

Verse 2: "And sent Timotheus, our brother, and minister of God, and our fellowlabourer in the Gospel of Christ, to establish you, and to comfort you concerning your faith."

The Acts of the Apostles traces Paul's footsteps from the city of Thessalonica to Berea, and from Berea to Athens (Acts 17:10–15). In Acts 17:14–16 Silas and Timothy were both left behind at Berea as Paul journeyed on to Athens, leaving instructions for them to follow him as soon as possible. If Paul's two fellow ministers ever arrived in Athens it is not clearly stated in Acts. Silas and Timothy are not mentioned again until their return together from Macedonia, and at that time they found Paul in the city of Corinth (Acts 18:1–5). However, it is clear in our present chapter (verses 1–3) that Paul sent Timothy to Thessalonica to comfort and encourage the believers there, and also to bring back a report on the status of the church.

There is no contradiction between Luke's account in Acts and Paul's account here in I Thessalonians. It is altogether possible that Silas and Timothy did follow Paul, and Luke did not record it. To him it may not have been important—or it could be that Luke did not *know* for sure whether or not they joined Paul in Athens; but you may rest assured that there is no conflict between these two writers, for the Holy Spirit dictated the words they penned down.

It is altogether possible that Paul, upon arriving at

Athens, immediately discovered that he could not return to Thessalonica and therefore sent directions to Timothy to return to the church there in his place. He could have had him to go there instead of coming to Athens, as formerly planned. It could be that Silas remained in Thessalonica, and after Timothy visited there he and Silas both could have rejoined Paul in the city of Corinth. It could also be that Timothy did travel to the city of Athens from Berea, and that Paul immediately sent him back to Thessalonica. If so, Paul was practically alone from the time he left Berea until Timothy and Silas joined him at Corinth.

It was certainly a trial and heartache to Paul to be left alone, particularly at this time; but he was so anxious about the Thessalonians that he was willing to suffer loneliness in order to send his fellow ministers to comfort and strengthen those who were being sorely tested and tried by the enemy.

Paul sent Timothy to do what he himself longed to do—and what he *did* do as best he could by writing the epistle to them. Above all, he prayed to God to establish the believers, to comfort and encourage them. In verses 12 and 13 in our present chapter Paul prays that the Thessalonians will be established in heart, unblameable in holiness before God unto the coming of the Lord Jesus with all of His saints. Also, in II Thessalonians 2:16 and 17 he prays from a heart of love, "Now our Lord Jesus Christ Himself, and God, even our Father, which hath loved us, and hath given us everlasting consolation and good hope through grace, comfort your hearts, and stablish you in every good word and work." Paul practiced what he preached in I Thessalonians 5:17: *"Pray without ceasing."* He did just that for his children in the Lord in the churches he established.

Verse 3: "That no man should be moved by these

afflictions: for yourselves know that we are appointed thereunto."

Later Paul said to the Romans, "Who shall separate us from the love of Christ? Shall tribulation, or distress, or persecution, or famine, or nakedness, or peril, or sword? As it is written, For thy sake we are killed all the day long; we are accounted as sheep for the slaughter. Nay, in all these things we are more than conquerors through Him that loved us. For I am persuaded, that neither death, nor life, nor angels, nor principalities, nor powers, nor things present, nor things to come, nor height, nor depth, nor any other creature, shall be able to separate us from the love of God, which is in Christ Jesus our Lord" (Rom. 8:35–39).

Paul sent Timothy to Thessalonica to remind the believers that afflictions and persecutions should not cause them to become discouraged or despondent, but rather should cause them to be more consecrated and dedicated to the cause of the Gospel. Read II Thessalonians 2:2 and Colossians 1:23. In II Timothy 3:12 Paul said, "Yea, and all that will live godly in Christ Jesus shall suffer persecution." The Thessalonians were to understand that if they lived godly lives they would be persecuted by the enemies of godliness. Jesus said, "If they hated me they will hate you." In John 16:33 He said, "These things have I spoken unto you, that in me ye might have peace. IN THE WORLD YE SHALL HAVE TRIBULATION: But be of good cheer; I have overcome the world." All believers may rest assured that God will never ask them to walk a path Jesus did not walk before them.

Verse 3 closes thus: ". . . We are appointed thereunto." It is natural for believers to suffer . . . it would be *unnatural* for Christians to live in this world and NOT suffer. The word "appointed" is the same word used in

98

Philippians 1:17, translated "*set* for the defence of the Gospel." It is also the same word used in Matthew 5:14, when in the Sermon on the Mount Jesus refers to a city that is "*set* on an hill," indicating the situation in which the believer is placed. The believers at Thessalonica were appointed this particular position (post) in the army of the Lord in defense of the Gospel against the enemies of Christ, and Paul is saying to them, "You know that you are called to fiery trials, and strange things will happen to you." Read I Peter 2:20, 21; 4:12, 13. I wonder how many true ministers we have today—ministers who would measure up to the standard set by the Apostle Paul in the Holy Spirit?

Verse 4: "For verily, when we were with you, we told you before that we should suffer tribulation; even as it came to pass, and ye know."

A more precise reading would be, "*used to tell you*," for this was no single warning, but one repeated and familiar. For other references to the Apostle's previous instructions read I Thessalonians 2:11,12; 4:1,2; II Thessalonians 2:5—15; 3:10.

In our present verse he reminds them that when he was with them he continually repeated the warning that believers are called to suffer, and that if we suffer with Christ we shall reign with Him; but if we deny Him He will deny us.

In Thessalonica there were fanatical priests who were not led by God but by their own personal religious convictions and motives. These were determined to destroy the Church of which Jesus said, "The gates of hell shall not prevail against it." In Thessalonica there were also the craftsmen who knew not God and cared for nothing save their own personal gain. They were not concerned about spiritual matters and would make merchandise of the souls of men. There were multitudes who knew nothing of things spiritual; they knew nothing of the law of God and *cared* nothing for the *grace* of God. They were intensely irritated by this strange group who called themselves Christians and preached the death, burial and resurrection of One named Jesus.

All these wicked men united their wicked minds to destroy the believers who were turning the world upside down. Then, *as now*, the masses were against true believers—but also then, as now, "If God be for us, who can be against us?" (Rom. 8:31). "Greater is He that is in you than he that is in the world" (I John 4:4). Paul assured the believers that they were on the winning side. They were *called to suffer*, and therefore they should rejoice and be glad to be *counted worthy* to suffer for the name of Jesus.

Verse 5: "For this cause, when I could no longer forbear, I sent to know your faith, lest by some means the tempter have tempted you, and our labour be in vain."

In this verse Paul repeats what he said in verse one, but expresses it in a different manner. Paul is saying to the believers, "You were in affliction so grievous that it could endanger your faith, and I felt unendurable anxiety for you. Therefore I sent Timothy to comfort you and bring back to me a report concerning your faith. Timothy came to you for two reasons: To comfort you in the Lord in this hour of persecution, and to relieve my own anxious heart, so sorely distressed and plagued with fears concerning your fiery trials, fearing that perhaps this continued and increasing persecution might cause some of the weaker brethren to stumble. God forbid that this should happen to my beloved children in the Lord in Thessalonica." Read Acts 18:5–10; I Corinthians 2:3. That his labour be in vain was the dark thought that plagued the mind of Paul, and it was that terrifying thought that he could no longer bear.

The sentence might be rendered in the interrogative, expressing the apprehension as it actually arose in the Apostle's mind: "I sent that I might know about your faith: had the tempter haply tempted you, and would our labor prove in vain?" The thought that all the labor bestowed upon the Thessalonians might be lost and the success that at first was so glorious should end in failure and disgrace wrung the Apostle's heart in fear. But even though the tempter who had hindered Paul from visiting the church had at the same time tempted the Thessalonians, they stood one hundred percent true to the faith.

Verse 6: "But now when Timotheus came from you unto us, and brought us good tidings of your faith and charity, and that ye have good remembrance of us always, desiring greatly to see us, as we also to see you."

With a heart filled with anxiety Paul had sent Timothy to Thessalonica and then anxiously awaited his return. The moment Timothy returned and gave the good report concerning the steadfastness of the believers at Thessalonica, Paul sat down and wrote the epistle to the church there. He wrote from a heart filled with gratitude and love, for Timothy brought glad tidings concerning the pure, steadfast faith and fervent love to other people manifested in the lives and stewardship of the Thessalonian believers.

"*Good tidings*" is a single word in the Greek, the same word used throughout the New Testament for "the glad tidings," meaning the good news of God's salvation and the coming of King Jesus to reign on earth. The Greek word used by Paul here signifies that the news Timothy brought back was Gospel news, declaring the truth and the unending, everlasting power of God's Gospel in the lives of true believers. Because of this the Apostle was exceedingly happy and exclaimed in verses 7 and 8, "Brethren, we were comforted over you in all our afflictions and distress by your faith. . . . NOW WE LIVE!" The encouraging message gave new life to Paul.

The good tidings Timothy brought to Paul concerned the faith and charity of the Thessalonian believers. Faith and charity make up Christian living, for Christianity *begins* when we exercise faith in the finished work of the Lord Jesus, and true faith produces charity (love). *We love Him because He first loved us*—and when we love Him we also love the brethren. If we cannot love our brothers whom we have seen, how can we love God, whom we have not seen? Our hope in the Lord Jesus Christ is based on faith in His finished work and demonstrated daily by our love for the brethren. Read I Thessalonians 1:3, II Thessalonians 1:3, Ephesians 1:15, Philemon 5 and 7, and I John 3:23. The heart of the Gospel message is that we should believe in the name of His Son Jesus Christ—and love one another. This is the heart and soul of pure religion.

Another thing that made Paul exceedingly happy was the report that the believers at Thessalonica still remembered those who had brought them the glad tidings of the Gospel: *"And that ye have good remembrance of US always*, desiring greatly to see us, as we also to see you." Paul unceasingly remembered the Thessalonians, and now—even though they were suffering, were being slandered daily by the enemy and even by their own countrymen, their minds had not been alienated from the dear missionaries who brought them the Gospel message; on the contrary, they remembered Paul and his fellow laborers *always*. Their feelings toward each other were mutual; Paul longed to see his children in the Lord, and they in turn longed to see their beloved Apostle.

102

Verse 7: "Therefore, brethren, we were comforted over you in all our affliction and distress by your faith."

The good report brought back by Timothy comforted Paul's aching heart. You will find a similar statement in II Corinthians 7:6,7: "Nevertheless God, that comforteth those that are cast down, comforted us by the coming of Titus; and not by his coming only, but by the consolation wherewith he was comforted in you, when he told us your earnest desire, your mourning, your fervent mind toward me; so that I rejoiced the more."

In his distress and affliction, Paul took courage: "We were comforted through your faith!" The faith of the Thessalonians was the essential point about which Timothy was to inquire; for if they were true to the faith once delivered to the saints, then all else would go well. Paul knew that if they were steadfast in true faith, all hell could not move them, regardless of the methods or schemes employed by the devil.

To Peter Jesus said, "Simon, Simon, behold, Satan hath desired to have you, that he may sift you as wheat: But I have prayed for thee, THAT THY FAITH FAIL NOT" (Luke 22:31,32). In II Corinthians 1:24 Paul said, "By faith ye stand." Paul preached, "By grace are ye saved through faith. . . . Faith cometh by hearing and hearing by the Word of God. . . . Whatsoever is not of faith is sin." John said, "Whosoever is born of God overcometh the world, and this is the victory that overcometh the world, EVEN OUR FAITH." Paul places the cap stone on the pyramid of true salvation by saying, "*Looking unto Jesus*, the author and finisher of our FAITH."

Verse 8: "For now we live, if ye stand fast in the Lord."

The good report brought by Timothy lifted from the

heart of Paul a tremendous load of anxiety and apprehension. He felt as though his life was wrapped up in this church. The heaviest burden borne by Paul was "the care of all the churches" (II Cor. 11:28). His entire life and his whole soul were wrapped up in the churches the Lord had used him to establish. He referred to the believers as his children, loved and longed for—his joy, his glory and his crown of boasting! Please read every word in II Corinthians 7:2–16. These verses give a picture of the heart of Paul, and you will see a vivid portrayal of his great love for those in the churches he had established.

Verse 9: "For what thanks can we render to God again for you, for all the joy wherewith we joy for your sakes before our God."

Paul is saying here, "The good news Timothy brought concerning your unshakeable faith has given me new life to such extent that *I cannot find words* to express my thanksgiving and my gratitude to the God of our Lord Jesus Christ. Joy floods my heart when I think that you have suffered so much—and yet, according to Timothy, you are steadfast and immovable in the faith! Words cannot express my joy and thanksgiving to God."

Verse 9 closes with the statement, *"before our God."* Paul always assured his readers and those to whom he ministered that God was his witness in all things; therefore God knew the exceeding joy that flooded his heart because of the good report of the church at Thessalonica. The joy he was now experiencing was more vivid because of the sorrow and suffering he had previously known due to the anxiety concerning the spiritual condition of the believers there. Only Christians who have suffered severely can know such joy unspeakable and full of glory—joy in its full capacity. Paul describes it thus in II Corinthians 6:9,10: ". . . As dying, and, behold, we live . . . as sorrowful, yet alway rejoicing."

Verse 10: "Night and day praying exceedingly that we might see your face, and might perfect that which is lacking in your faith."

The Greek word here for "exceedingly" carries a strong meaning, as of *"beyond measure"* or *"super-abundantly."* Paul uses this word in I Thessalonians 5:13 (translated *"very highly"*) and in Ephesians 3:20. Night and day beyond measure (exceedingly) Paul prayed for the believers in Thessalonica. "Praying" is here more strictly "begging or beseeching"—the same truth as is set forth in II Corinthians 5:20, where Paul said, "We beg you on Christ's behalf, be ye reconciled to God." (In other places the word for prayer indicates devotion and worship, as used in I Thessalonians 1:2 and II Thessalonians 3:1.) But in this particular verse Paul is greatly burdened and begs with all of his heart that God will keep, strengthen and deliver the Christians at Thessalonica.

The statement *"and might perfect that which is lacking in your faith"* does not mean that their faith had stopped short of the faith that saves . . . not at all. According to I Thessalonians 1:3–8, 2:13, 3:6–8 and II Thessalonians 1:3, the faith of the believers there was genuine, pure, and increasing: "Your faith groweth exceedingly." There is no such thing as exercising *partial saving faith.* When we have faith in God, when we believe on the Lord Jesus Christ, we are born into God's family, *saved instantaneously and completely,* nothing lacking from the standpoint of redemption or salvation; but we are to cry out with the man in the days of Jesus, "Lord, I believe; help thou mine unbelief!" We are commanded to grow in grace and in the knowledge of our Lord and Saviour, Jesus Christ.

105

We do not grow INTO faith nor INTO grace—but we grow IN faith and IN grace *after* we are redeemed. Paul is here telling the Thessalonians that they needed the teaching he could give them for added light and moral wisdom concerning Christian stewardship and daily practices of Christian life. As we continue our study you will note that chapters 4 and 5 of this letter are filled with pure doctrine and spiritual instruction.

The good report brought by Timothy made Paul glad and removed his great anxiety concerning their faith— but it also caused him to realize more than ever the need of this most promising of his young churches. Therefore he longed to visit them and *teach* them, that they might grow in grace and become stronger in the inner man.

The word *perfect* signifies "fully furnished, fully equipped, fully fitted out." The same word is translated *"mending* nets" in Matthew 4:21. It is also used in Romans 9:22 in connection with "vessels fitted for destruction," and in Ephesians 4:12—"perfecting saints for the work of administration (ministry)." Paul's desire for the Thessalonians was that they be fully equipped and perfectly fitted for whatsoever the tempter might hurl at them, as well as for whatsoever door of opportunity might open to them as witnesses of the truth and the pure Gospel of God's saving grace. He wanted them to be *full grown in the inner man.*

Verse 11: "Now God Himself and our Father, and our Lord Jesus Christ, direct our way unto you."

Paul's prayer in this verse has its ultimate goal in verse 13. The heart and soul of his teaching in all the churches was the coming of the Lord Jesus. He instructed all of his children in the Lord to look for "that blessed hope and the glorious appearing of the great God and our Saviour, Jesus Christ." And now he prays that God Himself, the Father of our Lord Jesus, direct him to Thessalonica for the singular purpose of furthering the preparation of those believers for the coming of their Lord Jesus in the air to receive them unto Himself and reward them for their faithful stewardship. Paul longed for the believers to receive a full reward. Note I Thessalonians 1:10 and 5:23.

The word *"direct"* in the statement "direct our way unto you" is the same word used in Luke 1:79 (*"guide* our feet into the way of peace") and also in Psalm 37:23: "The steps of a good man are *ordered* by the Lord: and he delighteth in His way." No doubt Paul had this verse in mind when he prayed the words in our present verse. He believed what the Lord Jesus said: "I and my Father are ONE. . . . If ye shall ask anything in my name I will do it" (John 10:30; 14:14). Paul asked God the Father and the Lord Jesus Christ to direct his steps to the beloved saints in the church in Thessalonica.

Verse 12: "And the Lord make you to increase and abound in love one toward another, and toward all men, even as we do toward you."

The Thessalonian believers excelled in brotherly love—a grace of which there can never be too much in the lives of believers (I Thess. 4:9,10; 1:3; II Thess. 1:3). Paul knew that *increased* love for one another would be the best supplement to their defects of faith (verse 10); and its increase lies in its own growth and enlargement . . . the growth of love in the heart. Love for one another is the basis of unblameable holiness, in which they were to appear at Christ's coming if they were full grown in the inner man (verse 13).

Paul also prays that they will ABOUND in love— and this abounding (abundance) is the overflowing of love in a believer's heart, thus blessing others through that overflow. These comparisons are used again in Romans 5:20: ". . . Where sin abounded (increased or multiplied) grace *superabounded.*"

This increased and abounding love was not to be confined to believers only, but was to extend "toward all men"—and includes unbelievers and even our enemies. For the Thessalonian church, this was very difficult and required extra grace, because they were sorely persecuted and had many enemies; but Paul wanted them to love their enemies and do good to those who despitefully used them. He wanted them to obey the command of Christ in Matthew 5:44.

Verse 12 closes with the words, *"even as we do toward you."* No doubt Paul was thinking of the words of Jesus in John 13:34: "That ye love one another, as I have loved you." Paul's love for his children in the Lord was not a stationary or stagnant love—it was a living, flourishing, growing devotion.

In verse 10 Paul prayed *concerning the faith* of these believers. In verse 12 he prayed *concerning their love toward each other.* Verse 13 reveals WHY he was so concerned about their faith and pure love. Such concern was not from a selfish motive, but for their sakes.

Verse 13: "To the end He may stablish your hearts unblameable in holiness before God, even our Father, at the coming of our Lord Jesus Christ with all His saints."

The phrase *"stablish your hearts"* is an Old Testament expression, found primarily in the Psalms. In Psalm 104:15 the psalmist speaks of "bread that strengtheneth man's heart." The Hebrew word for *strengthen* is the same word in the Greek for "stablish." Again in Psalms we read, "His heart is established. He shall not be afraid." James 5:8 tells us, "Be ye also patient; stablish your hearts: for the coming of the Lord draweth nigh." All of these passages signify the imparting of conscious strength; and the phrase denotes here, therefore, not so much a *making firm or making steadfast in character*, but *giving a firm confidence and a steadfast assurance to the heart*—or the inner man. Note II Thessalonians 2:2. This would be the result of abounding love in the hearts of the believers—the kind of love Paul prayed for in verse 11 of this present chapter.

Paul is using different words to express what John said in I John 3:18–21 and I John 4:16–18: "Herein is our love made perfect, that we may have boldness in the day of judgment. . . . Perfect love casteth out fear." The Thessalonian church believed in and looked for the imminent return of the Lord Jesus Christ, just as the true Church does today. The church had been taught by Paul that Jesus was coming again to catch them up in the air to meet Him and that there they would be judged *according to their stewardship*—not as to whether or not they were saved (I Cor. 3:12–15 and II Cor. 5:10). In order to "assure their hearts before Him" for this judgment, the Thessalonian believers must increase and abound in love. *"Love never faileth"* (I Cor. 13:8). From I Thessalonians 4:13–18 and 5:14 we conclude that some of the believers lacked this joyous confidence and courage; therefore Paul said, "Comfort one another with these words."

". . . *Unblameable in holiness* . . . ." The phrase appears to be anticipatory . . . *unblameable* carries our thoughts at once to "the coming of the Lord Jesus Christ." This statement, amplified, would read thus: "My heart's desire for you is that the Lord make you to abound in pure love—first to Him, then one to another—in order that you may have such confidence and strength of heart abiding in you that you will be found blameless in pure holiness before God at the coming of the Lord Jesus Christ for His saints.'' This blamelessness will be *manifest* at the coming of the Judge; but it is *imparted* already, and belongs to them whose hearts are filled with love to their fellow men, and so with confidence toward God.

In II Corinthians 1:12 Paul said, ''For our rejoicing is this: The testimony of our conscience that in simplicity and godly sincerity, not with fleshly wisdom, but by the grace of God, we have had our conversation in the world and more abundantly to you-ward.'' Such confidence as described here must always be carefully guarded by strict self-discipline (or self-scrutiny) and also by absolute and total dependence upon Christ. It is in Him that we live and move and have our being, and only in Him can we have such confidence.

The goal of Paul's prayers and labors for the church (I Thess. 2:19; 5:23; II Thess. 1:11,12) is that they will be full grown in the inner man—spotless, blameless and unashamed when they stand before the righteous Judge to receive their reward for the deeds done in the body (II Cor. 5:10). He prays continually that they may be able with a good conscience and an assuring heart to look forward with confidence toward that day of the glorious appearing of the great God and our Saviour Jesus Christ, and he desires that each child of God not ''be ashamed before Him at His coming'' (I John 2:28; 3:3).

Please notice that Christ is the agent of all that is declared in verses 12 and 13. It is Christ—and *only* Christ—who fills the hearts of His people with faith and love; it is Christ who sanctifies His people through the truth (John 17:17); it is Christ who gives His children the Holy Spirit to guide them into paths of righteousness so that at the end of life's journey He may present them

110

to the Father as His joy and crown. Then He (Christ) will be "glorified in His saints, and . . . be admired in all them that believe (because our testimony among you was believed) in that day. Wherefore also we pray always for you, that our God would count you worthy of this calling, and fulfil all the good pleasure of His goodness, and the work of faith with power: That the name of our Lord Jesus Christ may be glorified in you, and ye in Him, according to the grace of our God and the Lord Jesus Christ" (II Thess. 1:10–12).

"His saints" (His holy ones) are believers, "unblameable in holiness," whom the Lord Jesus Christ will acknowledge, receive, and associate with Himself at His coming in the Rapture. The last words in verse 13 have been shaping the Apostle's prayer all through the chapter. Believers who possess the Spirit, who are permeated by His love, having trusted in Him through faith, have the promise that they will be found among the holy ones approved by God because they have trusted in His only begotten Son, the Lord Jesus. These holy ones will be in that happy throng in the glorious Rapture, *when the dead in Christ will be raised first* and living saints will be changed in a moment—"in the twinkling of an eye"; and together all saints will be caught up to meet Jesus in the clouds in the air.

When Christ comes in the Rapture, He will bring with Him the *spirits* of all the saints who have died, their *bodies* will be raised incorruptible, the bodies of living saints will be changed instantaneously—and together this great host will meet the Lord Jesus in the air. We will sit with Him at the marriage supper and will be rewarded for our stewardship. Read Philippians 3:20,21; Colossians 3:4; I Thessalonians 4:13–18 and II Thessalonians 2:1.

The second coming of Jesus Christ is the hope of

the Church, the final hope of all believers, and the hope of all creation. In Romans 8:18–25 Paul said: "For I reckon that the sufferings of this present time are not worthy to be compared with the glory which shall be revealed in us. For the earnest expectation of the creature waiteth for the manifestation of the sons of God (the second coming in its second stage—the Revelation— as described in Revelation 1:7). For the creature was made subject to vanity, not willingly, but by reason of Him who hath subjected the same in hope. Because the creature itself also shall be delivered from the bondage of corruption into the glorious liberty of the children of God. For we know that the whole creation groaneth and travaileth in pain together until now. And not only they, but ourselves also, which have the firstfruits of the Spirit, even we ourselves groan within ourselves, waiting for the adoption, to wit, the redemption of our body. For we are saved by hope: but hope that is seen is not hope: for what a man seeth, why doth he yet hope for? But if we hope for that we see not, then do we with patience wait for it."

1. Furthermore then we beseech you, brethren, and exhort you by the Lord Jesus, that as ye have received of us how ye ought to walk and to please God, so ye would abound more and more.

2. For ye know what commandments we gave you by the Lord Jesus.

3. For this is the will of God, even your sanctification, that ye should abstain from fornication:

4. That every one of you should know how to possess his vessel in sanctification and honour;

5. Not in the lust of concupiscence, even as the Gentiles which know not God:

6. That no man go beyond and defraud his brother in any matter: because that the Lord is the avenger of all such, as we also have forewarned you and testified.

7. For God hath not called us unto uncleanness, but unto holiness.

8. He therefore that despiseth, despiseth not man, but God, who hath also given unto us his holy Spirit.

9. But as touching brotherly love ye need not that I write unto you: for ye yourselves are taught of God to love one another.

10. And indeed ye do it toward all the brethren which are in all Macedonia: but we beseech you, brethren, that ye increase more and more;

11. And that ye study to be quiet, and to do your own business, and to work with your own hands, as we commanded you;

12. That ye may walk honestly toward them that are without, and that ye may have lack of nothing.

13. But I would not have you to be ignorant, brethren, concerning them which are asleep, that ye sorrow not, even as others which have no hope.

14. For if we believe that Jesus died and rose again, even so them also which sleep in Jesus will God bring with him.

15. For this we say unto you by the word of the Lord, that we which are alive and remain unto the coming of the Lord shall not prevent them which are asleep.

16. For the Lord himself shall descend from heaven with a shout, with the voice of the archangel, and with the trump of God: and the dead in Christ shall rise first:

17. Then we which are alive and remain shall be caught up together with them in the clouds, to meet the Lord in the air: and so shall we ever be with the Lord.

18. Wherefore comfort one another with these words.

Chapter four begins the second of the two main divisions of Paul's letter to the church at Thessalonica, and changes from narrative to exhortation. Chapters 1, 2 and 3 are complete in themselves, carrying a complete message. I Thessalonians could have terminated at the close of the prayer in chapter 3:11–13. Paul had accomplished the chief objective for which he began the epistle—which was that of assuring the believers of his deep interest in their welfare (spiritually and otherwise), and to express to them heartfelt sympathy because of their persecution and bitter trials, as well as explaining how he had longed to return to them but Satan had prevented his doing so. These things were uppermost in his mind and rested heavily upon his heart. Thus the first three chapters carry a complete message to the Christians at Thessalonica.

However, Paul could not let the occasion pass without also admonishing and exhorting the believers concerning certain subjects and doctrines in which they needed further guidance and instruction. Chief among these was the misunderstanding that had arisen touching the second coming of the Lord Jesus (I Thess. 4:13; 5:11); but before Paul dealt with that subject there were a few things he wished to say to them about morals and about their conduct toward each other. We will find these subjects discussed in chapter four and, to some degree, in chapter five.

It is significant that Paul puts these things first in his exhortation, for surely his heart was bursting with the desire to instruct them concerning the Rapture,

114

which he calls *"the glorious appearing* of the great God and our Saviour Jesus Christ" (Titus 2:13).

In chapter 4:1–12 Paul discusses chastity and the sanctification of the body. He also discusses brotherly love and emphasizes diligence in secular work. We might say that chapters 4:1–12 and 5:1–15 supplement the main body of truth and purpose of this letter. This is shown by the introductory phrase:

Verse 1: "FURTHERMORE then we beseech you, brethren, and exhort you by the Lord Jesus, that as ye have received of us how ye ought to walk and to please God, so ye would abound more and more."

"Furthermore then" in the Greek means "finally . . . for the rest, therefore . . . for what remains." Read Philippians 3:1 and 4:8. The verb "beseech" (ask) is used frequently by John in his writings, but Paul only uses it here and in chapter 5:12, II Thessalonians 2:1 and Philippians 4:3.

He asks (beseeches) the believers at Thessalonica to consider these things because of himself; they are his converts, and he does not want them to disgrace him through immorality or any other sin of the flesh or sin against each other. He also exhorts them because of their duty to Christ, since they are children of God. In other words, "BECAUSE YOU ARE CHRISTIANS you should practice these things every moment of every day."

There are many things Christians can do and not lose their salvation and burn in hell; but there are many things Christians *should not do* because they ARE Christian. We are the children of God, and the world judges God by our daily living. Those who will not read the Bible will read every move we make and every word we speak. Someone has said, "You are the only Bible this careless world will read. You are the sinner's Gospel,

115

you are the scoffer's creed." Paul has this truth in mind as he begs the believers at Thessalonica to be sanctified in soul, spirit and body, to live blameless and above reproach, because they are in the church in the Lord Jesus Christ (I Thess. 1:1; 2:15–19).

Paul's deep love for the believers at Thessalonica and his burning desire to see them prompted him to pray as he did in the last part of chapter 3. He begged the Lord Himself to make them blameless in holiness at His coming. It is "therefore" in accord with Paul's prayer and his desires concerning the believers that he now urges them to earnestly pursue and practice every Christian virtue in every detail of their Christian living and conduct before those "who are without."

When Paul came to Thessalonica he not only preached the doctrine of the grace of God, but he also taught that men should *practice* the full teaching of the Gospel concerning morality, work, or whatsoever man may be found doing. The Thessalonians had been given moral teachings along with the theological elements of Christianity. Paul did not preach a one-sided Gospel; he preached the full Gospel to all to whom he ministered. He preached what we should believe, but he also preached how we as Christians ought to walk (chapter 2:12).

The duty of pleasing God day by day in every aspect of living was a part of Paul's admonition to the Thessalonians. He declared that all they did, all they said and all that they were should be in the light of pleasing God. In chapter 2:4 Paul speaks of himself and Silas as being governed in everything they did by the thought of pleasing God, and in verse 15 of chapter 2 Paul pours out judgment and condemnation on the Jews because they were *not* pleasing God. The conduct of the believer—always, in all things—should please God, and if we do NOT please Him we are automatically displeasing Him, because there is no middle-of-the-road with God.

Paul was *admonishing* the believers—not censuring them. He was sure they were walking in the true path, but he wished with all of his heart that they would continue in that straight and narrow way. He urged them to continue walking as they had walked; he did not want them to come to a spiritual standstill. He wanted them to "abound more and more," to become stronger and stronger and to launch more deeply into spiritual things, thereby becoming better soldiers in the great army of the Lord.

Verse 2: "For ye know what commandments we gave you by the Lord Jesus."

In this letter Paul is reminding the believers of the things he taught them while he was with them. In verse 11 we read, "And that ye study to be quiet . . . do your own business . . . work with your own hands . . . AS WE COMMANDED YOU." Also note II Thessalonians 3:4. Here the Greek word suggests an announcement (or advice) publicly delivered. In I Timothy 1:3 and 18 the heart and soul of practical teaching as having to do with Christianity is referred to as a "CHARGE."

The exhortation (or charge) is given "by the Lord Jesus." Notice II Thessalonians 3:6: ". . . in the name of our Lord Jesus Christ." This admonition appealed to the believers as having to do with their standing and relationship to Christ, who is coming in glory to reward each and every believer in righteousness. Since we know that He WILL come "as a thief in the night" we should be alert and blameless every moment of every day. These were not new charges or new commandments delivered unto the believers at Thessalonica, for they well remembered Paul's preaching while he was with them in person.

Verse 3: "For this is the will of God, even your sanctification, that ye should abstain from fornication."

Paul wanted the Thessalonians to know that it was not *his* counsel or *his* will that he pressed upon them, but that he wrote these things upon the authority of Christ; and therefore it was nothing less than "*the will of God.*" It was GOD'S will that they be sanctified in body as well as in spirit and soul. He begged them to observe these moral standards—first because it was God's will, and secondly for their own sakes; and this was a big double reason for such admonition.

The paramount reason we should live chaste lives is the fact that God has called us to pure and holy living (I Thess. 5:23,24). Sanctification is synonymous with consecration, full dedication, entire devotion to God. Sanctification is the act of making holy, or the state of one who is made holy in the Lord Jesus. "Ye have your fruit unto holiness and the end everlasting life" (Rom. 6:22). "Follow peace with all men, and holiness, without which no man shall see the Lord" (Heb. 12:14). ("Holiness" here is the same Greek word used for "sanctification" in the Thessalonian epistle.)

"*Holy*" is the single word used in the Bible as having to do with "holy God," and denotes divine character as it is revealed to us in its moral aspect of absolute perfection—perfection raised above all that is earthly and sinful in any way. Read I Samuel 2:2 and Isaiah 57:15. "Holy" defines the character of God, the Holy One of Israel. The only holiness you and I possess as believers is the holiness of God in Christ. Christ is made unto us wisdom, righteousness, sanctification and redemption (I Cor. 1:28–30). "Ye are complete in Him" (Col. 2:10). Our holiness is in Christ: "There is therefore now no condemnation to them which are in Christ Jesus" (Rom. 8:1). "Christ in you, the hope of

118

glory" (Col. 1:27). "And this is the record, that God hath given to us eternal life, and THIS LIFE IS IN HIS SON. He that hath the Son hath life; and he that hath not the Son of God hath not life" (I John 5:11,12).

God's will for our lives is *our sanctification*; and our sanctification is the acknowledgment of God's rightful claim upon us because He is the Holy One who made us—the Holy One who, in His Son, provided salvation from sin. What the Law could not do—what the Law could never have done—the Holy One of Israel, Jehovah God, did for us in His Son, the Lord Jesus Christ (Rom. 8:1–3).

God has a right to command our sanctification—our complete surrender and entire devotion. We should be completely set apart and dedicated to Him—soul, spirit and body—in every phase of life. When we are born again we are *sanctified positionally*; we are translated into the kingdom of God's dear Son (Col. 1:13); but sanctification is progressive and involves our assimilation of God's divine nature. "Sanctify . . . through thy truth: thy word is truth" (John 17:17). Jesus said, "Except ye eat my flesh and drink my blood . . ." (John 6:53). When we appropriate and assimilate the Word, we are eating His flesh and blood: "In the beginning was the Word, and the Word was with God, and the Word was God. . . . and the Word was made *flesh* . . ." (John 1:1,14a). Sanctification is the *ultimate fulfillment* of the divine command: *"Be ye holy, for I am holy"* (I Pet. 1:16; Lev. 11:44; 19:2; 20:7).

Paul is declaring to the Thessalonians that chastity is definitely a part of holiness, and apart from a life of chastity there can be no true holiness. Believers need to recognize and confess that the physical frame (as well as the spirit and soul) belongs to God, and will share in the glorious resurrection through Christ when He comes in the Rapture and the first resurrection.

"What? Know ye not that your body is the temple of the Holy Ghost which is in you, which ye have of God, and ye are not your own?" (I Cor. 6:19). The literal Greek of this verse reads thus: "Know you not, that *your bodies are limbs of Christ, a temple of the Holy Ghost,* which you have from God? Therefore glorify God in your body!" Here Paul is referring to bodily sanctification. True faith in Christ subdues and rules out sensual lust and passion.

History teaches that in Paul's day the vice of fornication was prevalent in Greek cities, and few people condemned it. Public opinion was generally in accord, and in that day pagan religions sponsored and practiced fornication. Therefore, Paul saw the urgent need to warn against this pagan practice; and since the believers had turned from idols to the living God, they were to completely sever all relations with pagan practices, and that certainly included the practice of fornication. Paul knew the purity of the Thessalonians was threatened by the terrible society in which they lived, especially since many of them had been converted from just such a life and would face the temptation to return to it. He therefore urgently admonishes them concerning the believer and fornication.

Verse 4: "That every one of you should know how to possess his vessel in sanctification and honour."

The Greek reads, "That each one of you know how to possess himself of his own vessel, or how to be wise in the mastery of his own body." In this verse we have the positive side of what is expressed negatively in verse 3. We are to *abstain from* fornication—but we are also to possess ourselves in such a way that we control the members of the body and their habits. The "vessel" is the body—the house in which we live. We might explain this by saying, "What the tool is in the hand of the carpenter, what the vase is to that which it holds, the body is to man." Read II Corinthians 4:7 and 5:1-4. Paul refers to the spirit as "treasure in earthen vessels," and again as "the earthly house of our tabernacle"—the first referring to the spirit, the second referring to the body which is the tabernacle of God; for when we are saved, divine nature then dwells within us (II Pet. 1:4). In II Corinthians 5:1-4 Paul teaches that the body is "the earthly house of our tabernacle"—the *clothing* . . . without which we should be "found naked." He was not praying to be unclothed—but *"clothed upon"* with immortality . . . the new body from heaven.

The new believer who is a victim to fornication or sensual passion is not the master of his own person; he is not the ruler of his own house (or tabernacle). What Paul is saying here is simply this: "Believers, *possess yourselves*; control your bodies. Master the vessel in which the Spirit lives. See to it that the inner man is on the throne and in control at all times, thus providing a vessel sanctified and fit for the Master's use."

In I Corinthians 9:27 Paul says, "I keep under (buffet) my body, and bring it into subjection." Read Luke 21:19, Romans 1:24-26 and I Corinthians 6:15. Lust dishonors and degrades the body, while a body wholly dedicated to God, in honor and devotion sanctified and fit for the Master's use, honors God and at the same time brings honor to the body. A believer should present his body a living sacrifice, holy and acceptable unto God—not only in reverence to God, but also out of self-respect and regard for the honor of his own person. Believers should forbid unchastity.

Verse 5: "Not in the lust of concupiscence, even as the Gentiles which know not God."

Concupiscence simply means "sensual or lustful."

A better reading here is, *"not to have the body in a state of lustful passion."* A person immersed in wicked desires is the exact opposite of one living a life of sanctification and honor. *Passion* signifies not so much a *violent* feeling as an *overpowering* feeling—one to which a man so completely yields himself that he is driven along by evil as if it were a slavemaster and he were a slave. Such a person has lost his dignity of self-rule and has become a slave to his lower appetites. Read Romans 7:5. When man willfully and willingly denies his Maker he automatically degrades himself (Rom. 1:18–32).

Verse 5 closes with the statement, *"Even as the Gentiles which know not God."* The God whom these degraded, ungodly Gentiles "knew not" is the true, all-powerful, living God (I Thess. 1:9,10) whom the believers at Thessalonica had received and to whom they turned from idols. They had come to know Him through the Gospel message delivered by Paul; they had surrendered themselves to Him, and through that surrender their bodies had been delivered from the vice, dishonor and lust they had formerly practiced. Their souls had been cleansed by the precious blood of Jesus, and since they turned to God from idols and practices of idolatry, their souls had a clean house in which to live and their bodies were clean vessels meet for the Master's use. Paul's deep desire was that they remain thus.

Verse 6: "That no man go beyond and defraud his brother in any matter: because that the Lord is the avenger of all such, as we also have forewarned you and testified."

"That no man go beyond and defraud his brother...." More exactly, *"that none overreach and take advantage of his brother."*

"Any matter" is undoubtedly that which occupies

the previous two verses—acts of impurity, social wrongs, sins having to do with marriage, practice of fornication before marriage. The warning may include any harm done to another concerning the relationships that belong to marriage . . . "the matter" concerned in the present charge—which is expressly violated by "fornication." The Apostle sets the wrong in the strongest light; hence the stern warning that follows: *"Because the Lord is the avenger of all such . . . ."* It is written, "Vengeance belongs to God"—and in this matter He is peculiarly bound to exercise it.

In I Corinthians 7 Paul clearly sets forth and outlines the New Testament doctrine having to do with marriage, and sternly warns that each believer is to have his own wife and each believing woman is to have her own husband. Please study that chapter carefully and prayerfully.

The sin of fornication is ugly, but I am afraid it has become one of the outstanding sins of our day. Believers need to be on guard at all times and under all circumstances. "Let him that thinketh he standeth take heed lest he fall" (I Cor. 10:12). We can be more than conquerors through the Lord Jesus; He is our victory (I John 4:4; I Cor. 10:13). "Marriage is honourable in all, and the bed undefiled: but whoremongers and adulterers God will judge" (Heb. 13:4).

Verse 6 closes with the words, ". . . *We also have forewarned you and testified."* On this subject it appears that Paul had spoken clearly and solemnly from the very first. Apparently fornication was the prevailing sin among the Gentiles in Thessalonica and many of the believers in the church there had practiced this vice and lust before they became Christians. For this reason, Paul preached fervently and frequently on the subject in the early days of his ministry there. He now reminds them that it is God by whom they would be judged if they practiced fornication or took advantage of a brother in any way.

Paul did not sugar-coat the Gospel, and he believed in using words easily understood. The admiration of men was not his goal; he was not attempting to please men. He said, "Woe is me if I preach not the Gospel!" He recognized the solemn, eternal fact that he would give an account to God for his ministry, and not to man; therefore, he cried aloud and spared not. He warned, he exhorted, he charged—but with all the tenderness of a mother toward a newborn babe he also admonished and led the believers into greater depths of spiritual living in true holiness and pure sanctification.

Verse 7: "For God hath not called us unto uncleanness, but unto holiness."

All true believers in Christ are saints. God called us to live lives of purity—sanctified lives (II Thess. 2:13). God's call forbids uncleanness; He never intended one of His children to live a life of impurity. We are called to His own kingdom and glory (I Thess. 2:12). The eternal purpose of God's love in permitting Jesus to die on the cross was to call out and redeem a people, to sanctify and set aside a people who would honor Him in all things to His praise and glory, that in the end the exceeding riches of His grace would be seen, recognized, and known by all creation (Eph. 2:7). All born again, blood-washed believers are true saints; and true sainthood forbids—yea, *excludes*—all impurity and wrongdoing.

According to the Gospel of the Apostle Paul, God's Gospel is the starting point—the beginning—of the Christian life (John 6:44, Heb. 12:1). No man can come to Jesus for salvation except God draw him by the Holy Spirit. Jesus is the Author and the Finisher of saving faith. Since God so loved us that He gave Jesus to die for us; since Jesus so loved that He willingly died for us; since the Holy Spirit so tenderly knocked at the door of our hearts until we opened the door and by faith invited Him in; since our salvation rests entirely upon the finished work of Jesus Christ, certainly we should walk worthy of the calling wherewith we were called (Eph. 4:1).

Verse 8: "He therefore that despiseth, despiseth not man, but God, who hath also given unto us His Holy Spirit."

The Greek word translated "despise" really should be "reject." It is the same word used in Luke 10:16, and in Galatians 2:21, where we read, "I do not frustrate (make void) the grace of God." The meaning points to *authority set at nought* or *engagement nullified*. What Paul is saying to the believers at Thessalonica is this: "God's call summons you to the new life you now possess and enjoy. HIS voice—not the voice of man—reached you through the message of the Gospel. (Note I Thessalonians 2:12,13.) It will therefore be God's authority, not man's, that you defy, nullify and reject, if this charge is disregarded by you. You ought to please God; this is God's will concerning you—even God who has placed within you His Holy Spirit."

The wording here is the same as that used in Ezekiel 37:14, where Jehovah said to the dry bones, "I will *put my Spirit into you* and you shall live and shall know that I am the Lord." In Galatians 4:6 we read, ". . . God hath sent forth the Spirit of His Son *into your hearts.*" In Ephesians 3:16 we read, ". . . strengthened with might by His Spirit (entering) into the inner man."

God gives His Holy Spirit to every individual believer, to dwell in the heart of the inner man (Rom. 8:9, 14,16; John 3:5; Eph. 4:30). Concerning the Holy Spirit

Jesus said to His disciples, ". . . That He may abide with you . . . and shall be in you" (John 14:16,17). Read also Luke 11:13. Through the indwelling of the Holy Spirit we know the love of God, we know we are the sons of God, heirs of God, and we know we are sealed until the day of redemption. Study Galatians 3:14; 4:6,7; Romans 5:5; 8:14–17; Ephesians 1:13,14.

"Know ye not that your body is the temple of the Holy Ghost which is in you, which ye have of God, and ye are not your own?" (I Cor. 6:19). "And grieve not the Holy Spirit of God, whereby ye are sealed unto the day of redemption" (Eph. 4:30).

Verse 9: "But as touching brotherly love ye need not that I write unto you: for ye yourselves are taught of God to love one another."

"*Have no need*" is an expression found in I Thessalonians 1:8; 5:1; and I John 2:27. There WAS a need for Paul to discuss the subject of verses 3 through 8 in our present chapter; but concerning the grace of brotherly love, the believers at Thessalonica excelled (I Thess. 1:3, II Thess. 1:3). In brotherly love they were God-taught; brotherly love was God-breathed into their hearts. Compare II Timothy 3:16, John 6:45 and Isaiah 54:13. "And all thy children shall be taught of the Lord: and great shall be the peace of thy children." The lesson of brotherly love so rapidly gripped the hearts of the Thessalonian Christians and was so perfectly practiced by them that it was evident they were "taught of God" to love one another.

Verse 10: "And indeed ye do it toward all the brethren which are in all Macedonia: but we beseech you, brethren, that ye increase more and more."

Such practice of brotherly love toward all men signified that they had been taught that divine lesson of

God—not of man. Thessalonica was the capital of Macedonia and was a very prosperous commercial city. It was the center of all the Macedonian churches, including those at Philippi and Berea. Therefore, the believers there were using this great opportunity to influence other believers and prove to them that they had learned the lesson of brotherly love . . . fruit that came as a result of saving grace.

When Paul wrote the first Thessalonian letter, Silas and Timothy had just returned from Macedonia (Acts 18:5; I Thess. 3:6) and had doubtless reported to Paul the tremendous impact of the testimony of the Thessalonians on the neighboring churches (I Thess. 1:7,8). However, Paul exhorts the believers not to become self-satisfied nor fall into self-righteousness through pride in their love for fellow Christians, but rather to *increase day by day* in greater love for the brethren in other churches throughout that area.

Jesus told His disciples that by manifesting love for one another they would prove to the world that they were saved. "And this commandment have we from Him, That he who loveth God love his brother also . . . and everyone that loveth Him that begat loveth him also that is begotten of Him" (I John 4:21; 5:1). If we cannot love our brother whom we have seen, how dare we say that we love God whom we have NOT seen? "We know that we have passed from death unto life, because we love the brethren. He that loveth not his brother abideth in death" (I John 3:14).

Verse 11: "And that ye study to be quiet, and to do your own business, and to work with your own hands, as we commanded you."

Thessalonica was a big city—a bustling metropolis with much activity. Therefore Paul admonishes the

Christians, "Make it *your* business and *your* ambition to live a quiet life." The Greeks were very active people, who had a love for personal distinction—and Paul knew there would be danger of their being occupied with secondary affairs, thus neglecting to give their best to spiritual matters. In I Timothy 2:1 and 2 Paul prays, ". . . that we may lead a quiet and peaceable life in all godliness and honesty."

A study of Paul's life convinces us that he was very active; it was his nature to be "on the move." Even so, he admired the quiet life and considered it an asset to the cultivation of Christian character and study. (Compare I Timothy 2:2.) Christians, in their zeal, sometimes attempt to do *too many things*. It is possible to sin by trying to do too much, attempting so much that we cannot do anything the way it should be done to the glory of God.

Paul also warns the Thessalonians that they should be occupied with their own affairs and not with the affairs of others. Probably some of them were busybodies and gadabouts, meddling hither and yon. Paul did not want the believers to live such a life. In II Thessalonians 3:11 he said, "For we hear that there are some which walk among you disorderly, working not at all, but are busybodies." You may rest assured that those who meddle in other people's business always wreck their own! If we take care of our own affairs and remain alert concerning our own life, we have little time to meddle in the affairs of others.

Verse 11 closes with the instruction, ". . . *work with your own hands, as we commanded you*." It is very probable that the majority of Thessalonian believers had learned some trade or other, and even considering that some were financially well-fixed, Paul believed that manual labor would be good for them, and he commanded them to work with their hands. Read I Thessalonians 2:9 and II Thessalonians 3:7–12. Paul recognized and acknowledged the danger of idleness.

The believers at Thessalonica were on fire for God. They were zealous, their testimony had reached throughout that entire countryside, and Paul knew that it was altogether possible for them to become so enthusiastic as to neglect the practical side of life and forget practical necessities. He therefore warns them not to be gadabouts and busybodies, lest they become lazy and adopt the attitude that the world owed them a living. (I wish Paul could deliver a message to some of the ministerial meetings of our day and hour. I wonder if he would not incorporate the truth of this verse in the message?)

I have known some believers who behave as though it were a sin for a Christian to work manually; but history reveals that some of the greatest spiritual leaders the world has ever known were men who earned their bread by the sweat of their brow as they proclaimed the Gospel of the grace of God. Paul declares, "If any provide not for his own, and specially those of his own house, he hath denied the faith and is worse than an infidel!" (I Tim. 5:8).

Verse 12: "That ye may walk honestly toward them that are without, and that ye may have lack of nothing."

Paul wanted his children in the Lord to "adorn the doctrine of God our Saviour in all things" (Titus 2:10), and in so doing, win the admiration and respect of unbelievers. In I Timothy 3:7 Paul said that those who are appointed to an office in a church should "have a good report of them which are without"—that is, we who are believers and who name the name of Jesus should live a life above reproach. Thus, even though unbelievers and sinners might not respect us or speak well of us in our presence, when they are away from us they will admit that we, like the apostles of Jesus, have been with the Lord.

Romans 14:7 says, "For none of us liveth to himself, and no man dieth to himself." God forbid that we "stand in the way of sinners or sit in the seat of the scornful." On the other hand, may God help us to be the salt of the earth and make men thirsty for the Christ who lives in us! We should let our light so shine before men that they may see our good works and glorify God, instead of ridiculing Christianity because of our poor advertisement of what Christ does for us. We are witnesses of His grace; and if we profess to be children of God, let us walk honorably, honestly, uprightly, and live blameless in the sight of all men.

The statement, *"them that are without,"* simply means those who are outside the Church . . . unbelievers. Read I Corinthians 5:12,13; Colossians 4:5 and Mark 4:11. If those who profess to be Christians and followers of Jesus are lazy, if they be busybodies and gadabouts, they will certainly hurt the cause of Christ. Paul wanted the Thessalonian believers to be good soldiers; he was ambitious that they have a good testimony, be good witnesses, and certainly that they not stand in the way of those without. He said, "I become as all men are, that I might win some." In other words, Paul would become a street sweeper, a ditch digger, or do any task that was honest and above reproach, in order to win someone to Christ. I do not doubt that Paul loved to eat meat—but he said, "If eating meat offends a weaker brother, then I shall eat no meat."

Verse 12 closes with a tremendous statement: ". . . *that ye may have lack of nothing."* That is, "Work, apply yourselves, be alert, live a quiet life, be honorable in all things; be honest, upright, decent—and do not allow yourselves to be dependent upon anyone. Love God with all your heart, work with your hands, live a blameless life; and let everyone inside the church—or outside of it—know that even though you are a believer, you have not set yourself above others just because you ARE a believer. Let your life prove that the difference between you and other men is *Christ in you*, sins washed away in His precious blood, and a new nature within."

Every person who names the name of Jesus should live such a life and should so conduct himself that he may win the respect of all inside or outside the church. God forbid that Christians be dependent upon any man, but rather that by honest labor they provide the things they need.

Paul could look the world in the face and say, "NEITHER DID WE EAT ANY MAN'S BREAD FOR NOUGHT; but wrought with labour and travail night and day, that we might not be chargeable to any of you" (II Thess. 3:8). Paul refused to bring reproach upon the Gospel by being lazy or depending upon others to do for him what God had given him the strength to do for himself. He trusted God in every detail of his life—but by the same token he believed in honorable independence, and *he preached it!*

What a day the rewarding day for believers will be! Some of those whom we expect to receive a great reward will be at the end of the line, while some of the insignificant, humble saints who never made headlines in the newspapers—perhaps did not even get their names in the church bulletin—will receive great rewards when God passes out the trophies! God's measuring stick does not measure like man's; but when God measures, that measurement is *right*, and every believer will get from the hand of God exactly what he earns by faithful stewardship—no more, no less. *Jesus Christ will judge and reward in righteousness.*

To the believers at Ephesus Paul said, ". . . But rather let him labour, working with his hands the thing which is good, that he may have to give to him that needeth" (Eph. 4:28). Paul preached that believers should be diligent in their secular work and that they should also demonstrate a spirit of love toward those who were truly in need. (Read Acts 20:34,35.) True Christianity does not render a man lazy, but makes him alert to witness with his mouth, labor with his hands, have faith in God and depend upon no man. We are to owe no man anything but to love him.

THE RAPTURE OF THE CHURCH

Chapter 4:13–18:

13. But I would not have you to be ignorant, brethren, concerning them which are asleep, that ye sorrow not, even as others which have no hope.

14. For if we believe that Jesus died and rose again, even so them also which sleep in Jesus will God bring with him.

15. For this we say unto you by the word of the Lord, that we which are alive and remain unto the coming of the Lord shall not prevent them which are asleep.

16. For the Lord himself shall descend from heaven with a shout, with the voice of the archangel, and with the trump of God: and the dead in Christ shall rise first:

17. Then we which are alive and remain shall be caught up together with them in the clouds, to meet the Lord in the air: and so shall we ever be with the Lord.

18. Wherefore comfort one another with these words.

The coming of the Lord Jesus is the principal theme of both Thessalonian epistles. Paul is not presenting the doctrine of the Rapture as though the believers had not already heard about it; he is simply *reminding* them of the things he preached when he was with them in person. Evidently some of the weaker saints had misunderstood some of his teachings concerning the Lord's return, and false teachers had attempted to cause the believers to think Paul had let them down. They had misunderstood his teaching on the resurrection of the saints who had died, and the translation of living saints; and because of the terrible persecution they were undergoing, some of them had concluded that they were in the tribulation and that the day of the Lord was upon them. Paul wrote the second Thessalonian epistle almost in its entirety to clear up this misunderstanding.

In the verses just quoted, Paul assures the believers that their dead loved ones are safe with Jesus and will come with Him in the clouds in the air. He explains that those who have died in the Lord will be raised first—and then we who are alive will be changed and this corruptible will put on incorruption. He further assures them that what he is saying is *by the word of the Lord.*

In chapter 5:1—3 Paul warns them that no man knows the hour or the moment of the Lord's return. He will come as a thief in the night; and therefore they are to be ready at all times, as a good soldier standing guard—fully armed and ready for that blessed hope and the glorious appearing of the great God and our Saviour Jesus Christ.

Verse 13: "But I would not have you to be ignorant, brethren, concerning them which are asleep, that ye sorrow not, even as others which have no hope."

"I would not have you to be ignorant, brethren" is a term Paul often uses in his writings. In this way he calls sharp attention to the topic he is about to discuss. There is no excuse for ignorance on the part of believers, for every believer has in his heart the Teacher of the Word of God (Rom. 8:9); and since the Spirit dictated the Word of God to holy men who penned it down, He is

133

the best teacher. In I John 2:27 we are told that we need not that any man should teach us, for we are taught of the Holy Spirit. "The Spirit searcheth all things, yea, the deep things of God." Paul commands, "Study to shew thyself approved unto God, a workman that needeth not to be ashamed, rightly dividing the Word of Truth" (II Tim. 2:15).

You may have a good reason for not finishing high school, college or a university. You may not have a diploma from any formal institution of learning; but *you can have a degree* in spiritual matters—a degree that only God can grant. We understand the things of the Bible only as we compare Scripture with Scripture and spiritual things with spiritual. Study carefully I Corinthians 2:10–14. The doctrine of which Paul desired the believers not to be ignorant was "concerning them which are asleep, that ye sorrow not, even as others which have no hope."

To the Christian, death is *sleep*. No, the believer does not become unconscious in spirit; the body returns to dust, but the spirit goes back to God who gave it. To be absent from the body is to be present with the Lord. The beggar Lazarus died and was carried by the angels into Abraham's bosom. Jesus said to the penitent thief on the cross, "*Today* shalt thou be with me in Paradise." He used the term "sleep" as referring to the death of the body: "And all wept, and bewailed her: but (Jesus) said, Weep not; she is *not dead*, but *sleepeth*" (Luke 8:52). He made the same statement concerning Lazarus, the brother of Mary and Martha (John 11:11). Sleep indicates a restful condition of the body; in sleep the body relaxes and is rebuilt . . . but *sleep is a temporary state.*

The early Christians called their burial grounds "cemetery." (The Greek word means *dormitory* or *sleeping chamber.*) In the true sense of the word, the believer's body is put in a grave ("dormitory")—a cript or sleeping chamber in a mausoleum—and it will remain there until the resurrection, at which time it will be raised an incorruptible body that will never die. Sleep, therefore, is not permanent. The body returns to dust, only to be raised incorruptible when Jesus comes.

The Bible does not teach "soul sleep." The spirit of man will never cease to be conscious—no, not for one second! Fifty billion years from now you and I will be either living with Jesus and rejoicing . . . or we will be roasting with the devil in the lake of fire; and from this moment forward, neither you nor I will be unconscious in spirit . . . we will be conscious throughout eternity. If we die before the Lord's return, our bodies will return to dust, but our spirits will remain conscious and will rest with Jesus until the first resurrection. When a wicked person dies, the body returns to dust and the spirit goes into the flames of hell. The rich man in Luke 16 cried, "I am tormented in this flame!"

Believers are not to be sorrowful: *"That ye sorrow not, even as others which have no hope."* These words should comfort believers: ("Wherefore comfort one another with these words"—verse 18.) When we stand beside the casket of a loved one who dies in the Lord, we should not behave as those who have no hope, hysterically begging that loved one to speak, trying to call him back. If a loved one dies in the Lord, that one would not return even if it were possible to do so, because when saints depart this earthly body they are immediately present with the Lord—and to be with Him is far, far better than anything earth can offer. Paul said, "For I am in a strait betwixt two, having a desire to depart, and to be with Christ; which is far better" (Phil. 1:23).

This phrase in the Greek reads, "That you sorrow

not—as the rest." *The rest* is synonymous to *"those without"* in verse 12 and occurs here in the same sense as in Ephesians 2:3—*"even as others,"* referring to those among whom "we also had our conversation in times past in the lusts of our flesh, fulfilling the desires of the flesh and of the mind; and were by nature the children of wrath, *even as others.*" *Job* had the assurance that he would see Jesus. He said, "Though . . . worms devour this body, yet *in my flesh* shall I see God" (Job 19:26).

These "others" have no hope. In Ephesians 2:11—13 Paul described them thus: "Wherefore remember, that ye being in time past Gentiles in the flesh, who are called Uncircumcision by that which is called the Circumcision in the flesh made by hands; that at that time ye were without Christ, being aliens from the commonwealth of Israel, and strangers from the covenants of promise, *having no hope*, and without God in the world: but now in Christ Jesus ye who sometimes were far off are made nigh by the blood of Christ."

Jesus clearly taught, "I am the resurrection and the life: he that believeth in me, though he were dead, yet shall he live: and whosoever liveth and believeth in me shall never die" (John 11:25,26).

The *believers* in Thessalonica had embraced Christianity, had turned to God from idols, and therefore *had a hope* . . . in Jesus they had hope even beyond the grave, *"hope in our Lord Jesus Christ."* Our hope is in Jesus—He who tasted death for every man and removed the fear of dying (Heb. 2:9,14,15). Therefore, "Whether we live . . . or die, we are the Lord's" (Rom. 14:8). ". . . That whether we wake or sleep, we should live together with Him" (I Thess. 5:10).

It seems that the Thessalonian believers were not

so much disturbed about whether or not they would be resurrected, as they were concerned about whether or not they would have part in the Rapture. They were anxious on behalf of their departed loved ones. Probably they had sent an inquiry to Paul concerning this subject, and he is answering their question in our present passage.

Verse 14: "For if we believe that Jesus died and rose again, even so them also which sleep in Jesus will God bring with Him."

In that one short statement the faith of the believer is set forth in brief, understandable form. The same message is found in Romans 10:9 and 10—the verses that assured me of my salvation and my hope of spending eternity with the Lord Jesus: "That if thou shalt confess with thy mouth the Lord Jesus, and shalt believe in thine heart that God hath raised Him from the dead, thou shalt be saved. For with the heart man believeth unto righteousness; and with the mouth confession is made unto salvation."

If we believe that Jesus died on the cross and God raised Him from the dead, all the fundamentals of Christianity are wrapped up in this declaration of faith. If we believe that God raised up Jesus from the dead, we believe Christ is divine (Rom. 1:4); we also believe that through His death we have justification (Rom. 4:25), and that if Jesus was raised from the dead, His blood was divine and *through His shed blood* we have redemption and remission of sins (Col. 1:14,20; I John 1:7). The resurrection is the heart and soul of Christian faith. If we refuse to believe in the bodily resurrection of Jesus, our preaching is vain, our faith is vain, our hope is vain, we are of all men most miserable, and we are traveling day by day, step by step, toward the lake that will forever burn with fire and brimstone. Read carefully I Corinthians 15:20—34. We DO believe: *"But now is Christ risen from the dead, and become the firstfruits of them that slept."* Read Romans 8:29 and Colossians 1:18.

In the Greek, the words "even so them also which sleep in Jesus" read, "them which *fell asleep* in Jesus." Because of His death and resurrection from the dead, the sting and fear of death have been removed for believers. Those in the Thessalonian church who had died in the Lord had not fallen into death—but had simply *fallen asleep in Jesus.* In I Corinthians 15:55—57 Paul cries out, "O death, where is thy sting? O grave, where is thy victory? The sting of death is sin; and the strength of sin is the Law. But thanks be to God, which giveth us the victory through our Lord Jesus Christ!" To the believer, death has no sting, no power—and the fear of death is removed in the fact that Jesus conquered death and emerged victorious from the tomb. Therefore, all who fall asleep in Jesus are not dead, but are resting from their labors. The works they leave behind will continue to bear fruit until the Church is complete and caught up to meet Jesus in the clouds in the air, where we will receive our rewards at the marriage supper of the Lamb (Rev. 14:13; II Cor. 5:10).

Verse 14 closes with, "Even so them also which sleep in Jesus *will God bring with Him."* Believers who have fallen asleep in Jesus, God will bring with Him—for the God who raised His Son from the dead will also raise up all believers who fall asleep in Jesus (II Cor. 4:14; Eph. 1:19,20). In this statement Paul gives assurance to believers whose loved ones have died in the Lord, that God will not forget them when He comes in the blessed hope and the glorious appearing. When He comes to set up His kingdom on earth, His bride will reign with Him for one thousand glorious years.

"*IF we believe*" in the beginning of verse 14 does not suggest that there were some who did NOT believe that Jesus died and rose again; but rather, the meaning is, "SINCE we believe that Jesus died and rose again, we also believe that because of the resurrection of Christ, God will raise the bodies of believers who have fallen asleep in Jesus and will bring them with Him when He comes in the air." Paul is proclaiming the tremendous truth that the resurrection of Jesus not only guarantees resurrection of the righteous dead, but also guarantees that all of the righteous—the "quick and the dead"—will participate in the glorious second coming and in the reign of Christ here upon this earth.

At the very outset of this epistle Paul says, "You turned to God from idols, to wait for His Son from heaven whom He raised from the dead" (I Thess. 1:10). The divine union between true believers and the Lord Jesus is such that whatever Christ as head of the Church does or experiences, He carries the members of His body (the Church) with Him. The Christian dead are "dead in Christ" (verse 16) and therefore have the divine guarantee that in due time they will be raised and glorified in Christ (II Thess. 1:12; II Tim. 2:11).

The tremendous truth Paul is attempting to get across to the believers at Thessalonica is that *Jesus died* and *rose again*, and *because* He died and conquered death, He made a pathway through the grave. By this pathway true believers who fall asleep before the Rapture will be conducted into the place where they will be at rest until Jesus comes, and at that time they will appear with Him in the air.

David did not have the glorious epistles we now have; neither did he hear the Apostle Paul preach. Yet he said, "The Lord is my Shepherd, I shall not want . . . Yea, though I walk through the valley of the shadow of

139

death I will fear no evil, for thou art with me; thy rod and thy staff they comfort me" (Psalm 23). David did not say, "Yea, though I walk *into* death," nor did he say, "Yea, though I walk *into* the valley of the shadow." He said, "Yea, though I walk THROUGH the valley of the shadow of death." David knew he would enter that valley—but he also knew he would come out on the other side, through the pathway Jesus provided through His death, burial and resurrection. Believers do not die, in the true sense of death. The *wages of sin* is death; but Christians fall asleep in Jesus to rest until the first resurrection . . . the body returns to dust, the spirit returns to God. When the Rapture takes place the *bodies* of believers who have fallen asleep will be raised incorruptible, Jesus will bring their spirits with Him in the air, and the spirit will unite with the resurrected, glorified body; the living saints will be changed (translated), and together we will be caught up to meet Jesus in the clouds in the air.

Verse 15: "For this we say unto you by the word of the Lord, that we which are alive and remain unto the coming of the Lord shall not prevent them which are asleep."

Paul assures his children in the Lord that the word he is giving to them is coming from the mouth of the Lord. He uses similar terms many times in his epistles: "And unto the married I command, YET NOT I, BUT THE LORD . . ." (I Cor. 7:10). In I Thessalonians 2:13 he thanked God that the Thessalonians received the Gospel, *"not as the word of men, but as it is in truth, the Word of God."*

Paul is not quoting something the Spirit had revealed to Matthew, Mark, Luke, John, Peter, James or Jude. He declares that the message of verses 13 through 18 is a direct revelation from the Lord. In Galatians

2:2 and also in Ephesians 3:3 Paul assures his readers that the message is a direct revelation given expressly to him. Paul was a chosen vessel, ordained of God as an apostle and a minister to the Gentiles, to reveal unto them the mystery that was hidden from the beginning. To Paul God gave very special and singular revelations concerning His dealings with the Church, the bride of Christ.

The direct revelation here has to do with "we which are alive and remain unto the coming of the Lord." Paul believed in the imminent return of Jesus, although he did not at any time state that Christ would come during his earthly sojourn nor during the lifetime of the believers at Thessalonica—for he was aware that no man knows the day or the hour when the Son of man will come. Jesus said to His disciples, "It is not for you to know the times or the seasons, which the Father hath put in His own power" (Acts 1:7). Read also Matthew 24:36.

In Paul's day he knew in part and prophesied in part (I Cor. 13:12); but now, that which is perfect is come (the perfect law of liberty, the Word of God in its entirety), and many things are set forth in the Word that definitely point—not to the day or the hour, but to the times and the seasons. With these things beginning to come to pass, and with the fig tree (the nation of Israel) budding, we know that Jesus is near, "even at the door"— and when one is at the door he is just as close as he can be until he enters!

I believe ministers today should preach that *every sign in the Bible having to do with the revelation of Jesus is with us, all around us and upon us*. We are not date setters nor religious fanatics when we say that surely this is the end-time. We know not the day nor the hour, but we do know that the Word of God is fulfilled—and *surely Jesus is at the door!*

141

The statement, "*we which are alive and remain until the coming of the Lord*" does not mean that Paul expected to be alive nor that he expected the Thessalonians to be yet living when Jesus comes in the Rapture; it simply means those who belong to the New Testament Church. When Paul uses the word "we" as he uses it here, he is speaking of all born again believers, members of the one Church of which Jesus is the head (I Cor. 12:12, 13; Eph. 5:25–30).

". . . *Shall not prevent*" means "*shall in no case precede*" them which are asleep in Jesus. (The word "prevent" is an old English word and means "to precede or hinder.") Some of the teachers of error had undoubtedly told the believers at Thessalonica that their dead loved ones would have no part in the glorious appearing of the Lord Jesus, about which Paul preached so much. Now Paul passes on to them the revelation Jesus gave to him—that not only would they share in His glorious appearing, but that the dead in Christ *will rise first* and will occupy the *foremost place* in His glorious appearing. The "dead in Christ" were absent from the body but were at home with the Lord, and therefore, when the Rapture occurs they will come with Him in the air only seconds before the translation of the living saints (II Cor. 5:6–8; Phil. 1:23).

In this glorious revelation Paul assured the living believers that they would in no case precede or go before their believing loved ones who had fallen asleep in Jesus; for since those loved ones *were* fallen asleep in Jesus, they were with God and would be with Him when He comes in the Rapture. God revealed much to the Apostle Paul concerning the great beyond, but he was forbidden to tell all of it. Study carefully II Corinthians 12:1–5.

Verse 16: "For the Lord Himself shall descend

from heaven with a shout, with the voice of the arch-angel, and with the trump of God: and the dead in Christ shall rise first.''

I repeat . . . Paul is not quoting what someone else said, he is not writing what someone else had written; *he is giving to us what God, by revelation, gave to him.* "Let God be true, but every man a liar" (Rom. 3:4). Paul said, "FOR THE LORD HIMSELF shall descend . . . .'' Today there are many preachers who refuse to believe in or preach a personal return of Jesus to this earth; they spiritualize His coming. Thousands of church members have been told that the second coming took place at Pentecost. Others have been told that the second coming is the conversion of a sinner, while still others have been told that the second coming is *death*. The second coming of Christ has many times been spiritualized in one way or another; but we must believe God! *Jesus Christ will return to this earth "in His personal, august presence."*

On the day of Pentecost the Holy Spirit came to call out a people (Acts 15:13–18; John 6:44; 16:7–15). But God will not send the Holy Spirit to receive the bride, nor will He send death to receive the bride: JESUS IS COMING AGAIN IN PERSON TO RECEIVE HIS OWN BRIDE. Before His ascension the Son of God instructed His disciples to tarry in Jerusalem until the day of Pentecost. They obeyed; and when the day of Pentecost "was fully come,'' they were filled with the Holy Ghost and were commanded to preach the Gospel in Judaea, Samaria, and then to the uttermost parts of the earth. "And when (Jesus) had spoken these things, while (the disciples) beheld, He was taken up; and a cloud received Him out of their sight. And while they looked stedfastly toward heaven as He went up, behold, two men stood by them in white apparel; which also said,

143

Ye men of Galilee, why stand ye gazing up into heaven? *This same Jesus*, which is taken up from you into heaven, *shall so come in like manner as ye have seen Him go into heaven!*" (Acts 1:9—11).

In other words, did they not remember that Jesus had told them He would return to the Father? He had instructed them to tarry until they were filled with power, and then they were to tell the good news. They were commissioned to preach the Gospel to the uttermost parts of the earth. Therefore—with such a glorious command and with the assurance that He would be with them even to the end, why stand gazing after Him? They were to get busy and occupy until this same Jesus comes exactly as they saw Him go away.

Beloved, you may believe whom and what you choose to believe; but as for ME, "Let God be true and every man a liar!" Regardless of who the preacher or the teacher may be, regardless of the educational degrees he may have, God is still true. *Jesus Christ is coming back to this earth in a body, exactly as He went!*

The Lord Himself will descend from heaven (from the Father's house) with a shout; but when Jesus comes in the air with a shout He will not touch this earth, nor will those on earth see Him at that time. He will descend in the air in the clouds and call us up to meet Him. Later, at the end of the tribulation and reign of Antichrist, Jesus will stand on the Mount of Olives as recorded in Zechariah 14:4.

The statement "with a shout" in the original language means "with the *word of command*." The shout with which the general gives a command to his troops, ordering them into battle or to march, or the command a captain gives to the crew of his ship is in mind here. *That shout will be the command of the One who is in Highest Authority*.

144

There will be not only a shout, but also *"the voice of the archangel and the trump of God."* Some Bible authorities suggest that the shout, the voice of the archangel and the trumpet could all three be *one*—that is, the shout expressing the command of Christ could be in the voice of the archangel, sounding as a trumpet. In Revelation we read that the divine voice is constantly uttered by an angel—*"a mighty angel"* (Rev. 5:2; 7:2). Also in Revelation we read that the voice is as the voice of a trumpet. John uses this statement to describe the glorified Son of man: "I heard behind me a great voice AS OF A TRUMPET talking to me" (Rev. 1:10; 4:1). Jesus said in Matthew 24:31, "He shall send His angels with a great sound of a trumpet." In I Corinthians 15:52 we read, ". . . The trumpet shall sound, and the dead shall be raised incorruptible . . . ." The original language suggests a military trumpet that sounds out "the word of command." *"The voice of the archangel"* signifies the majesty and power of the summons. In Jude 9 we read of Michael the archangel; in Daniel 12:1 he is called "Michael the great prince," and in Revelation 12:7 we read that Michael and his angels fought against the dragon (Satan).

Certainly this has nothing to do with our salvation nor with our going in the Rapture. The shout could be one voice, the archangel could be another, and the trumpet could actually be the blast of a real trumpet. Or, the shout could be the voice of the mighty archangel, *sounding* as a great trumpet. But we do know the command will be, *"Come up hither!"*

This word of command by which the Lord will announce His coming for His saints will rouse the sleeping bodies of believers who have fallen asleep in Christ. They will shake off the fetters of the grave, they will rise to be glorified in a body like unto His own glorious

145

body (I John 3:1–3); "then we which are alive and remain" will instantaneously be caught up with them to meet the Lord in the air—*and it will all be over in the twinkling of an eye!*

This glorious sixteenth verse closes with the statement, ". . . *The dead in Christ shall rise first.*" Since Paul received this message from the Lord there was no reason for the Thessalonians to sorrow over the premature death of the sleeping believers, nor to doubt but that those who had died in the Lord would certainly have a foremost part in the glorious appearing of the great God and our Saviour, Jesus Christ.

This verse as a whole is tremendous. We learn that "the Lord Himself"—not an angel, not a cherub, not a seraph, but *Jesus in person*—will descend from heaven. Jesus said, "In my Father's house are many mansions . . . I go to prepare a place for YOU. And if I go, I will come again and receive you unto myself, that where I am, there ye may be also" (John 14:2,3). He has been in the Father's house for more than 1900 years now, preparing that "place"; and one of these glorious days He will descend with a shout, the voice of the archangel and the trumpet of God will sound out the command, "Come up hither!"——and all of the believers who have fallen asleep in Jesus will rise first. The bodies of our dead loved ones now in the grave will be raised—and then *together* we will be caught up to where Jesus is waiting in the clouds! No wonder Paul said, ". . . the GLORIOUS appearing of our great God and Saviour, Jesus Christ!" No wonder he said, "Comfort one another with these words!"

Verse 17: "Then we which are alive and remain shall be caught up together with them in the clouds, to meet the Lord in the air: and so shall we ever be with the Lord."

146

As I pointed out earlier, the statement "We which are alive" does not necessarily mean that Paul thought he would be living when the Rapture took place. He is speaking of the Church—of the living believers when the Rapture takes place. They will be changed in a moment, in the twinkling of an eye—and then, together with the resurrected saints, will be caught up in the clouds to meet the Lord in the air; "and so shall we ever be with the Lord!"

The Greek "caught up" implies a sudden, powerful, irresistible force. Our English word "*seized*" describes the meaning—to be "snatched up." The same word is used in Matthew 11:12 where it is translated "the violent take it by force." In II Corinthians 12:1–5 Paul describes his being caught up into the third heaven, and declares that he saw and heard things not lawful to tell. The Rapture will be sudden; we will be removed from this earth by a powerful, irresistible force, seized and snatched up to meet our Saviour in the clouds.

The statement "*in the clouds*" in the Greek signifies "amid clouds." The suggestion here is that the saints will be surrounded by clouds which will act as a giant chariot, and we will be borne away on their downy softness. The angels at Christ's ascension promised He would come again as He went away (Acts 1:9–11). On the Mount of Transfiguration "a bright cloud" overshadowed, and a voice from the cloud said, "This is my beloved Son, in whom I am well pleased" (Matt. 17:1–8). There is something majestic, wonderful and mystical about the clouds. Nahum tells us that clouds are "the dust of (God's) feet" (Nah. 1:3). The glorious event of the Rapture will be surrounded by clouds, and the curtains of the atmosphere will hover about us as we are raised into the air to be with our blessed Lord.

"*And so shall we ever be with the Lord.*" Paul

does not say that we will remain in the AIR forever; he says we will be *with the Lord* forever—and that statement is sufficient comfort for me, just to know that I will always be with the Lord. Wherever He is, is heaven, peace and joy. Jesus said, "Where I am there shall also my servant be" (John 12:26). To be with Jesus is good enough for me, whether it be in the air, on the earth or in the Father's house. Hallelujah! We will never again be separated from the Lord, from our precious loved ones, nor from our brothers and sisters in Christ!

Verse 18: "Wherefore comfort one another with these words."

This chapter closes with words of comfort. The believers in Thessalonica had been disturbed concerning their loved ones who had died. Some teachers had led them to believe that they would not have part in the resurrection and in the glorious kingdom Jesus promised; but Paul assures the living believers that their loved ones who have fallen asleep in Jesus will have the foremost place on God's giant elevator that will literally raise us up in the air to meet our Lord and Saviour Jesus Christ.

One thing that made the message of verses 15 through 17 so very comforting was the fact that Paul assured the believers that he had received the message by revelation from God, and that he was not conveying to them words that another mortal had communicated to him.

Notice how Paul longed that his children in the Lord should minister to one another: "Comfort one another with these words." That is, "Read them to each other, say them to each other, quote them over and over again, assure and reassure each other."

The Greek word for "comfort" is the same as "exhort" in verse 1 of this chapter and other places in the letter. It means to encourage or assure through comforting words, to exhort through words that give strength. It suggests cheering one another, and that was the desire of Paul's heart for the believers who had suffered severe persecution and bereavement. The teachers of error were attempting to rob them of their spiritual birthright of full joy, abundant life, peace that surpasses all understanding, and the blessed hope that He who died and rose again will bring with Him all who have fallen asleep in Jesus.

I THESSALONIANS — CHAPTER FIVE

1. But of the times and the seasons, brethren, ye have no need that I write unto you.

2. For yourselves know perfectly that the day of the Lord so cometh as a thief in the night.

3. For when they shall say, Peace and safety; then sudden destruction cometh upon them, as travail upon a woman with child; and they shall not escape.

4. But ye, brethren, are not in darkness, that that day should overtake you as a thief.

5. Ye are all the children of light, and the children of the day: we are not of the night, nor of darkness.

6. Therefore let us not sleep, as do others; but let us watch and be sober.

7. For they that sleep sleep in the night; and they that be drunken are drunken in the night.

8. But let us, who are of the day, be sober, putting on the breastplate of faith and love; and for an helmet, the hope of salvation.

9. For God hath not appointed us to wrath, but to obtain salvation by our Lord Jesus Christ.

10. Who died for us, that, whether we wake or sleep, we should live together with him.

11. Wherefore comfort yourselves together, and edify one another, even as also ye do.

12. And we beseech you, brethren, to know them which labour among you, and are over you in the Lord, and admonish you;

13. And to esteem them very highly in love for their work's sake. And be at peace among yourselves.

14. Now we exhort you, brethren, warn them that are unruly, comfort the feebleminded, support the weak, be patient toward all men.

15. See that none render evil for evil unto any man; but ever follow that which is good, both among yourselves, and to all men.

16. Rejoice evermore.

17. Pray without ceasing.

18. In every thing give thanks: for this is the will of God in Christ Jesus concerning you.

19. Quench not the Spirit.

20. Despise not prophesyings.

21. Prove all things; hold fast that which is good.

22. Abstain from all appearance of evil.

23. And the very God of peace sanctify you wholly; and I pray God your whole spirit and soul and body be preserved blameless unto the coming of our Lord Jesus Christ.

24. Faithful is he that calleth you, who also will do it.

25. Brethren, pray for us.

26. Greet all the brethren with an holy kiss.

27. I charge you by the Lord that this epistle be read unto all the holy brethren.

28. The grace of our Lord Jesus Christ be with you. Amen.

The first part of this chapter is closely connected with the last six verses in chapter four. Verses 13–18 in chapter four and verses 1–6 in chapter five are the most distinctive and weighty verses in the epistle, and they contain the heart of Paul's message to believers wherever he preached.

In verses 13 through 18 of chapter four, Paul gives the message God revealed to him to comfort believers concerning friends and loved ones who had departed this life, while the first six verses in chapter 5 contain words of exhortation and admonition concerning the model walk of believers on earth as having to do with the return of Jesus. All believers should be prepared, waiting and watching, because His coming for the Church is imminent; but *we are not to be idle.* We are to "occupy" until He comes!

Verses 1 and 2 in chapter 5 indicate that in the church in Thessalonica Paul had often taught the doctrine of the second coming.

Verse 1: "But of the times and the seasons, brethren, ye have no need that I write unto you."

The Greek word for "times" denotes *stretches of time* or *that particular time.* In other words, "Brethren, you need not that I write to you concerning the times and seasons of the Lord's return. When I was with you

151

I fully instructed you concerning the return of our Lord for His own, and you already know as much as can be known."

Paul was a "Second Coming preacher." He followed the same line of teaching that Jesus followed when He was on earth. Jesus told His disciples, "It is not for you to know the times or seasons, which the Father hath put in His own power" (Acts 1:7). In Mark 13:32 Jesus said, "Of that day and hour knoweth no man, no, not the angels which are in heaven, neither the Son, but the Father." According to these clear, understandable statements from the Word of God, such knowledge is not for us—and certainly we are not to indulge in idle speculation concerning the precise time when the Lord will come. Date-setters are false prophets, and we should pay no attention to any man who sets a date when the Lord will return for His own.

Verse 2: "For yourselves know perfectly that the day of the Lord so cometh as a thief in the night."

Paul believed in thoroughly instilling the fundamentals of the faith into the hearts and minds of those to whom he preached. The word "perfectly" in the statement *"For yourselves know perfectly"* can be translated "precisely," "accurately" or "carefully." It could be that the Thessalonian believers had sent Paul a message saying, "We would like to know more *precisely*, we would like to be taught more *accurately*, concerning the times and seasons when the day of the Lord will be." (Notice II Thessalonians 2:1–3.)

In essence, Paul answered, *"You already know* precisely that nothing precise *can be known* concerning the Rapture, for this glorious event will come upon the world as a thief in the night. Precise dates and precise events cannot be known. We dare not speculate

152

concerning this glorious day."

"*The day of the Lord so cometh as a thief in the night.*" What Paul is saying here is, "There is coming such a day as I spoke of when I was with you in person—a day when Jesus will come for His jewels, when the dead in Christ will be raised, the living will be changed, *and together we will be caught up* to meet the Lord in the clouds in the air. Such a day is coming—yea, it is on the way! And it is certain to be; but no man can know WHEN this day will arrive. No man can be exact or precise, and there should be no speculation concerning those things that God has not seen fit to reveal unto His own."

Why did the Holy Spirit compare the Rapture to a thief coming in the darkness of night? The answer is clear: Even a child knows what a thief is, what he does and how he does it. When Jesus comes in the Rapture, His coming will be unexpected by the world. *Believers* are looking for Him, waiting for Him and praying for His soon return; but "as it was in the days of Noah, so shall it be in the days of the coming of the Son of man." In Noah's day the people ate, they drank, they bought, they sold, they married wives—and "KNEW NOT UNTIL THE FLOOD CAME AND TOOK THEM ALL AWAY."

The days of Noah were marked by extreme wisdom and knowledge on one hand, and by extreme ignorance on the other. The fourth chapter of Genesis reveals that they were business men—they were building cities, they were in the iron and brass business, the music-making business . . . *and wholesale killing!* Genesis 6:4 tells us that "*there were giants in the earth in those days.*" This does not necessarily mean physical giants, even though there might have been those; but it refers primarily to men who were giants mentally. The Scripture says, "They became mighty men . . . men of renown."

The days before the flood were marked by unusual wisdom and knowledge on the part of man. The same is true today. We are seeing all around us a repetition of Noah-days. When we see these things coming to pass all around us, we do not set a date for the Lord's return, we do not name an hour when He will come—*but we know that His coming draws very near*!

A thief usually comes in the darkest hour of the night, and he does not announce his coming. He comes quietly into the house, catches up diamonds, rubies, pearls, silver—whatever is of value—and leaves immediately. He takes with him the precious stones and jewels, but leaves the kitchen chairs and table, the brooms and mops. *A thief comes for that which is valuable*; and when he gets what he came for, he disappears at once—and in the majority of cases he is not seen by anyone.

When Jesus comes in the Rapture, He will take the jewels (the born again ones), but He will not be seen by unbelievers. They may hear the shout; it is possible that they will hear the trumpet blast—*but they will not see Jesus*. Neither will WE see Him until we are with Him in the clouds in the air. *And the entire event will be over in the twinkling of an eye*!

When Jesus walked this earth, He taught in words easily understood. He talked about the sower, the seed, the lily of the field, the grass, the fowls of the air. He talked about little children. Jesus came down to earth to bring salvation to man, and He *explained* salvation in language that could be understood—even by a little child. It is a strange thing that ministers in this day like to see just how much they can learn, in order to preach in high-sounding words and phrases, seemingly advertising their own ability instead of holding forth the Christ who called them! God forbid that I judge, but most churches do not seem to be interested in how *spiritual* a minister is, nor how much he loves the Lord and the people he serves. The focal point of interest seems to be, "Where did he attend school? What universities has he attended? How many degrees does he have—and is he an eloquent man?" God give us preachers who love souls and preach down-to-earth sermons that can be understood by ordinary people!

Writing to the Corinthians, Paul declared that ministers should speak in understandable language: "So likewise ye, except ye utter by the tongue words easy to be understood, how shall it be known what is spoken? for ye shall speak into the air" (I Cor. 14:9). I am afraid some of our eloquent sermons of this day are "spoken into the air."

The Rapture of the Church is compared to the coming of a thief in the night so that ordinary people—even children—can understand what the Rapture is and how it will occur. Jesus spoke of the thief in His sermon on judgment (Matt. 24:43; Luke 12:39,40). Peter also uses the word in II Peter 3:10. John uses it in Revelation 3:3.

Let me again point out that there are no signs (as such) pointing to the *Rapture only*. By that I mean, the signs in the New Testament—things that must and will occur before the Day of the Lord—do not point to the Rapture (the thief-coming of Jesus for His saints), but to the *revelation* spoken of by Jude, John and Zechariah—the time when Jesus will come with tens of thousands of His saints: "Behold, He cometh with clouds; and every eye shall see Him, and they also which pierced Him: and all kindreds of the earth shall wail because of Him. Even so, Amen" (Rev. 1:7). That could not be the coming of which Paul speaks when he says to Titus, "For the grace of God that bringeth salvation hath appeared to all men, teaching us . . . (to look) for that blessed hope, and the glorious appearing of the great God and our Saviour Jesus Christ; who gave Himself for us, that He might redeem us from all iniquity, and purify unto Himself a peculiar people, zealous of good works" (Titus 2:11–14).

The Rapture is a *blessed day*, but the *Day of the Lord* is a day of darkness, as we will see when we study the second chapter of II Thessalonians.

Verse 3: "For when they shall say, Peace and safety; then sudden destruction cometh upon them, as travail upon a woman with child; and they shall not escape."

To me it seems that these words could be the headlines in any newspaper tomorrow morning. When people are saying, "Peace and safety," when the world talks of security and peace; when governments imagine they have drawn up councils of nations who will set up rules and regulations through which peace will come—*that is the very hour in which God is about ready to throw the switch and lower His great boom of judgment upon mankind!*

I am not a prophet of gloom, nor am I a pessimist. I am definitely an optimist—but my optimism is not in man or earthly rules. *My optimism is in the Son of Righteousness, the Lord Jesus Christ.* You may rest assured that so long as the devil is out of the pit there will be no lasting peace on earth. Jesus said that the days just before His return to this earth will be days marked by wars and rumors of wars, with nation rising against nation and kingdom against kingdom (Matt. 24).

Such is the case today. I believe we have suffered our last world war until after the Rapture; but there are many little wars, and these will increase more and more. Yet all the while, as tribes and kingdoms fight, the rulers of earth (heads of Communist governments and even those

156

at the head of our own Republic) will be talking "Peace, peace!" The Christian knows deep down in his heart that *there is no peace.* The devil never changes his line of lies. In Ezekiel's day men were saying, "Peace!"— and there was no peace. When the wicked feel in their hearts that they have discovered and manufactured sufficient planes and bombs to guarantee peace, that is the hour when Jehovah God will laugh at them and will have them in derision. (Please read the entire second Psalm.)

Immediately after the Rapture, the false Messiah will make his appearance. He will be riding upon a white horse (a symbol of peace) with a bow—but no arrow—in his hand (another symbol of peace). A crown will be given to him, and he will go forth—"conquering and to conquer." The crown denotes authority; and since he has a bow but no arrow, he will conquer the world without bloodshed. He will conquer by flatteries and vain promises as described in Daniel concerning the "little horn," who is the Antichrist.

The first three and one-half years after the Rapture will be years of peace—false security. On the surface there will be peace, but underneath will be turmoil eating away as a cancer destroys the human body. In the middle of Daniel's second week of prophecy, after three and one-half years of peace, the Antichrist will break every covenant, every promise—and all hell will break out. The nation of Israel, back in her own land at that time, will suffer a deluge of blood such as she has never known.

When Pilate asked at the trial of Jesus, "Whom shall I release unto you?" the Jews shouted, "Release Barabbas!" Pilate then asked, "What shall I do with Jesus, who is called the Christ?" and they cried out, "Crucify Him! LET HIS BLOOD BE UPON US AND UPON OUR CHILDREN!"

Jesus said to the Jews, "I am come in my Father's name, and ye receive me not; if another shall come in his own name, him ye will receive" (John 5:43).

When the world is talking peace, declaring that at last man has done away with war and bloodshed and brought in Utopia, thus making earth a paradise, at that very moment "SUDDENLY OVER THEM STANDS DESTRUCTION!" Thus reads the Greek. Without one second of warning, all hell will break out; and such torment, persecution, bloodshed, misery and woe will be upon this earth as man has never known.

In the last part of verse 3 Paul describes this day of terror in another way: "... *as travail upon a woman with child; and they shall not escape.*" The Greek reads, "As the birth-pain upon her that is with child." This illustration signifies suddenness, terrible agony, intense pain; and the event is inevitable—it cannot be escaped. Once the birth pang is felt, the woman must be delivered. When the appointed hour (known only to Jehovah God) arrives, judgment must fall; there is no stopping the hand of justice and righteousness: "And they shall not escape!" Read II Thessalonians 1:9 and Revelation 6:15–17.

When this terrible Day of the Lord comes, Jesus will be revealed from heaven with multiplied millions of His mighty angels. With His angels He will come in flaming fire, taking vengeance on them that know not God and who obey not the Gospel. These unbelievers, wicked men, will be punished with everlasting destruction from the presence of the Lord and the glory of His power. This will take place when Jesus comes to be glorified in His saints and to be admired in all them that believe. This day will be the day when Jesus returns with His bride, after the marriage supper in the sky and the rewarding of believers for their stewardship.

158

Verse 4: "But ye, brethren, are not in darkness, that that day should overtake you as a thief."

Paul is reminding the believers at Thessalonica that when they turned to God from idols, to serve the true and living God, they began that moment to wait and look for His Son from heaven. The grace of God that brings salvation teaches us to deny ungodliness and worldly lusts, and that "we should live soberly, righteously, and godly in this present world; looking for that blessed hope, and the glorious appearing of the great God and our Saviour Jesus Christ" (Tit. 2:11–13). All born again people believe in the second coming of Jesus Christ. The grace of God that saves us also teaches us to deny ungodliness and to live righteously; *and that same grace teaches us to look for the blessed hope and the glorious appearing of our great God and Saviour, Jesus Christ.* If you are not looking for that glorious day, according to the Word of God you are not saved by grace.

We do not all agree on every detail of the second coming, but all believers *do* agree that *He is coming*— because He said, "I go . . . I will come again!" . . . and Jesus cannot lie (Heb. 6:18; Titus 1:2). Paul had carefully instructed the Christians in Thessalonica concerning the Rapture of the Church, and therefore they were not in darkness. They were in the light because he had carefully taught them in the true doctrine of the Lord's return.

Verse 5: "Ye are all the children of light, and the children of the day: we are not of the night, nor of the darkness."

All believers are "children of light . . . *sons* of light." We are translated into the kingdom of God's dear Son when we believe (Col. 1:13). We are literally taken from the kingdom of darkness and placed over into the kingdom of light, and therefore we are sons of light.

By a common Hebrew idiom, a man is said to be a son of any influence that dominated the character of that man. For instance, "son of Belial" means *worthless*. In the New Testament Jesus spoke of "sons of thunder," "sons of the resurrection." Here Paul is saying that those who are the "*sons of light*" cannot be "*in darkness*." Light is a favorite figure of speech with Paul—he uses it frequently. (Read Romans 13:11-14; Ephesians 5:8-14; Colossians 1:12,13.) John the Beloved uses the same term frequently in the Gospel that bears his name. Jesus refers to Himself as *the Light of the World* (John 8:12).

Light is used to describe the righteousness and truth of God as compared to the wickedness of the devil and the lie that he is. John 3:19: ". . . Men loved darkness rather than light, because their deeds were evil." In I John 1:5-7 we read, "This then is the message which we have heard of Him, and declare unto you, that God is light, and in Him is no darkness at all. If we say that we have fellowship with Him, and walk in darkness, we lie, and do not the truth: But if we walk in the light, as He is in the light, we have fellowship one with another, and the blood of Jesus Christ His Son cleanseth us from all sin."

The Psalmist cried out, "THE LORD IS MY LIGHT AND MY SALVATION" (Psalm 27:1). (Read also John 8:12 and II Corinthians 4:6.) Jesus is the LIGHT of the world, and those who know Him as Saviour and Lord do not live in the *darkness* of the world nor walk in paths of unrighteousness. He is the light of our life, and the Holy Spirit leads believers into paths of right living.

"*Children of the day*"—sons of the day—are born of God, are therefore sons of God, and are of the resurrection. Believers are also *sons of the DAY of the Lord*—

160

that is, we are part of that day when we will return with
Him to judge the wicked and to reign with Him in peace.
Read Luke 20:34–36, II Thessalonians 1:7, Romans 8:
18–24 and Colossians 3:4.

"*We are not of the night, nor of darkness.*" Note
that Paul passes from the second person to the first.
The verse begins with "Ye," referring to the believers
in Thessalonica, and closes with "we," having to do
with Paul AND the believers there, thus proving that all
believers belong to the same Church (the same body),
and all believers will go in the Rapture. There is no
such thing as a partial Rapture.

Night is darkness; day is light. The night is opposite the day. The same is true in the spiritual realm.
Night signifies spiritual darkness, unbelief and ignorance;
day signifies light. All born again believers have been
translated out of darkness into light, out of spiritual ignorance into spiritual truth. Therefore no believer is of
the night nor of the darkness.

Verse 6: "Therefore let us not sleep, as do others;
but let us watch and be sober."

This verse begins with "*Therefore.*" (Since the
preceding is true, the following should automatically be
true.) The Greek reads, "*Accordingly then.*" Paul uses
this same statement in II Thessalonians 2:15. He uses
it eight times in his epistle to the Romans, and he uses
it on other occasions in his other writings. The meaning here is, "Therefore (since we have been translated
out of darkness into light) it is logical and practical that
we should not sleep as do unbelievers, nor should we
walk in darkness as do they. We should be watchful at
all times—alert and sober. We should be awaiting and
expecting the imminent return of the Lord Jesus. *All
this should be true—since we are children of the day*

161

rather than children of the night."

In Romans 13:11,12 Paul admonishes, "And that, knowing the time, that now it is high time to awake out of sleep: for now is our salvation nearer than when we believed. The night is far spent, the day is at hand: let us therefore cast off the works of darkness, and let us put on the armour of light."

Luke 12:36,37: "And ye yourselves like unto men that wait for their Lord, when he will return from the wedding; that when he cometh and knocketh, they may open unto him immediately. Blessed are those servants, whom the Lord when He cometh, shall find watching: verily I say unto you, that He shall gird Himself, and make them to sit down to meat, and will come forth and serve them."

"*Be sober.*" Sobriety is the exact opposite of drunkenness. Paul is telling the believers at Thessalonica that Christians should be the exact opposite of unbelievers.

Verse 7: "For they that sleep sleep in the night; and they that be drunken are drunken in the night."

Since believers are sons of the day, they should at all times be wakeful and sober. Those who demonstrate the opposite advertise that they are sons of the night—unbelievers and children of wrath. In Paul's day, for one to be drunken by day was almost unheard of. Read Acts 2:15. These words look beyond the literal sense of "sober" in verse 6. Here, drunkenness signifies the condition of a soul besotted and enslaved by sin, and Paul warns against such. In Luke 21:34 Jesus said, "And take heed to yourselves, lest at any time your hearts be overcharged with surfeiting, and drunkenness, and cares of this life, and so that day come upon you unawares."

162

Verse 8: "But let us, who are of the day, be sober, putting on the breastplate of faith and love; and for an helmet, the hope of salvation."

In Ephesians 6:13-17 Paul gives almost the same instructions, but in greater detail. He is instructing us here, "Since we believers are of the day, it is understood that we are to be watchful and ready at all times. We are to put on the breastplate of faith and love—and for a helmet we are to wear the hope of salvation."

Good soldiers are always alert when the dawn begins to break. If a soldier sleeps and gets his rest during the hours of darkness, he is ready to awake and be on his toes at the crack of dawn. On the other hand, if he spends the night in drunkenness and revelry, he is NOT alert at the bugle call, his armor is not ready—and he enters into battle unprepared.

Paul had much to say about being a good soldier for the Lord Jesus Christ. Christians are in the greatest army known to earth or heaven—the army of the Lord. We are commanded to put on the whole armor of God and be alert and diligent at all times, under all circumstances. According to Romans 13:12,13 we are to put off the shameful garments of darkness and night, and put on the armor of light. We are to walk in the day—and we are to be careful HOW we walk. We are to be alert and walk with the dignity becoming to the Christ we represent and in whose army we serve.

Paul sets forth the *breastplate and helmet* as the two main pieces of our defensive armor because they protect the most vital parts of the body. The *breastplate of faith and love* guards the heart, the center of life. From the heart proceed the issues of life, and to this quarter *"faith and love"* are naturally assigned as protection from the arrows of the wicked one.

163

The helmet of the believer is the hope of SALVA-TION. Paul here quotes from Isaiah 59:17: "For He (Jehovah) put on righteousness as a breastplate, and an helmet of salvation upon His head; and He put on the garments of vengeance for clothing and was clad with zeal as a cloke." (In this Old Testament quotation, Jehovah God is preparing to fight for His people.)

Observe Paul's favorite combination of graces—the well-known trio of Faith, Hope and Love (see chapter 1:3)—but the greatest of these is love (I Cor. 13:13).

Believers who are dressed according to the spiritual pattern will never succumb to the fiery darts of the devil, for *He who saves also keeps*. He has promised a way of escape; He has promised final victory. Study carefully I Corinthians 10:13, I John 4:4 and Romans 8:35–39. If you are living a defeated life as a believer, it is your own fault, for it is God's good pleasure to give complete victory to each and every one of His children. God is no respecter of persons (Rom. 2:11); and what He does for one of His children, He will do for all if they will only let Him. Many believers are enjoying only second best in the spiritual realm, when it is God's good pleasure to give them *abundant life*. The Psalmist describes it thus: "No good thing will He withhold from them that walk uprightly" (Psa. 84:11b).

THE CHURCH WILL NOT ENTER THE TRIBULATION

Verse 9: "For God hath not appointed us to wrath, but to obtain salvation by our Lord Jesus Christ."

There are those who believe in the doctrine of Pre-millennialism—the belief that the Rapture will take place before the Tribulation. There are those who believe the Rapture will occur in the *middle* of the Tribulation period, thus teaching that the Church will go through the first half of the Tribulation. Still others believe and teach that the Rapture will take place *after* the Tribulation, and thus the Church will go through the entire Tribulation period.

Be not deceived by the teachers of error who advocate Mid-tribulation or Post-tribulation Rapture. The Lord Jesus will take His bride out of this earth before the appearing of Antichrist, as we will clearly see in the Second Thessalonian Epistle. Here Paul assures the believers that God has not appointed believers to wrath—the word *wrath* as used in this verse pointing to the Tribulation period, the time when the Antichrist will reign.

John the Beloved adds an "Amen" to this truth in Revelation 3:10: "Because thou hast kept the word of my patience, I also will keep thee from the hour of temptation, which shall come upon all the world, to try them that dwell upon the earth."

Not one drop of flood water fell until Noah and his family had entered the ark and God had shut them in. Surely God did not love Noah more than He loves the New Testament Church—the Bride of His only begotten Son! Not one spark of fire and brimstone fell upon Sodom and Gomorrah until Lot was safely outside the city. In the nineteenth chapter of Genesis we learn that after God gave solemn warning, Lot spent the night and next morning in the city of Sodom. Finally, the messengers of God took Lot, his wife and his two daughters *and literally set them outside the city*, saying that God could not send judgment upon the city until Lot was safe.

II Peter 2:7 tells us that Lot was a *just* man, vexed with the filthy conversation of Sodom. It is true that he had backslidden—he had sinned grievously—but nevertheless, not one spark of fire and brimstone touched Sodom until Lot was safe outside the city. *The Antichrist will not appear*, the Tribulation will *not* begin, *until the Church is seated at the marriage supper in the sky*. When the Great Tribulation comes, the Bride (the Church) will have a ringside seat with Jesus in the sky!

The statement *"but to obtain salvation"* does not mean that we will finally be redeemed in the end. The moment we believe we are fully redeemed, we are fully saved, we are a child of God—but it means that "He who hath begun a good work in us is able (and will) perform it" until we are conformed to the image of "His dear Son" (Rom. 8:29). Our salvation will be full and complete when we "see Him as He is" (I John 3:1–3).

Salvation in the New Testament includes all the benefits and all the blessings of the Gospel. God is our salvation, and in Him we possess redemption—sins forgiven and forgotten; we are guaranteed deliverance from the world, the flesh and the devil, from death, hell and the grave; we know that we will be raised to be like Him; because He lives, *so shall we live*. Salvation guarantees the fulfillment of every promise Jesus made—all of which He has a right to give because He paid redemption's price in full. He satisfied the heart and holiness of God and stands today to confess us to the heavenly Father. He is the One who will see that we safely reach our heavenly abode. He will never leave us nor forsake us, so that we may boldly say, "The Lord is my helper; I shall not fear what man may do unto me." We can say, "IN HIM we are more than conquerors! We WILL overcome, because greater is He that is in us than he that is in the world." The Christ who abides in the bosom of every born again believer is very capable of keeping that which we have committed unto Him against that day.

"God hath not appointed us to wrath, but to obtain salvation . . . ." Here Paul makes a solemn contrast

166

between the anger and righteous judgment of God upon the wicked, and the glorious salvation to be revealed in its fulness in the Rapture, when believers will receive glorified, incorruptible bodies like unto the Lord's resurrection body. In I John 4:8 we learn that God is love, but in Hebrews 12:29 we are assured that God is a consuming fire. We know that it is not God's will that any perish, but that all come to repentance—yet the Psalmist clearly tells us, "God is angry with the wicked every day" (Psa. 7:11). "The wicked shall be turned into hell, and all the nations that forget God" (Psalm 9:17). In Romans 2:5,6 Paul said, "But after thy hardness and impenitent heart treasurest up unto thyself wrath against the day of wrath and revelation of the *righteous judgment of God*; who will render to every man according to his works." God is love, God is righteous, God is long-suffering—*but God will also judge the wicked*!

"But God commendeth His love toward us, in that, while we were yet sinners, Christ died for us. Much more then, being now justified by His blood, WE SHALL BE SAVED FROM WRATH THROUGH HIM. For if, when we were enemies, we were reconciled to God by the death of His Son, much more, being reconciled, WE SHALL BE SAVED BY HIS LIFE. And not only so, but we also joy in God through our Lord Jesus Christ, by whom we have now received the atonement" (Rom. 5:8–11).

When the precious blood of Jesus is applied to our hearts by faith, *redemption is the result*. His blood gives us the assurance of God's favor instead of His anger. The Christian *fears* God ("The fear of the Lord is the beginning of wisdom"—Psalm 111:10) . . . but not in that we are afraid to meet Him, because we know that we are covered by the precious blood that cleanses from all sin. Paul could say, "I know whom I have believed, and am persuaded that He is able to keep that which I have committed unto Him against that day" (II Tim. 1:12). Study carefully Romans 8:31–39. These precious words bring assurance, hope—and stability that produces joy unspeakable and full of glory.

Verse 9 closes with the words, *"by our Lord Jesus Christ."* Salvation is of the Lord—yea, salvation IS the Lord Jesus Christ, who loved us and willingly gave Himself for us. He came not to be ministered unto, but to minister, and to give His life a ransom for many. *"Neither is there salvation in any other: for there is none other name under heaven given among men, whereby we must be saved"* (Acts 4:12). Jesus said, "I am the door: by me if any man enter in, he shall be saved . . ." (John 10:9a). To Thomas He said, "I am the way, the truth, and the life; no man cometh unto the Father, but by me" (John 14:6).

"And this is the record, that God hath given to us eternal life, and THIS LIFE IS IN HIS SON. He that hath the Son hath life; and he that hath not the Son of God hath not life" (I John 5:11,12). "Christ in you, the hope of glory" (Col. 1:27).

If you have not received the Lord Jesus Christ, receive Him this moment as your personal Saviour. He will save you, and you will know it!

Verse 10: "Who died for us, that, whether we wake or sleep, we should live together with Him."

The death of Jesus was a *must*, that we might have redemption. We are redeemed through His shed blood. Jesus died on the cross to save souls. In His first coming, He paid the sin-debt in full; however, the *first coming* of Jesus (the cross) demands the *second coming* (the Rapture). Our salvation will be complete when we see Jesus. The righteous dead are resting now in Paradise—they are conscious, they know what is going on around them; and they rejoice: "There is joy in the *presence* of the angels of God over one sinner that repenteth" (Luke 15:10).

Moses and Elijah descended in a body to the Mount of Transfiguration. But the body—whatever form it may be—that the righteous have now in Paradise is not the body we will have and in which we will dwell throughout eternity.

"Beloved, now are we the sons of God, *and it doth not yet appear what we shall be: but we know that, when He shall appear, we shall be like Him*; for we shall see Him as He is" (I John 3:2). ". . . Christ the firstfruits; afterward they that are Christ's at His coming" (I Cor. 15:23). Paul's overwhelming statement, "CHRIST DIED FOR US . . . THAT WE SHOULD LIVE TOGETHER WITH HIM," wraps up the entire doctrine of redemption by the death and resurrection of Jesus and encompasses the fact that we will live with Him where He is *throughout eternity*. Study carefully Romans 3:21–26; 4:25; 5:2; 8:1–4; Gal. 2:10–21; 3:9–14; II Cor. 5:14; I Thess. 4: 13–18; I Cor. 15:51–57; I John 3:1–3.

Paul preached atonement and salvation from sin by simple faith in the finished work of the Lord Jesus Christ. He preached that when one believes, the Holy Spirit comes into the heart crying, "Abba, Father," thus denoting sonship. He preached our abiding union with Christ in His risen and heavenly life, where He now sits at the right hand of God the Father, making intercession for us (I Tim. 2:5).

Verse 10 closes: ". . . *That, whether we wake or sleep, we should live together with Him*." The meaning is simply, "Living or dead, awake or asleep—when Jesus comes we will go to meet Him in the clouds in the air, and so shall we ever be with our Lord." The death of Jesus on the cross guarantees deathless, eternal life for every believer.

In Romans 14:8,9 Paul said: "For whether we live, we live unto the Lord; and whether we die, we die unto the Lord: whether we live therefore, or die, we are the Lord's. For to this end Christ both died, and rose, and revived, that He might be Lord both of the dead and living." Christ died for us, that we who receive Him might live an eternal life in spiritual union with Him, who is the head of the New Testament Church. Believers are members of His body; therefore, as long as the head lives, WE will live, and we know that Christ is alive to die no more!

To His disciples Jesus said, "I am come that they might have life . . . I am the living bread which came down from heaven: if any man eat of this bread, he shall live forever: and the bread that I will give is my flesh, which I will give for the life of the world" (John 10:10; 6:51).

The grave could not hold Him; He died, but the third day He arose, and He lives at the right hand of God the Father. Death cannot touch Him. Read Romans 6:9,10. Those of us who are born again are joined to the Lord—we are one body. We enter that body through the baptism of the Holy Spirit; we are all baptized by one Spirit into one body (I Cor. 12:13). Because He lives, we live also. We are in Christ in God (Rom. 8:1; Col. 3:3).

THE GUARANTEED CURE FOR BACKSLIDING

In the following verses we have Paul's prescription for a sure cure for backsliding. Any believer or any church practicing the truth set forth in these verses will never, *never*, NEVER backslide!

Verse 11: "Wherefore comfort yourselves together, and edify one another, even as also ye do."

That is, "Encourage one another. Build each other up by fellowshipping, demonstrating unselfishness, being kind, affectionate, tender, merciful. Exhort each other, and by so doing, spiritual encouragement and strength will be the result."

In I Corinthians 12 Paul declares that the Church is one body made up of many members; thus, when one member suffers, the whole body suffers; and when one member is blessed, the whole body is blessed. He therefore fervently preached Christian unity and brotherly love, holding that especially in the church should Christians meet together unto edification, exhortation and comfort.

In Ephesians 2:22 Paul refers to the Church as the habitation of God through the Spirit. Each member of the Church contributing one to another in every way (especially in love, exhortation and edification), strengthens the whole Church, thereby glorifying God, which is the real mission of the Church on earth.

In Ephesians 5 Paul likens the Church to husband and wife. He admonishes a wife to love her husband and then admonishes the husband to love his wife. In the Church Paul ascribes edifying graces to the *whole body*—not to just a select few or an appointed group. "*The whole body*, fitly joined together and compacted by that which every joint supplieth, according to the effectual working in the measure of every part, maketh increase of the body unto the edifying of itself in love" (Eph. 4:16). Here Paul is speaking of the New Testament Church.

Verses 12 and 13: "And we beseech you, brethren, to know them which labour among you, and are over you in the Lord, and admonish you; and to esteem them very highly in love for their work's sake. And be at peace among yourselves."

We combine these verses because they carry a very important message for born again church members. A believer should unite with a Bible-believing church where the pastor preaches the Word of God in all its fulness. There are too many preachers today who preach to please a denomination, a religious group or fellowship. Paul admonishes Timothy, *"Preach the word*; be instant in season, out of season; reprove, rebuke, exhort with all longsuffering and doctrine"* (II Tim. 4:2). We are to preach the Word, and we are to preach ALL of the Word—not just the part we like or the part that suits our particular denomination. Bible preachers preach the Word of God from Genesis to Revelation. If you do not belong to a Bible-believing church, let me urge you to pray much, and let the Lord lead you to some church where God's man preaches God's Word in its fulness.

"To know them which labour among you." You should not support any minister until you know him well enough to know what he believes and preaches. You should not blindly support any religious group, nor should you support any radio minister until you investigate and know that he is preaching the pure, unadulterated Word of God. Never give your money just to be *giving*, nor with the attitude that by giving in the right spirit it is up to the one *to whom* you give, to use that gift to the glory of God. *God will hold you responsible*—not only for *what* you give, but for *where* you give His money. Know the man who is your pastor—know what he believes and what he stands for. If you belong to a church and do not know what the minister stands for, make it your business to find out! Ask him if he believes in the Virgin birth, the blood atonement, the verbal inspiration of the Bible and the second coming of the Lord Jesus. *Ask him* what he believes. If he is your spiritual advisor, if he is to read and interpret the Scriptures (the Road

172

Map that leads from this life to life eternal), then you need to be sure that he reads it correctly, comparing spiritual things with spiritual. You should not be concerned with what he thinks or what he has been taught in some seminary—but with what the *Spirit* teaches. Know your pastor—and support no pastor who does not believe the Word of God in its entirety.

Not only should Christians know their pastor—but parents should know the men and women who teach their children in Sunday school. Certainly you do not want someone teaching your child if that person does not believe all of the Word of God. Neither should you allow someone to teach your child if that teacher does not live a clean life. If YOU do not drink, smoke and practice sins of the flesh before your children, certainly you do not want them to be under the instruction of a Sunday school teacher who participates in such worldly amusements and lusts. *You should "know them that are over you in the Lord, and admonish you."*

I like verse 13. We should esteem our pastor, our Sunday school teachers and spiritual leaders very highly. We should love them, we should follow them, and we should, in the right spirit, *express our appreciation* for them. Believers should belong to a church pastored by a man whom they can praise and honor—someone about whom they can tell friends and neighbors. No believer should belong to a church he cannot invite his friends and loved ones to join. By like token, believers should not belong to a Sunday school class that has a teacher who cannot be honored and praised in the spirit of sincere love and appreciation.

We should esteem the leaders of our church "very highly in love for their work's sake," for if they are what they should be in the church, they are God's representatives on earth; they are working for our good, and

173

we should thank God for them. They are to us *spiritually* what our natural family is to us *physically*. The church is our spiritual hospital, our spiritual cafeteria and our spiritual drug store. What the hospital, the family doctor and the drug store are to the body, the church, the pastor, the Sunday school teacher and other church officials are to the soul. You should not belong to any church, Sunday school class or young people's group where the leader is not worthy of esteem, love, honor and wholehearted support.

Verse 13 closes: *"And be at peace among yourselves."* God have mercy on our local churches today! How many churches do you know, where there is perfect peace and harmony among the members? Today churches are divided. They are like children at play—choosing up sides against church authorities and different sections of the membership. I sometimes preach a sermon on the subject, *"Cannibal Christians,"* using the text of Galatians 5:15: "But if ye bite and devour one another, take heed that ye be not *consumed* one of another." In the preceding verses, Paul admonishes the Galatians to love one another, declaring, "For all the law is fulfilled in one word, even in this: THOU SHALT LOVE THY NEIGHBOR AS THYSELF" (Gal. 5:14). If church members bite and devour one another, they are spiritual cannibals, always destroying instead of building up God's Word in the church. Thus Paul's admonition to the Thessalonians, "Be at peace among yourselves."

Verse 14: "Now we exhort you, brethren, warn them that are unruly, comfort the feebleminded, support the weak, be patient toward all men."

Church discipline is almost a thing of the past. Many years ago the old-time Baptists, Methodists, Presbyterians and others believed in church discipline; on Saturday nights they held a business meeting and dealt with those members who were living in such manner as to bring reproach upon the name of Christ and the church. According to Paul, for the sake of peace in the church the "unruly" *must not be left unreproved*. Only a false and cowardly peace will allow disorder to continue in the church, unchecked and unreproved.

It is imperative that every community, church, school, nation or home have the right kind of discipline in order to succeed. The unregenerate, if left alone, will continually evolve in reverse—not upward, but downward—until sin claims them in physical death and eternal damnation. Christians must be led by the Holy Ghost in their own heart, and they must also be admonished and disciplined by men appointed of God—pastors, teachers, evangelists—who are filled with the Holy Ghost.

Occasionally when I go into a church for revival services, I am told that there has been no disturbance there in ten, fifteen, or perhaps twenty years. Such a statement is proof positive that that church is dead! Any church that is winning souls and spreading the Gospel will be attacked by the devil—from without and from within; and there will be disorderly conduct even among Christians unless they are warned, rebuked and disciplined. That is a Bible fact. Read the Scriptural account of the disciples—Paul, Barnabas and others—and you will find that human nature, regardless of how saved, sanctified, consecrated and dedicated one may be, must be buffeted and crucified daily. The old nature must be starved, it must be *policed* by the individual and by the right kind of spiritual leaders.

Paul reminded the Thessalonians how he had exhorted and comforted them. He had acted toward the believers as a father toward his own children—and consoled them accordingly. His instructions to *"support the weak"* had already been practiced by Paul in Acts

20:35.   He had set the example before preaching it to the Thessalonians:

"I have shewed you all things, how that so labouring ye ought to support the weak, and to remember the words of the Lord Jesus, how He said, It is more blessed to give than to receive" (Acts 20:35).   Read also Ephesians 4:28.   The weak and the fainthearted are to be comforted; they need a stimulant; they need to be stirred, built up and pushed on.   The unruly and the disorderly are to be rebuked.   They are self-confident and over-proud, and they need to be held in check.   Many times we pass the weak believers by and do not speak to them. Sometimes we even accuse them of being unfriendly or proud, when all the time they are just self-conscious, despondent and weak.   They need to be encouraged and brought out into the open.   We could do it, if we would only speak to them, shake their hand and encourage them, instead of passing them by.

Verse 14 closes: ". . . *Be patient toward all men*." Please notice—this is a command, and the subject of the sentence is YOU—each and every believer.   Christians should show patience toward all men, whether weak or strong, whether they try us with presumption or timidity, by rude aggressiveness or feebleness and incapability. To be patient and longsuffering is one of the special marks of real Christian grace. "Charity suffereth long. . ." (I Cor. 13:4).

Verse 15:   "See that none render evil for evil unto any man; but ever follow that which is good, both among yourselves, and to all men."

What Paul is saying here is simply this: "See that no believer renders unto anyone evil in return for evil. It takes grace to return good for evil; but believers are *saved* by grace, and the grace that SAVES also TEACHES that we should live righteously and godly in this present world."

176

The believers in Thessalonica were receiving much evil from their enemies. They were sorely tempted, tried and persecuted. They were wronged—many times by their own loved ones, friends and neighbors. Paul felt the need to admonish them to be very careful in that they not return evil for evil, but follow that which is good— not only in the church, but *"to all men."*

A believer certainly brings reproach on the church and upon the name of the Lord, as well as discrediting himself, when he returns evil for evil, wrong for wrong, dirt for dirt; but it is commendable, it honors God the Father, Son and Holy Spirit and brings honor to the name of Christian when we return good for evil.

In Romans 12:19—21 Paul said, ". . . Avenge not yourselves, but rather give place unto wrath: for it is written, Vengeance is mine; I will repay, saith the Lord. Therefore if thine enemy hunger, feed him; if he thirst, give him drink: for in so doing thou shalt heap coals of fire on his head. *Be not overcome of evil, but over-come evil with good."* This is the teaching of Christ in Matthew 5:38—48 in His sermon on the mount, and I Peter 2:18—25 also admonishes us against returning evil for evil.

The statement in our present Scripture, *"ever follow that which is good,"* means follow—not by imitation, as in chapter 1:6 and 2:14—but by way of *aim and pursuit.* The good here is that which benefits the fellowman. It follows, and is closely associated with, the command, "See that none render evil for evil." We might say it this way: "Christians, always make the good of your fellowman your aim; do not let the unworthiness and carelessness on their part turn you aside from it."

This line of conduct is to be followed *"both among yourselves, and to all men"* . . . not only believer toward believer, but believer toward those who are not believers—one toward another *and toward all*. The man or woman who is a true believer following in the steps of Jesus will not wilfully harm anyone, for the love of God worketh no evil against one's fellowman. Jesus made this distinction in Matthew 5:43,44: "Ye have heard that it hath been said, Thou shalt love thy neighbour, and hate thine enemy. But I say unto you, Love your enemies, bless them that curse you, do good to them that hate you, and pray for them which despitefully use you, and persecute you."

We who name the name of Jesus can prove to the world that Jesus is everything the Bible says He is—and more—by living consecrated, dedicated lives . . . lives permeated by the love of God and filled to overflowing with His love. When we prove to the sinner that we love him and that we want him to be saved, that God loves him and gave Jesus to die on the cross to save him, that sinner will make a path to our door to learn about the Saviour who saves and gives peace that surpasses all understanding. He will want to learn of the salvation that removes the fear of dying, the fear of meeting God, and gives assurance and boldness, both in this life and in death.

The greatest need in the average church and in the life of the average Christian today is not a better education from the secular standpoint, but a thorough baptism of the love of God. We should pray that God will fill *us*, in order that we may bless others. Paul said, "And now abideth faith, hope, and charity (love), these three; but the greatest of these is charity (LOVE)" (I Cor. 13:13).

Verse 16: "Rejoice evermore."

It seems a little strange that Paul would admonish the believers in Thessalonica to "rejoice evermore," knowing that they were severely afflicted and persecuted by the enemies of the Gospel (I Thess. 1:6; 2:14; 3:2–4; II Thess. 1:4). But Paul had learned to rejoice even under heavy fire from the enemy, and he taught Christians to rejoice when persecuted.

In Romans 5:3–5 we read, ". . . We glory in tribulations also: knowing that tribulation worketh patience; and patience, experience; and experience, hope: And hope maketh not ashamed; because the love of God is shed abroad in our hearts by the Holy Ghost which is given unto us." In II Corinthians 12:9,10 Paul says, ". . . Most gladly therefore will I rather glory in my infirmities, that the power of Christ may rest upon me. Therefore I take pleasure in infirmities, in reproaches, in necessities, in persecutions, in distresses for Christ's sake: for when I am weak, then I am strong." In the Beatitudes Jesus teaches rejoicing when tested by the tempter. I Peter 4:12–14 also admonishes believers to rejoice when persecuted for righteousness' sake.

There is no joy and no reward in being persecuted for the sake of ignorance or because of our carelessness; but when we are persecuted for righteousness' sake we should rejoice and be exceeding glad. In the world we will have tribulation; but Jesus said, "Be of good cheer: I have overcome the world!"

A rejoicing Christian will never backslide. One who is so completely yielded to the Lord Jesus that he has a spirit of joy and rejoicing at all times will never entertain the thought of returning to the beggarly elements of the world. Therefore, *Christian, rejoice!*

I do not believe in foolishness in God's house. I do not believe in a religious barn dance or show; but I DO believe the Church of the Lord Jesus Christ should be alive with joy and rejoicing that is decent and in order—joy that comes from a heart overflowing with gratitude and worship to God and to the Lord Jesus for the wonderful salvation we have. Salvation is not "feelings"; salvation is not emotions; but according to Peter, salvation does produce "joy unspeakable and full of glory" (I Pet. 1:8).

Verse 17: "Pray without ceasing."

I am sure someone is saying, "I cannot pray without ceasing. I work eight hours a day; I have other duties." Dearly beloved, Paul is not speaking here of going into a closet, shutting the door, falling upon one's knees and crying to God in prayer. He means that we should at all times be in an ATTITUDE of prayer—a spirit of prayer forming an undercurrent of all our thoughts. I am convinced that some of the most effective praying done by this preacher is done while I am traveling, or when I wake in the night or in the wee small hours of the morning and talk to God in silence, in the Spirit! *Pray without ceasing.* We cannot afford to do less, because if our prayer life weakens, the devil will drive a wedge between us and our spiritual birthright of abundant life.

Paul and his co-laborers were men of prayer. In Acts 16, before Lydia was converted, they prayed. A little later, just before the fortune teller was saved, they prayed. In prison, at midnight, they prayed—and God answered with an earthquake that opened every door in the prison! If you will study Paul's epistles, you will find that he prayed always. He was not preaching what he did not practice; he said, "Pray without ceasing," and he did just that. He was in an attitude of prayer at all times (I Thess. 1:3; 2:13). A believer who prays without ceasing will not backslide—he cannot backslide while praying in the Spirit.

Verse 18: "In every thing give thanks: for this is

the will of God in Christ Jesus concerning you."

"*In everything give thanks.*"   Again—Paul is not
preaching what he did not practice (I Thess. 1:2; 3:9,10;
Phil. 4:6; Col. 4:2).   In *everything*—even in persecution
and shame, humiliation, heartache and pain, in jail or
out of jail—in EVERYTHING give thanks!   Read Philippians 1:29 and II Corinthians 12:9,10.

It is easy to be thankful when everything goes well—
when all the children are healthy and there is money in
the bank; when we have just gotten a raise in salary,
we have a new car, and the home is paid for; when we
have good clothes, plenty to eat, and everybody speaks
well of us.   ANYONE could give thanks and praise God
under those conditions.   But the Thessalonian Christians were being severely persecuted, they were suffering sorely, they were being tried and tested on every
hand.   Yet in spite of such trials, Paul said, "In everything *give thanks.*   You are suffering temptation, you
are afflicted, despondent, your heart is breaking—but in
spite of it all, be thankful!   Thank God that you are
counted worthy to suffer for the Lord Jesus, who suffered
so much for you."

A normal, healthy, productive spiritual life is a
life of prayer ("Pray without ceasing"); constant joy
("Rejoice evermore"); and constant thanksgiving ("*In
everything give thanks*").

In I Thessalonians 3:3 Paul declares that the believers in Thessalonica had a special appointment from
Almighty God—*they were appointed to suffer.*   Very few
of us who name the name of Jesus today know the meaning of that word.   Very few of us have EVER suffered
for the sake of the Gospel.   Sometimes we speak of being persecuted; but compared with the persecution of Paul
and the early Christians, we know nothing of persecution.

In II Corinthians 11:24–30 Paul tells his personal story of suffering for Christ: "Of the Jews five times received I forty stripes save one. Thrice was I beaten with rods, once was I stoned, thrice I suffered shipwreck, a night and a day I have been in the deep; in journeyings often, in perils of waters, in perils of robbers, in perils by mine own countrymen, in perils by the heathen, in perils in the city, in perils in the wilderness, in perils in the sea, in perils among false brethren; in weariness and painfulness, in watchings often, in hunger and thirst, in fastings often, in cold and nakedness. Beside those things that are without, that which cometh upon me daily, the care of all the churches . . . *If I must needs glory, I will glory of the things which concern mine infirmities.*"

Yet—with such a personal testimony of persecution, that great apostle could say, *"Rejoice evermore! In everything give thanks!"* Paul practiced what he preached; he knew what he was talking about. He knew by experience what it meant to endure suffering and persecution for the sake of the Gospel, and he finally sealed his testimony with his own blood under the headsman's ax. All of this came because he preached grace to the Gentiles and declared that Jew and Gentile, slave and master, rich and poor, bond and free—ALL belong to the same body, of which Jesus Christ is the head. He was hated and persecuted until at last his enemies claimed his life. His indomitable courage endured to the end; and just before he faced Nero's chopping block he declared, "I have fought a good fight, I have finished my course, I have kept the faith: Henceforth there is laid up for me a crown of righteousness, which the Lord, the righteous judge, shall give me at that day: and not to me only, but unto all them also that love His appearing" (II Tim. 4:7,8). In Philippians 1:21 he said, "For to me to live is Christ, and to die is gain!"

Verse 18 closes: ". . . *This is the will of God in Christ Jesus concerning you.*" According to this Scripture, it is a sin to be unthankful. Regardless of what we may suffer or be called upon to sacrifice, it is a sin to grumble or to be despondent and discouraged when we know that Jesus said, "I will never leave thee nor forsake thee." "*If God be for us, who can be against us?*" Knowing these tremendous truths, we should be thankful and rejoice, even in the darkest hours.

Many people say, "I would like to know God's will for my life." Here is part of it: *It is God's will for you to be thankful in all things.* If ever you come to the place where you think God has put more on you than you can bear, *remember Jesus.* As He saw the cup in the Garden He cried out, "O my Father, if it be possible, let this cup pass from me: nevertheless not as I will, but as thou wilt" (Matt. 26:39). On Calvary's rugged cross He bore our sins in His own body. Because of your sins and mine He lost sight of the Father's face—everything turned dark and Jesus cried out, "My God! My God! Why hast thou forsaken me?"

The answer is plain: *We know that God Almighty could not look upon sin*—and Jesus was paying the sin-debt of the world. He carried your sins and mine to His cross and nailed them there. He spoiled principalities and powers, He won the victory over the world, the flesh and the devil, death, hell and the grave. Jesus paid it all—and what a price He paid!

The next time you become discouraged, remember the words of Paul. Christians should be ashamed of grumbling because of a little suffering for the Gospel's sake. "And what shall I more say? for the time would fail me to tell of Gedeon, and of Barak, and of Samson, and of Jepthae; of David also, and Samuel, and of the prophets: Who through faith subdued kingdoms, wrought righteousness, obtained promises, stopped the mouths of lions, quenched the violence of fire, escaped the edge of the sword, out of weakness were made strong, waxed valiant in fight, turned to flight the armies of the aliens. Women received their dead raised to life again: and others were tortured, not accepting deliverance; that they might obtain a better resurrection: And others had trial of cruel mockings and scourgings, yea, moreover of bonds and imprisonment: They were stoned, they were sawn asunder, were tempted, were slain with the sword: they wandered about in sheepskins and goatskins; being destitute, afflicted, tormented; (Of whom the world was not worthy:) they wandered in deserts, and in mountains, and in dens and caves of the earth. And these all, having obtained a good report through faith, received not the promise: God having provided some better thing for us, that they without us should not be made perfect.

"Wherefore seeing we also are compassed about with so great a cloud of witnesses, let us lay aside every weight, and the sin which doth so easily beset us, and let us run with patience the race that is set before us, looking unto Jesus the author and finisher of our faith; who for the joy that was set before Him endured the cross, despising the shame, and is set down at the right hand of the throne of God. For consider Him that endured such contradiction of sinners against Himself, lest ye be wearied and faint in your minds. Ye have not yet resisted unto blood, striving against sin" (Heb. 11:32 – 12:4).

When we read these verses, we should be ashamed of ourselves if we grumble because of the little insignificant suffering we are called upon to bear for Jesus today—and especially, *"For consider Him that endured such contradiction of sinners against Himself . . . YE HAVE NOT YET RESISTED UNTO BLOOD, STRIVING*

The time may come before the Rapture when Christians will again be imprisoned for their faith. In some parts of the world this situation exists today. But in America we do not know the meaning of suffering for the Gospel's sake! God help us to be good soldiers, rejoicing and giving thanks in all things. God help us to be good examples of born again believers, for this is the will of God. When we are unthankful and grumble, we are sinning: *"Whatsoever is not of faith is sin,"* and if we have faith in God we know that He will put nothing on us that will not work to our good and to His glory.

Verse 19: "Quench not the Spirit."

There are many who do not realize the tremendous importance of the work and ministry of the Holy Spirit as having to do with believers. We know that His primary work is to draw us to Christ (John 6:44; 16:7—11). The Holy Spirit convicts us, convinces us and draws us to Jesus; He then is the attending Physician at the new birth (John 3:3,5). The Holy Spirit baptizes us into the body of Christ (I Cor. 12:12,13); He indwells us (Rom. 8:9); He leads us (Rom. 8:14); He assures us (Rom. 8:16); He seals us (Eph. 4:30). It is altogether possible to *grieve* the Holy Spirit. It is also possible to *quench* the Spirit.

The word *quench* means "to extinguish, subdue, suppress, to make an end of." That is the definition given in Webster's dictionary. Whatever obstructs, hinders or dampens the work of the Holy Spirit in the souls of men is *forbidden*. "Quench" is used here in the sense of putting out a fire—i.e., we are not to extinguish the influence of the Holy Spirit in our hearts.

If the Spirit bids "Go," then GO—asking no questions.

When the Holy Spirit directs you to a ministry or mission to the glory of God, do not request a road map, for when it is time to alter course, the Holy Spirit will make it known. He speaks "with groanings which cannot be uttered"; He directs in many ways. ". . . Not by might, nor by power, but by my Spirit, saith the Lord of hosts" (Zech. 4:6). Anything that will tend to quench the ardor of worship in the soul, to render us lifeless in the service of God, may be regarded as "quenching" the Spirit. Worldliness, pride, ambition, will do it.

When we are willing to be led by the Spirit of God, we will not fulfill the lusts of the flesh; we will not follow a selfish, self-centered, self-glorying path, for the Holy Ghost came to glorify Jesus and to speak—not of Himself—but of Jesus. He leads us into paths of right living—paths which, even though they may be paths of suffering, will glorify the Lord Jesus.

A believer can grieve and quench the Holy Spirit even in personal work. I have seen this happen. I do not believe in walking up and down the aisles in a church, asking people at random, "Are you saved?" But I DO believe the Holy Spirit directs us to speak to certain individuals in meetings. If the Holy Spirit directs, you will know it; and if the Holy Spirit directs you, He will be working in the heart of the one to whom He leads you to speak. To refuse to follow His leading, for one reason or another, is to quench the Spirit—and that is sin. We should go where the Spirit leads, we should say what the Spirit directs us to say, and we should minister wherever the Holy Spirit leads us to minister.

On several occasions Paul said that the Spirit forbade his going to certain communities to preach, but led him in an altogether different direction. The Spirit will lead us if we will only permit Him to direct us in our daily living. We should never begin a day without praying to God to lead us by the Holy Spirit that day. We should never teach a Sunday school class, preach a sermon, or even speak to a person about his salvation without first praying for the Holy Spirit to lead and direct us in what we should say. When the Holy Spirit leads, you may rest assured that the victory will be won and good will be accomplished, although we may not see it at that moment. But the outcome will be glory to God and victory over the devil.

There will be no backsliding for a believer who is thankful in everything and all things, and who does not quench the Spirit, but follows His bidding.

Verse 20: "Despise not prophesyings."

To prophesy is to foretell things that will happen many years from now—but it is also to *forthtell* things that have *already been foretold*. Every minister and Sunday school teacher is a prophet in one sense . . . not as Daniel and Ezekiel were prophets——but we are *forth*telling what they *foretold*. Every minister is a prophet, and believers are not to despise prophesying. In the days of Paul the "perfect law of liberty" had not come; the Bible was not complete. All the books of the Bible had not been given, and in that day God's prophets (including Paul) had the power of declaring the mind of God by direct inspiration. It seems that in the Thessalonian church this great gift of prophesying was being despised by some of the more sober-minded men. Therefore, Paul gives a direct command that *believers were not to despise what the prophets said*. They might not like it, they might not agree with it—but they were to receive what God's man prophesied.

Today, we have "that which is perfect"—the Word of God. We have the Bible in its completeness—the "perfect law of liberty"—and we need no extra epistles or chapters. In this Book of books we have all that we need to know about God and the devil, heaven and hell, salvation and sin, time and eternity. All we need to know of things eternal we find in the sixty-six books of our Bible. All Scripture is given by inspiration, and the Bible we now have is ALL the Scripture there is!

Dear Christian, do not despise what you do not like in a Gospel message. *Ask yourself WHY you do not like what the preacher said.* It could be that there is sin in your life and you are convicted by what your pastor is giving you from God's Word. If you would let the Holy Spirit lead you (instead of quenching the Spirit and criticizing the minister), you might find yourself at an old-fashioned altar, pouring out your soul to God in repentance. When the minister preaches, if he is God's preacher you should hear his message—and be not a hearer only, but *do what he tells you to do*, for he is led of the Holy Ghost in preaching the Word of God.

If he is NOT God's man, then you have no business *listening* to him! You should not listen to any minister who is not a man of God. Someone may ask, "How can I KNOW if a preacher is a man of God? How can I know if he is preaching the Word of God?" Beloved, if you cannot discern a true minister of the Gospel from a liberal and a counterfeit, my advice to you—in kindness and love—is that you need to be saved!

When a God-fearing, born again minister enters the pulpit to preach God's Word, if you are born again *your* spirit will witness with *his* spirit; and if that be not true as he preaches, then dearly beloved, either you are not saved or he is not God's preacher! God's man feeds both the children and the adults in the spiritual family. The Word of God is milk, bread and meat to the hungry hearts of the believers; and when God's preacher preaches God's Word, *believers know it.* If you cannot know whether a

188

minister is a true man of God or a counterfeit of the devil, I fear you do not have the Holy Spirit; because the Spirit searcheth all things, yea, the deep things of God.

". . . The anointing which ye have received of Him abideth in you, and ye need not that any man teach you: but as the same anointing teacheth you of all things, and is truth, and is no lie, and even as it hath taught you, ye shall abide in Him" (I John 2:27).

"Wherefore also it is contained in the Scripture, Behold, I lay in Sion a chief corner stone, elect, precious: *and he that believeth on Him shall not be confounded*" (I Peter 2:6).

In these words the Holy Ghost is telling us that those who are in Christ will not be confused, confounded or led astray by false teachers and false prophets. *A true child of God will not follow error*: ". . . When (the Shepherd) putteth forth His own sheep, He goeth before them, and the sheep follow Him: for they know His voice. And a stranger will they not follow, but will flee from him: for they know not the voice of strangers" (John 10:4,5).

According to these words of Jesus, Christians know the voice of Jesus—and the voice of strangers *they will not follow*. Therefore, if you do not know the true Word of God when you hear it, surely the Spirit of the Good Shepherd is not leading you. Check up; search the Scriptures! Make your calling and election sure. KNOW that you are truly born again and covered by the blood.

Verse 21: "Prove all things; hold fast that which is good."

Just how are we to prove all things? *By the Word of God*. In other words, *prove the denomination you belong to by the Bible*—not by books of doctrine, catechisms, traditions of men or church covenants. *Read the Bible.*

Put your denomination beside the Bible and see if it measures up to God's specifications. No preacher (or layman) has any right to make the Word of God fit what he believes. Preachers are to believe the Bible and preach the unadulterated Word of God, and Christians are to believe the Word. Weigh any doctrine in the scales of the Bible, and pray for God to give you the spirit of understanding and discernment. (Read I Corinthians 12: 3,10.) Hear John the Beloved as he admonishes, "Beloved, believe not every spirit, but try the spirits WHETHER THEY ARE OF GOD" (I John 4:1–3).

You have probably heard the statement, "There is a little *good* in all religions." That may be true. There is some good bread in the garbage can, but I do not want to get my bread there! I had rather go to the supermarket and buy a loaf of good clean bread than to pluck it from a garbage can from among the other garbage, even though the bread might be wholesome and good. By like token, I do not want a little bit of Gospel mixed with a barrel or error, and I refuse to support any man or any denomination where there is deviation from the fundamentals of the faith!

Every minister should hear Paul's charge to Timothy: "I charge thee therefore before God, and the Lord Jesus Christ, who shall judge the quick and the dead at His appearing and His kingdom; Preach the word; be instant in season, out of season; reprove, rebuke, exhort with all longsuffering and doctrine. . . . But watch thou in all things, endure afflictions, do the work of an evangelist, make full proof of thy ministry" (II Tim. 4:1–5).

"Study to show thyself approved unto God, a workman that needeth not to be ashamed, rightly dividing the word of truth" (II Tim. 2:15).

Every believer should prove all things by the Bible— we should prove our habits, the places we go, the things we do, the language we use, the songs we sing, the company we keep, the job we hold, the church we join, the evangelists and missionaries we support, the tracts we give out on the street or from house to house.

If you are doing something about which there is a question in your mind, place that "something" beside the Word of God, weigh it in the scales of the Bible; and if it cannot be proved right, according to Scriptures, *let it alone*! Do not ask preachers if it is harmful to do this or that—*search the Scriptures*: for preachers do not agree. One minister may tell you that it is a sin to dance, while another will tell you that he *sponsors* dances in the church he pastors! Whatsoever you do, wheresoever you go, prove it by the Word of God. Hold fast to the good, let go the chaff.

Verse 22: "Abstain from all appearance of evil."

That verse of Scripture contains only six words—but in those words we find the answer to thousands of questions! For instance: "Is it a sin to attend modern movies? Is it a sin to drink beer? Is it a sin to gamble or go to the races?" The Bible says to every believer, *"Abstain from all appearance of evil."*

Eve first looked at the forbidden fruit—and saw that it was beautiful. She did not abstain from the appearance. David walked out on the roof of his house and looked at his neighbor's wife in her own private bathing pool in her back yard. He did not abstain from the appearance of evil—and you know what followed: adultery, murder, heartbreak, tears, the death of his illegitimate child and a commentary of grief that followed David until God called him home.

The devil tempts through three avenues: (1) the lust of the flesh; (2) the lust of the eye; (3) the pride of life. Through these avenues Satan tempts, draws souls away from God, and damns them. It was through the lust of the flesh, the lust of the eye and the pride of life that Jesus was tempted. A personal devil met a personal Christ—but Jesus did not succumb to temptation. Eve fell, Adam fell, David fell, others have fallen—but not Jesus!

You may ask, "Preacher, is this thing wrong?" I ask you, "Is it evil from the standpoint of stirring the emotions of lust, the desires of the flesh and of the world?" No Christian should look at anything, go anywhere, keep company with anyone that will bring about a tendency to desire evil. If we would be victorious, if we would receive a full reward and enjoy our spiritual birthright, we must "abstain from all appearance of evil." A person who does this, along with other things we have named thus far, will never backslide.

Verse 23: "And the very God of peace sanctify you wholly; and I pray God your whole spirit and soul and body be preserved blameless unto the coming of our Lord Jesus Christ."

The Greek language here reads, "The God of peace Himself sanctify you wholly." Note also chapter 3:11 and II Thessalonians 2:16. Paul is here stressing divine power, contrasting God's divine ability with the limited ability of man. Notice also Philippians 2:12,13.

"The God of peace" is a term often used by Paul in his epistles. God IS the God of peace, and Isaiah said, "Thou wilt keep him in perfect peace, whose mind is stayed on thee: because he trusteth in thee" (Isaiah 26:3). Read also Hebrews 13:20, II Thessalonians 3:16 and Romans 16:20.

We have peace with God through our Lord Jesus Christ (Rom. 5:1). We also "joy in God" through our Lord Jesus Christ (Rom. 5:11), who through His shed blood made peace between God and man—that is, if man will put his trust *in the finished work* of the Lord Jesus. Peace is God's distinguishing gift in the Gospel through the sacrifice of His only begotten Son. God makes Himself known in the hearts of men through the peace that He gives. In Romans 15:5 Paul refers to our God as "the God of patience and consolation." In Romans 15:13 He is the *"God of our hope."* In II Corinthians 13:11 He is the *"God of love and peace."* In I Peter 5:10 He is the *"God of all grace."* There IS no peace apart from the GOD OF PEACE; true peace is "THE PEACE OF GOD." Please read Philippians 4:7–9.

All believers are sanctified in Christ Jesus when they are born again (II Thess. 2:13; I Cor. 1:2); but Paul is praying here that the very God of peace *"sanctify you wholly"*—sanctify you unto completeness or full perfection (full grown, in the spiritual sense). Sanctification is *progressive* as well as *positional*. Paul is praying here that the sanctification of the Thessalonian saints will increase, bringing them to the full stature of the spiritual man.

Please note the word *"wholly"*—spelled W-H-O-L-L-Y— not "holy." Our God is a holy God, and it is true that *"without* holiness no man shall see God." He accepts nothing less than holiness because HE is holy; but our holiness is in Christ (I Cor. 1:29,30). The word "wholly" means *entirely*—from head to foot, within, without, in every detail.

Paul continues, "I pray God that your whole *spirit* and *soul* and *body* be preserved blameless unto the coming of our Lord Jesus Christ." Please note:

      (a) "your whole spirit

      (b) and soul

      (c) and body . . . ."

When God created man, He said, "Let us make man in our own image." We know that there are no two human beings who are identical. We hear the term, *"identical twins"*; but there have never been twins so alike that the mother could not distinguish between the two. Man lost much, physically, in the fall; but I personally believe that when the Bible speaks of man being created in the image of God, the Scriptures teach that that image is not so much in *physical appearance* as in *spiritual likeness.*

God is a Trinity—Father, Son and Holy Ghost. In the beginning . . . GOD! In John 1:18 the Word tells us, "No man hath seen God at any time; the only begotten Son, which is in the bosom of the Father, He hath declared Him."

In John 1:1, 14 we read, "In the beginning was the Word, and the Word was with God, and the Word WAS God . . . and the Word was made flesh . . . ."

Jesus was God in flesh (II Cor. 5:19); yet He said to Peter, "Flesh and blood hath not revealed this to thee, but my Father which is in heaven." Jesus was on earth; yet He said, "The Father is in heaven." I cannot explain the sovereignty of God, neither His omnipotence, omniscience nor omnipresence. I *believe it all*—but I cannot explain it.

Anyone who wants to see the truth of the Trinity—one God manifest in three persons—can clearly see it in the Gospel of Matthew, when Jesus was baptized. Jesus came to John the Baptist and requested to be baptized of John: "And Jesus, when He was baptized, went up straightway out of the water: and, lo, the heavens were opened unto Him, and He saw the Spirit of God descending like a dove, and lighting upon Him: And lo a voice from heaven, saying, This is my beloved Son, in whom

I am well pleased'' (Matt. 3:16,17).

> (1) *Jesus* came up straightway out of the water.
>
> (2) *The Spirit* in bodily form (like a dove) came upon Him.
>
> (3) *A voice* from heaven said, "This is my beloved Son . . . ."

Jesus came up out of the water. The Holy Spirit came upon Him and remained upon Him—and the Father from heaven spoke in an audible voice saying, "This is my beloved Son, in whom I am well pleased." Anyone who is not defending a cult, a denomination or a religion can clearly see the Trinity in these two verses: God the Father in heaven, God the Son in the water, God the Holy Spirit in the form of a dove, the symbol of peace, upon Jesus.

I repeat—I cannot explain the Trinity, and I dare not speculate. But I believe it because the Bible teaches it. Neither can I explain the trinity of man—but man IS a trinity. We are created in the image of God in that we are trinitarian. We have a *spirit*, we have a *soul*, we have a *body*—and the Scriptures clearly differentiate between the three.

"For the Word of God is quick, and powerful, and sharper than any twoedged sword, piercing even to the dividing asunder of *soul* and *spirit*, and of the *joints and marrow*, and is a discerner of the thoughts and intents of the heart" (Heb. 4:12).

In this verse of Scripture we clearly see that soul and spirit are not identical; they are divisible. Paul clearly distinguishes between the soul and spirit in the burial and resurrection of the body—sown a natural body, raised a spiritual body (I Cor. 15:44).

The spirit is the part of man that KNOWS: "For

195

what man knoweth the things of a man, save the spirit of man which is in him? Even so the things of God knoweth no man, but the Spirit of God. . . . But the natural man receiveth not the things of the Spirit of God: for they are foolishness unto him: neither can he know them, because they are spiritually discerned" (I Cor. 2:11,14).

Please notice: "For what man knoweth the things of a man, SAVE THE SPIRIT OF MAN WHICH IS IN HIM?"! According to the Word of God, it is the *spirit* of man that KNOWS. The spirit is the part of man that is capable of knowing and capable of reasoning. When Jesus stood at the tomb of Lazarus the Word of God tells us that He "groaned in His spirit and was troubled." At the tomb of Lazarus Jesus was thinking and weeping with two broken-hearted sisters over the death of their brother. He knew the broken hearts of Mary and Martha because of the death of Lazarus, and He was thinking with them in sorrow.

However, when Jesus was in the garden of Gethsemane pouring out His soul for the sins of the whole world, He said to His disciples, "MY SOUL IS EXCEEDING SORROWFUL UNTO DEATH: tarry ye here and watch" (Mark 14:34). He was loving two sisters and weeping with them at the tomb of Lazarus; but in the Garden He was loving the whole world and paying the sin-debt for the whole world. Therefore, His soul was about to die within Him because of the grief sin had brought upon mankind—for He bore our grief. (Read Matt. 26:38; Mark 11:29; John 12:27.) The soul is the seat of affections and emotions. The soul is the part of man that loves and hates. The soul of Jesus was crushed with the load of sin. He loved the world so much that He took the sin of the whole world upon Himself and nailed it to His cross.

There is a definite distinction between soul and

spirit in man. The Word of God clearly teaches that the spirit makes man capable of being God-conscious. Through the spirit we communicate with God. Read Job 32:8, Prov. 20:27 and Psalm 18:28.

It is absolutely imperative that man think right about God before he can think right about God's Word. It is absolutely imperative that man think right about God's Word before he can be saved, because salvation becomes ours by faith—and saving faith can come only by the Word of God (Rom. 10:17, John 5:24, I Pet. 1:23). Man has a spirit, and through that spirit we can communicate with God when we believe His Word. Believing His Word, we love the Lord with all our soul. When we think right about God, we automatically love Him.

The *body* is the house in which the *spirit* and *soul* live. And when the individual believes on the Lord Jesus Christ, the Holy Spirit takes up His abode in our heart; the heart is the seat of life, and therefore the Holy Spirit abides in our body and our body becomes the temple or tabernacle of the Holy Spirit. "What? Know ye not that your body is the temple of the Holy Ghost which is in you, which ye have of God, and ye are not your own? For ye are bought with a price: therefore glorify God in your body, and in your spirit, which are God's" (I Cor. 6:19,20).

Paul said to born again believers, "I beseech you therefore, brethren, by the mercies of God, that ye present your bodies a living sacrifice, holy, acceptable unto God, which is your reasonable service" (Rom. 12:1). These Romans were already saved, but Paul begged them to present their *bodies* to God—a living sacrifice. To teach that the soul, spirit and body are one and the same is gross ignorance.

In verse 23 Paul is begging the believers at Thessalonica to be sanctified, set apart, dedicated *wholly*—meaning from head to foot, from the tips of their toes to the top of their head—whole spirit, whole soul and whole body—ENTIRE, holding back nothing in their thinking, loving or living. And when we have done all that is commanded, we are to say, "We are altogether unprofitable servants. We have done that which is our duty" (Luke 17:10).

Notice the last words in verse 23: "... *be preserved blameless unto the coming of our Lord Jesus Christ.*"

Please note that Paul did not say "sinless," but "BLAMELESS." According to the Word of God, "If we (little children) say that we (little children) have no sin, we deceive ourselves, AND THE TRUTH IS NOT IN US" (I John 1:8). This does not give believers a license to sin; but when the *best* of us have *done our best*, we still fall far short of the glory of God. Many believers need to learn the definition of sin. If they fully understand what sin is, they will never again boast that they are sinless. Paul says, "Whatsoever is not of faith is sin" (Rom. 14:23). James says, "To him that knoweth to do good and doeth it not, to him it is sin" (James 4:17). The Bible clearly teaches, "The thought of foolishness is sin" (Prov. 24:9).

Since we are, as believers, to do all that we do to the glory of God, it stands to reason that if we do anything that is NOT to the glory of God, we have sinned. But *we can live blameless*, we can be examples to the unbelievers—in the words of Paul, "*to those who are without.*"

I like the word "*preserved*" used here. When I use this verse of Scripture I like to use an illustration that is very real to me: When I was a boy we lived on a farm, and in spring and summer my mother canned enough fruit and vegetables to feed the family through the winter months. She also made many kinds of *preserves*—peach, pear, plum, strawberry—and these were enjoyed in the winter time.

In the process of canning vegetables and fruits, there was always a small percentage of spoilage, and those cans or jars must of necessity be thrown out. But there was one place where the sound of spoiling and spewing was never heard—and *that was the corner where Mother kept her preserves*! Any dear lady who knows how to prepare preserves knows that preserves do not spoil. The older they become, the sweeter they grow— and if kept long enough will eventually turn to sugar. That is the reason why the dear old saints of God, saved for fifty years or more, stand in testimonial and say, "The way with Jesus grows sweeter day by day!" Those blessed saints were not "canned"—they were genuinely *saved and preserved* in the Lord.

The reason some church members cannot live right is simply because they were spiritually "canned" when they joined the church, instead of being "preserved" in the grace of God! I love verse 23 of this chapter: "And the very God of peace sanctify you wholly; and I pray God your whole spirit and soul and body be preserved blameless unto the coming of our Lord Jesus Christ!"

The last part of that verse, *"Unto the coming of our Lord Jesus Christ,"* sums up the heart of the message of both Thessalonian letters. According to Paul, the coming of the Lord Jesus Christ is the hope and highest goal of the believer. *When Jesus comes*, our stewardship will be put to the final test. According to Paul's letter to the church at Corinth, "Every man's work shall be made manifest: for the day shall declare it, because *it shall be revealed by fire*; and the fire shall try every

199

man's work *of what sort it is.* If any man's work abide which he hath built thereupon, he shall receive a reward. If any man's work shall be burned, he shall suffer loss: but he himself shall be saved; *yet so as by fire*" (I Cor. 3:13–15).

Paul's desire was that believers have a full reward. He did not want them to build "wood, hay and stubble." He wanted them to be sanctified entirely, in order that they might build upon the true Foundation—the Lord Jesus Christ—"gold, silver and precious stones."

I am so thankful that I am saved. I am not expecting a *great* reward, but I DO trust and pray that I shall receive a FULL reward; and when we crown Him Lord of all, I pray that I will have some trophies to lay at His precious, nail-scarred feet!

Dear believer, are YOU sanctified—spirit, soul and body? If not, I trust this will be the moment when you will bow your head and sincerely ask God to sanctify you wholly, and from this day forward give God your best. "Whatsoever ye do, do it heartily, as to the Lord . . ." (Col. 3:23).

Verse 24: "Faithful is He that calleth you, who also will do it."

Often in this epistle, Paul appeals to the faithfulness of God. God has *pledged* faithfulness; *and because He IS God, He must BE faithful.* God will keep every promise He has made in His Word (I Cor. 1:9; II Tim. 2:13). The believers in Thessalonica were keenly conscious that God had called them to a consecrated, separated, sanctified life (I Thess. 2:12). For believers to live the kind of life God wants them to live requires the full surrender of every power—soul, spirit AND body. We must commit our members to the leadership of the Holy Spirit, or we cannot live as God would have us live.

God calls the unbeliever to salvation through the Spirit and His Word. No man can come to Jesus except the Father draw him, and God draws *through* the power of the Holy Spirit (John 16:7–11). The Spirit applies the Word, and faith results when the unbeliever *hears* the Word (Rom. 10:17). When the unbeliever then exercises faith in God, that unbeliever will call on God for salvation (Rom. 10:13–17). The God who *calls* us will also do (in us and for us) everything He has promised— *if we are willing.* God wants to give unto us His best. "No good thing will He withhold from them that walk uprightly" (Psalm 84:11); but "he that covereth his sins shall not prosper . . ." (Prov. 28:13).

In the Old Testament we read, "God is not a man, that He should lie; neither the Son of man, that He should repent: hath He said, and shall He not do it? or hath He spoken, and shall He not make it good?" (Num. 23:19). God here speaks through Moses to assure us that God is not as man; man can and does lie—but God cannot (Heb. 6:18; Titus 1:2). Our God is not only a great GIVER— He is also a great DOER. God gave His only begotten Son that we might be saved; but He is willing, ready and able to do for us any and all things that we cannot do for ourselves. God expects us to work out our own salvation with fear and trembling (Phil. 2:12); but there are many things we cannot do and must depend upon God to do for us:

"For it is God which worketh in you both to will and to do of His good pleasure" (Phil. 2:13).

"For with God nothing shall be impossible" (Luke 1:37).

"If God be for us, who can be against us?" (Rom. 8:31).

No wonder Paul cries out in Romans 5:11: "And not

only so, but we also joy IN GOD through our Lord Jesus Christ, by whom we have now received the atonement."

Verse 25: "Brethren, pray for us."

The conclusion of Paul's first letter to the believers at Thessalonica is very brief. He has assured them many times that he is faithfully and untiringly praying for them (chapter 1:2; 3:10; and verse 23 in our present chapter). His one desire and urgent request to them concerning himself is *that they should pray for him.*

In II Thessalonians 3:1,2 Paul definitely requests prayer: "Finally, brethren, pray for us, that the word of the Lord may have free course, and be glorified, even as it is with you: And that we may be delivered from unreasonable and wicked men: for all men have not faith."

Note also Ephesians 6:19; Colossians 4:3,4; Philippians 1:19; Romans 15:30. You will find words similar to these many times in Paul's epistles: ". . . That ye strive together with me in your prayers to God for me." Paul prayed for the believers, and he wanted them in turn to remember him and strive together with him in prayer always.

It is altogether possible for a church to grow and win souls without a pastor (although God ordained pastors to represent Him as undershepherds in the local church)— but *NO church can go forward without prayer!* The disciples of Jesus never requested Him to teach them how to preach—but they did beseech Him, "Teach us to *pray.*" One of the greatest needs among preachers and in the church today is that of prayer; prayer is the key that unlocks the storehouse of God, and *without prayer* it is utterly impossible for an individual or a church to be what God would have them to be.

Verse 26: "Greet all the brethren with an holy kiss."

In the first days of the Church, the kiss was a common sign of affection among kinsmen and close friends; they kissed upon meeting and again upon parting. The practice was universal in the Christian assemblies in Paul's day, and is still used in the Greek and oriental churches—especially when communion is observed. In the western world the "holy kiss" has all but disappeared. Had the custom continued until our present hour, it would be abused and would create much suspicion; but during the primitive Christian era the holy kiss was not abused, and the simple lives of faith lived by early Christians proved that the heart was pure and that the kiss placed upon the cheek of the brethren was "an holy kiss." Such practice would be definitely out of line in our present society, but Paul wanted the holy kiss to be exchanged by the brethren at Thessalonica as an expression of his love to each member of the church.

To the Romans Paul said, "Salute one another with an holy kiss. The churches of Christ salute you" (Rom. 16:16). He uses the same term in I Corinthians 16:20, and closes that epistle with the words, "My love be with you all in Christ Jesus. Amen." In II Corinthians 13:12 he says, "Greet one another with an holy kiss." In I Peter 5:14 the salutation is called "a kiss of charity (love)."

A much needed grace in the church today is pure love one for another. The church needs a baptism of the love of God that would fill us to overflowing and convince our fellow Christians that we love them sincerely and tenderly in the Lord. This is a cold, selfish, loveless age. Most of us are so busy satisfying ourselves that we have no time to love our fellowman.

Verse 27: "I charge you by the Lord that this epistle be read unto all the holy brethren."

It is noteworthy that Paul requested this epistle to be read to the entire congregation. He wanted to be sure that every believer in the church at Thessalonica was present when it was read. The dearest doctrine to his heart was the imminent return of Jesus to receive His bride, and someone had attempted to poison the minds of the Thessalonian Christians concerning the truth he had preached about the return of Christ in the Rapture. Therefore, Paul wanted this epistle read to each and every member of the church there.

It is as if Paul said, "I put you on your oath before the Lord to do this" . . . an extraordinary expression. It is unlikely that there was such jealousy existing in the Thessalonian church that the letter would intentionally be withheld from any of its members. Two circumstances come to mind which might in some cases cause neglect of the epistle: the sincere desire on the part of the members for Paul's presence in Thessalonica, and the fact that they had undergone great disappointment because of his failure to return. The feeling might lead some to say, "This is only a letter; why does he not come himself?"

Then too, since some of the believers had lost their loved ones in death, they were in deep sorrow; and unless the letter was read to them in their home they might miss the consolation that Paul desired to be theirs through his writing. Since this is Paul's first letter to any of the churches, and the custom of reading such communications to the church in assembly had not been established at that time, he therefore charged the ones in authority to be certain the letter was read and heard by all the holy brethren.

Verse 28: "THE GRACE OF OUR LORD JESUS CHRIST BE WITH YOU. AMEN."

This is Paul's usual form of benediction. In some

of his later epistles he uses the Trinitarian blessing (II Cor. 13:14). Sometimes he simply says, "Grace be with you" (Col. 4:18). The benediction used here ("the grace of our Lord Jesus Christ be with you") contains all the spiritual good and all the blessing possible for one believer to wish for another. The grace of our Lord Jesus Christ saves us, teaches us and directs us. The grace of our Lord Jesus Christ provides the light in which we walk, guiding and sustaining us in our daily living. So Paul wishes GRACE for the believers at Thessalonica.

You remember I said verses 11−28 contain a spiritual prescription for the sure cure for backsliding. I promise a positive guarantee to all who will obey the admonition here, that they will never, never backslide. Here is the outline:

1. Comfort yourselves together; edify one another.

2. Know them which labor among you and are over you and admonish you. Esteem them very highly—that is, ministers, teachers, church leaders. Love them, honor them, respect and cherish them, and pray for them.

3. Warn the unruly, comfort the feebleminded, support the weak, be patient toward all men. Any believer who practices this will be on guard at all times, and the devil will not have a chance to edge into his daily living.

4. See that none render evil for evil unto any man. Follow that which is good—among yourselves and to all men.

5. Rejoice evermore!

6. Pray without ceasing.

7. In everything give thanks, for this is the will of God in Christ Jesus concerning you. *"In everything"*—

not just the things that bless and bring profit, gain and encouragement—but also the heartaches, heartbreaks and disappointments. In EVERYTHING give thanks.

8. Quench not the Spirit. When the Spirit speaks and directs, follow that leading.

9. Despise not prophesyings. When your spiritual advisor admonishes you from the Word of God, do not despise it. Accept it, whether you like it or not.

10. Prove all things; hold fast good. A believer who puts everything with which he has to do, to the Bible test—taking the good, leaving the bad, accepting the righteous, rejecting the unrighteous—that believer will never backslide.

11. Abstain from all appearance of evil. That statement speaks for itself.

12. The very God of peace sanctify you wholly—spirit, soul and body preserved blameless unto the coming of our Lord Jesus Christ. A believer who is sanctified in his *spirit* (mind), *soul* (heart) and *body* (the tabernacle in which spirit and soul live) will never backslide.

13. "FAITHFUL IS HE THAT CALLETH YOU, WHO ALSO WILL DO IT." God is faithful; God cannot be unfaithful or untrue.

He promised to supply every need: "Seek ye first the kingdom of God, and His righteousness; and all these things shall be added unto you" (Matt. 6:33). ". . . For He hath said, I will never leave thee, nor forsake thee. So that we may boldly say, The Lord is my helper, and I will not fear what man shall do unto me" (Heb. 13:5,6). "There hath no temptation taken you but such as is common to man: but God is faithful, who will not suffer you to be tempted above that ye are able; but will with the temptation also make a way to escape, that ye may be able to bear it" (I Cor. 10:13). ". . . Grieve not the Holy Spirit of God, *whereby ye are sealed unto the day of redemption*" (Eph. 4:30).

The God who loved us so much that He gave His only begotten Son to die for us, that grace might be ours, will do for us everything He has promised. He is faithful; *He cannot be unfaithful.*

Practice the things I have outlined here, and you may rest assured that you will never backslide!

The Second Epistle of Paul
the Apostle
to the Thessalonians

II THESSALONIANS — CHAPTER ONE

1. Paul, and Silvanus, and Timotheus, unto the church of the Thessalonians in God our Father and the Lord Jesus Christ:

2. Grace unto you, and peace, from God our Father and the Lord Jesus Christ.

3. We are bound to thank God always for you, brethren, as it is meet, because that your faith groweth exceedingly, and the charity of every one of you all toward each other aboundeth;

4. So that we ourselves glory in you in the churches of God for your patience and faith in all your persecutions and tribulations that ye endure:

5. Which is a manifest token of the righteous judgment of God, that ye may be counted worthy of the kingdom of God, for which ye also suffer:

6. Seeing it is a righteous thing with God to recompense tribulation to them that trouble you;

7. And to you who are troubled rest with us, when the Lord Jesus shall be revealed from heaven with his mighty angels,

8. In flaming fire taking vengeance on them that know not God, and that obey not the gospel of our Lord Jesus Christ:

9. Who shall be punished with everlasting destruction from the presence of the Lord, and from the glory of his power;

10. When he shall come to be glorified in his saints, and to be admired in all them that believe (because our testimony among you was believed) in that day.

11. Wherefore also we pray always for you, that our God would count you worthy of this calling, and fulfil all the good pleasure of his goodness, and the work of faith with power:

12. That the name of our Lord Jesus Christ may be glorified in you, and ye in him, according to the grace of our God and the Lord Jesus Christ.

There can be no doubt that Paul wrote this second epistle, for the opening verse of chapter 1 clearly states, "*Paul*, and Silvanus, and Timotheus, unto the church of the Thessalonians *in God our Father and the Lord Jesus Christ*." By this we know that Paul is the author, and that the Holy Spirit spoke through him. He names Silas and Timothy here, as in verse one of his first epistle to the Thessalonians.

This second letter was written very soon *after* the first epistle, and it is possible that the bearer of that letter brought back to Paul questions from the church concerning the condition of some of the believers there.

This second letter was written to correct error concerning *the Day of the Lord.* Some of the Christians there were shaken in mind and troubled in heart, supposing that the persecutions and stern testings they were suffering were those of the great and terrible Day of the Lord (Isa. 2:12). Paul had taught them that they would be caught up to meet Jesus in the clouds in the air before the terrible Day of the Lord should come upon them. From a statement Paul makes in this epistle ("Nor by letter as from us"), it would seem that someone had forged his name to a letter and sent it to the believers at Thessalonica. Probably some of the enemies of the grace of God had done this evil thing in an attempt to upset and tear down the work Paul had been used of the Lord to begin there: so the second epistle was written to assure the Christians that they were NOT in the Great Tribulation period (the Day of the Lord), and that they would certainly be delivered "from the hour of temptation that shall come upon the whole world." Christians are not the children of wrath. We are not appointed unto tribulation, but unto salvation—full and complete.

II Thessalonians was written to clear up in the minds of the believers the difference between the *Rapture* (our gathering together unto Him) and the *Revelation* (the time when "every eye shall see Him and all the kindreds of the earth shall wail because of Him").

Verse 1: "Paul, and Silvanus, and Timotheus, unto the church of the Thessalonians in God our Father and the Lord Jesus Christ."

The salutation of this second epistle is almost

identical to that of the first. Here the Apostle writes, "Unto the church of the Thessalonians in God our Father and the Lord Jesus Christ." In the first letter he writes, "Unto the church of the Thessalonians which is in God the Father and in the Lord Jesus Christ." The only difference between the two is that in the first letter he referred to *THE Father*, and here he uses the term, "*OUR Father*"—that is, "the Father of us who are believers." (Read Romans 1:7 and Luke 12:32.) We also see the same statement in chapter 2, verse 16, of our present study: "Now our Lord Jesus Christ Himself, and God, even our Father, which hath loved us, and hath given us everlasting consolation and good hope through grace."

Thus Paul points out the source of all spiritual blessings—that source being twofold, yet ONE: *God the Father* is the *spring* from which all living water and spiritual blessings proceed. *The Lord Jesus Christ* is the *mediating cause* of grace and peace. "In the beginning was the Word, and the Word was with God, and the Word was God" (John 1:1). "And the Word was made flesh, and dwelt among us, (and we beheld His glory, the glory as of the only begotten of the Father,) full of grace and truth" (John 1:14). No man could ever look upon God or appear before Him—and live; he would be utterly consumed. But Jesus brought God down to man in flesh and said, "I and my Father are one . . . they that have seen me have seen the Father also." Jesus did not hesitate to say, "I am in the Father, and the Father in me." Nor did He blush when He said, "I am the Light of the world." He did not apologize to the Pharisees when He said, "Your fathers did eat manna in the wilderness, and are dead . . . I AM THE BREAD OF LIFE . . . Except ye eat the flesh of the Son of man, and drink His blood, ye have no life in you" (John 6:48, 49, 53).

When Jesus said this, many of His followers "went

back, and walked no more with Him. Then said Jesus unto the twelve, Will ye also go away? Then Simon Peter answered Him, LORD, TO WHOM SHALL WE GO? THOU HAST THE WORDS OF ETERNAL LIFE. And we believe and are sure that thou art that Christ, the Son of the living God'' (John 6:66–69). Jesus did not rebuke Peter for asking, *"TO WHOM shall we go?"*—for what Peter said is true: *There is life in none other!* Jesus is the *one Mediator* between God and men. God loved us, and Jesus brought grace down to us, presenting grace to us on our own level . . . *God in flesh*, reconciling the world unto Himself (II Cor. 5:19). Please study the sixth chapter of John's Gospel in its entirety.

I like the statement, *"Unto THE church of THE Thessalonians, in God our Father and the Lord Jesus Christ."* Today as never before we need to see this tremendous truth—today when certain ones are declaring that *their* group composes the bride of Christ, and all others are outside the bride. They maintain that those not baptized into *their church by their ministers* will not sit at the marriage supper, but will be servants and guests; but after reading this verse from the inspired pen of Paul, no person with an open mind, desiring to know the truth, walk in the light and be true to the Gospel, can say that the local church is THE Church. It is true that there was *a local assembly* in Thessalonica; but Paul said, "the church of the Thessalonians IN GOD OUR FATHER AND THE LORD JESUS CHRIST." The *meeting house* of the assembly was in Thessalonica; the believers were abiding in *bodies of flesh* in Thessalonica; but *the true Church is in God and in Christ!*

To the Colossians Paul said, "Ye are dead, and your life is hid with Christ in God" (Col. 3:3). To the Ephesians he said, "For we are members of His body, of His flesh, and of His bones" (Eph. 5:30). The New

Testament Church is a living organism made up of all born again, blood-washed believers. The local assembly is ordained and recognized by God—but no local church has any right to claim to be THE Church. ALL local churches wherein are members who are truly born again, are a part of the invisible body of which Jesus is the head; but *the Church of the living God is IN God NOW*; we sit together in heavenly places in Christ Jesus NOW. We are pilgrims here; we are on a journey, and our citizenship is in heaven—even NOW, *this moment!*

Verse 2: "Grace unto you, and peace, from God our Father and the Lord Jesus Christ."

Paul knew there was no peace (and certainly no grace) apart from God, through the Lord Jesus Christ. Grace is God's unmerited favor, God's unearned gift; and that gift is the Lord Jesus Christ. Paul knew, as most of us will *never* know, what it means to be delivered from religious bondage into the liberty of grace. Paul was a Pharisee of the Pharisees, and he lived after the straitest sect of the Pharisees. He was in bondage to religion, and what he did against the Church, he did in ignorance (Acts 26:2–11). He persecuted the Church; but he did so "in all good conscience," believing the Church to be the enemy of God.

Since Paul was exceedingly glad and joyous because HE had found the grace of God (and, through that grace, PEACE), he prays that God's grace and peace will be abundant in the hearts of the believers in Thessalonica—especially during the days of intensive testing by the enemy.

Verse 3: "We are bound to thank God always for you, brethren, as it is meet, because that your faith groweth exceedingly, and the charity of every one of you all toward each other aboundeth."

Here, as in the first epistle, Paul expresses sincere thanksgiving for the believers in Thessalonica. He first expresses thanksgiving for their growth in faith and love—especially in brotherly love toward each other in the church.

He is also exceedingly thankful in his own heart that the believers are patient during the persecutions and tribulations through which they had been and were passing (verse 4). In the third place, Paul is thankful that God will judge the enemies of the church in righteousness. It is a righteous thing with God to recompense tribulation to them that trouble His children, and for this, Paul expressed thanksgiving (verses 5–10).

Notice the opening words of verse 3: *"We are bound to thank God always for you, brethren."* Also, in chapter 2:13 we read, "But *we are bound to give thanks* alway to God for you, brethren . . . ." Paul does not use this statement in any other epistle. It seems that he feels a special debt of gratitude to God for the grace given to the Thessalonians—the grace that had caused them to stand true to the faith during a time of suffering and anguish so intense that some of them actually thought they were in the very midst of the Great Tribulation period.

Paul was *also* going through testing and heartbreak at this time, and the stedfastness of the believers in Thessalonica seemed to encourage him and bring cheer to his heart, thus sustaining and strengthening him in the inner man at a time when he sorely needed sustenance. (Read Acts 18:9,10 and I Corinthians 2:3.) In I Thessalonians 3:8 Paul says, *"Now we live, if ye stand fast in the Lord"*! It would have broken his heart had the Thessalonian believers forsaken God and the truth he had preached to them.

"As it is meet" signifies that Paul's thanksgiving

was not just a personal feeling, but because they were due to be honored and praised in the right sense. In other words, "Your growth in grace deserves such acknowledgement to God." To the believers at Philippi Paul said, "Even as it is meet for me to think this of you all" (Phil. 1:7). His heart was not filled with pride in the wrong way, but with *spiritual* pride and with thanksgiving because of the faithfulness of the saints; and it was right to send up praises and thanksgiving to God because of their stedfastness and growth in faith.

In I Thessalonians 3:2 and 6 Paul sent Timothy to Thessalonica to get a report on the faith of the Thessalonians, and the report Timothy brought back encouraged Paul in great degree because Timothy testified that the Thessalonians were true to the faith once delivered to the saints and that they manifested extraordinary, unusual growth in the faith.

I think the outstanding reason for this growth can be attributed to the *character of their initial faith* . . . they turned *completely to God* and in so doing turned *completely away from their idols*, "to serve the living and true God; and to wait for His Son from heaven." James tells us that "faith without works is dead." The faith of the Thessalonians was genuine, and they exercised that faith—not only in turning to God from idols, but also in SERVICE. They demonstrated a "work of faith" (I Thess. 1:3).

Persecution also increased their faith. If faith is not genuine, then trials, persecutions, heartaches, heartbreaks and warfare from the underworld will destroy it; but if faith is the faith once delivered to the saints, persecution will only serve to strengthen it in like manner as the storms that beat upon the great oak trees in the forest cause their roots to go deeper into the earth, thereby securing a firmer grip to sustain the tree in the hour of tempest.

217

Paul said to the Romans, "Who shall separate us from the love of Christ? shall tribulation, or distress, or persecution, or famine, or nakedness, or peril, or sword? As it is written, For thy sake we are killed all the day long; we are accounted as sheep for the slaughter. Nay, in all these things we are more than conquerors through Him that loved us. For I am persuaded, that neither death, nor life, nor angels, nor principalities, nor powers, nor things present, nor things to come, nor height, nor depth, nor any other creature, shall be able to separate us from the love of God, which is in Christ Jesus our Lord" (Rom. 8:35-39).

Since the faith of the Thessalonians was genuine, persecution did not tear them from the love of Christ, but rather drove their roots of faith deeper into the foundation of Christianity—that foundation being the finished work of Jesus, His death, burial, resurrection and imminent return. Trials strengthened them instead of destroying them, and the same is true today in the lives of truly born again believers.

Verse 3 closes with the statement, ". . . *The charity of every one of you all toward each other aboundeth.*" Certainly this is the result of believers growing in faith. FAITH and LOVE are the *siamese twins* of the graces of the theology of the New Testament and Christianity. The only person who can love aright is the person who has exercised faith in God. No mother can love her children as fervently as she should until she has exercised faith in God. No love is complete if it is not preceded by true faith. Paul speaks of "faith, hope, charity, these three; but the greatest of these is charity" (I Cor. 13:13). Read also I Thessalonians 1:3; 5:8 and Galatians 5:5,6.

The Thessalonian believers excelled in pure love—love that could be produced only by faith that was a growing faith. In Paul's first letter to the Thessalonians he acknowledged their excellent love one for another, and exhorted them to ABOUND YET MORE IN LOVE. *The very essence of Christianity is love*—first to God, and then to our kinsmen in the Lord.

Verse 4: "So that we ourselves glory in you in the churches of God for your patience and faith in all your persecutions and tribulations that ye endure."

The victory won by the Gospel of grace in Thessalonica had given Paul a peculiar sense of satisfaction and joy. As previously pointed out, the city of Thessalonica was strategically located and had great advantages from the standpoint of trade and commerce. Travelers came to the city from all over the surrounding area, and the testimony of the believers there had spread throughout the neighboring provinces.

If you will read all of Paul's epistles you will find that he took great joy in commending one church to another. Here he is thinking of the churches in Judaea (note I Thessalonians 2:14) and also of the assemblies in Syria. He and Silas were in correspondence with the churches there, and to these assemblies they had sent good news, expressing joy and satisfaction over the faith and devotion of this new church in Thessalonica.

In II Corinthians 9:2 Paul speaks of "boasting to the Macedonians" about the liberal offerings of the Corinthians. There was no selfishness, jealousy or partiality in his heart, and he sincerely recommends one church to another.

Notice the term, *"We ourselves."* Paul is here stressing the fact that it is not only he—but also Silas and Timothy—who sent salutations. This trio of devoted missionaries were very careful not to boast about anything that would bring credit or honor to themselves. This is clearly proved in Galatians 6:14, II Corinthians

12:1–6 and also in I Thessalonians 2:6,7. These men of God did not glory in themselves, but they freely boasted concerning the believers in the churches the Lord had used them to establish.

The *patience* of the believers at Thessalonica was one thing that caused Paul to point them out to other churches. They were patient and faithful—even under the severest persecution. Under heaviest fire from the enemy they showed such endurance and faith that Paul was led to express his gratitude to them "for your patience and faith in all your persecutions and tribulations that ye endure."

The major element in the sufferings of the believers at Thessalonica was persecution (I Thess. 2:14; Acts 17:5–9). They had endured afflictions of many kinds, but persecutions tormented them most of all. Hebrews 10:32,33: ". . . Ye endured a great fight of affliction . . . whilst ye were made a gazingstock both by reproaches and afflictions; and . . . companions of them that were so used." The literal Greek for this passage reads, "Ye endured a great conflict of suffering . . . being made a gazingstock by reproaches and afflictions . . . and partaker of those so used." The same Greek word used here for "afflictions" is also used in I Thessalonians 1:6; 3:3,4,7.

These believers had proved to be good soldiers under massive attacks from the enemy, and this fact caused Paul to rejoice "with joy unspeakable and full of glory." He never ceased to give thanks and praise God for the faithfulness of his converts in Thessalonica.

Verse 5: "Which is a manifest token of the righteous judgment of God, that ye may be counted worthy of the kingdom of God, for which ye also suffer."

As we study the remaining verses in this chapter,

we will see further reasons why Paul was so thankful for the believers in Thessalonica. He knew that the true God would justly recompense the enemies of the Gospel, and he had some understanding of what that would mean— for to the Hebrews he said, "It is a fearful thing to fall into the hands of the living God!" He knew that God in His righteousness would reward the teachers of error and the persecutors of the Gospel who had tormented the Thessalonian Christians continuously since the church there began.

The retribution the Apostle foresees is twofold, consisting of *rest* and *glory* for the persecuted saints (verses 5, 7, 10 and 12), and the *punishment* of the persecutors according to their works (verses 6, 8 and 9). In these verses we will learn that Jesus is coming for a twofold purpose:

First—*for the glorification of His people.* When Christ, who is our life, shall appear, then shall we also appear with Him in glory. The dead in Christ will be raised incorruptible; living saints will be changed as this corruption puts on incorruption; and together we will be caught up to meet the Lord in the clouds in the air.

Second—*He is coming in judgment.* Vengeance will fall upon the oppressors of the Gospel—and the judgment God pours out will be *righteous judgment.* Justice will be meted out to every man—the righteous and the unrighteous. The suffering of the Thessalonian believers was not in vain. If we suffer with Christ we will also reign with Him.

In the Philippian letter Paul said, "Only let your conversation be as it becometh the Gospel of Christ: that whether I come and see you, or else be absent, I may hear of your affairs, that ye stand fast in one spirit, with one mind striving together for the faith of the Gospel;

221

and in nothing terrified by your adversaries: which is to them an evident token of perdition, but to you of salvation, and that of God" (Phil. 1:27,28).

The fact that the Thessalonians had stood true to the faith under heavy fire from the enemy testified that they were genuinely born again. Their heroic faith proved that God was on their side. It was God who had inspired them to stand true to the Gospel under such severe persecution (I Thess. 1:6); and He, the righteous Judge, had already declared that His judgment was sure to fall upon the enemies of the Gospel. Paul and Silas knew what it was to be persecuted for preaching the Gospel. They knew what it meant to be beaten, thrown in jail, having their feet fastened in the stocks; but in spite of their pain and the darkness of the dungeon, they sang and prayed at midnight! (Please read the entire chapter of Acts 16.) Stephen was stoned—but the Word of God tells us that when he stood before the council that condemned him, his face shone "as it had been the face of an angel" (Acts 6:15).

Verse 5 closes with the words, *"that ye may be counted worthy of the kingdom of God, for which ye also suffer."* Paul is saying, "Your faithfulness under severe persecution and testing is a token of God's righteous judgment, given with the purpose that you may be counted worthy of His kingdom." The very fact that these believers stood true and unshakeable under such terrible persecution assured Paul that they were worthy of the kingdom of God.

The believers at Thessalonica were enduring suffering *for the kingdom's sake.* They had strong hope of the coming of the Lord Jesus Christ in great victory over the enemies of the Gospel. They were awaiting the glad cry, "Come, ye blessed of my Father, inherit the kingdom prepared for you from the foundation of the world!"

222

(Matt. 25:34). Read also I Thessalonians 2:12 and II Thessalonians 2:13. We have God's promise that if we suffer with Him we shall also reign with Him.

The kingdom of God is prepared for those who prepare for that kingdom (Matt. 20:23); those who are counted worthy (II Thess. 1:11); also I Thessalonians 2:12; 3:13; Luke 20:35 and Matthew 22:8. The kingdom of God will be shared and enjoyed by those who are worthy *through the shed blood of the Lord Jesus Christ and true faith in His finished work.* Jesus said, "The wedding is ready, but they which were bidden were not worthy. Go ye therefore into the highways, and as many as ye shall find, bid to the marriage" (Matt. 22:8,9). Of course, "they which were bidden" refers to the Jews, His own people. They refused to accept Christ as their Messiah, and therefore He turned to the Gentiles—the poor, the halt, the withered, the lame—yea, Gentile "dogs"; "whomsoever" were invited to the marriage supper.

Heaven is a prepared place, and only people who are prepared will go there (John 14:1-6). The inheritance of the righteous is reserved in heaven, ". . . an inheritance incorruptible, and undefiled, and that fadeth not away, RESERVED IN HEAVEN FOR YOU" (I Pet. 1:4). Dear reader, if you do not make reservation, you will not enter the Paradise of God that is now being prepared for those who accept the finished work of Jesus for the remission of sins. Read carefully the solemn words recorded by John the Beloved in Revelation 22:10-15.

To Timothy Paul said, "If we suffer, we shall also reign with Him: if we deny Him, He also will deny us" (II Tim. 2:12). Read carefully Hebrews 10:34-39; Romans 8:16-19 and Philippians 1:20.

Verse 6: "Seeing it is a righteous thing with God to recompense tribulation to them which trouble you."

In verse 5 Paul has just declared that the judgment to be poured out upon the persecutors of the saints in Thessalonica would be *God's righteous judgment.* The things that will come upon the enemies of the Gospel will come from a righteous God and will be *"a righteous thing."* The justice of the affliction that will be meted out to the wicked is evident: Affliction will be poured out upon *"them that trouble you"*; and to the afflicted saints will come *ease*—(the Greek word suggests *relaxation,* as when a taut string on a violin is released). So the Apostle speaks of his own "relief" from anxiety. (Note II Corinthians 2:13; 7:5.)

In Romans 2:9 Paul said, "Tribulation and anguish, upon every soul of man that doeth evil"—and the term used here, as in our present verse, indicates personal suffering and torment. The same words are also used in Luke 16:25, referring to the rich man and Lazarus: "Now (Lazarus) is comforted, and thou art tormented." "He that doeth wrong shall receive for the wrong which he hath done: and there is no respect of persons" (Col. 3:25). The same principal of retribution in kind is set forth in Revelation 13:10 and Matthew 26:52. Judgment from God is just, for the true and righteous God cannot do anything UNRIGHTEOUS. To bring peace, rest and relaxation to the righteous is the common rule of justice with God; to bring misery, anguish, woe and torment to the wicked and upon those who hate God is also the common rule of justice with God. It stands to reason that if this law demands suffering to those who are wicked, by the same righteous law shall surely come relief and relaxation to those who are tormented by the rulers of spiritual darkness and the underworld. The Psalmist cried out, "The wicked shall be turned into hell, and all the nations that forget God" (Psalm 9:17). Paul said to the Hebrew Christians, "There remaineth therefore a rest to the people of God" (Heb. 4:9).

Verse 7: "And to you who are troubled rest with us, when the Lord Jesus shall be revealed from heaven with His mighty angels."

I doubt that anyone on earth could have sympathized with the suffering Thessalonians more sincerely than the Apostle Paul, for no man but Jesus ever suffered as Paul suffered. His was a life of harassment, fatigue, pain, floggings, stonings and sufferings; but he had the blessed hope of a day of rest! *To think of that day* was indeed sweet to this man who bore in his body the marks of the sufferings he had undergone for the Gospel. In Galatians 6:17 he cries, "FROM HENCEFORTH LET NO MAN TROUBLE ME: FOR I BEAR IN MY BODY THE MARKS OF THE LORD JESUS!"

In spite of his suffering, Paul had joy unspeakable and full of glory. I think no man ever came nearer walking in the footsteps of Jesus than did the Apostle Paul. His epistles are interlaced with words of joy pertaining to the resurrection, the crowning day, the rewarding day, the day of gain (II Cor. 4:14; II Tim. 4:8; Phil. 1:20–23). JESUS endured the cross, despising the shame, *for with joy He looked to the glory beyond the cross* (Heb. 12:1–4); so PAUL suffered untold agony for the sake of the Gospel, but beyond that agony he saw the glory of sharing the crown!

In verse 7 Paul reminds the believers that the Lord Jesus is coming: He will be revealed from heaven, He will come with His mighty angels . . . and *when He comes He will execute judgment upon the wicked.* The hope of the Church is the coming of the Lord Jesus. Paul said, "Yea, and all that will live godly in Christ Jesus shall suffer persecution." Jesus Himself said, "In the world ye shall have tribulation." For the Church and the believer there is no relief from the standpoint of suffering, heartache, disappointment and persecution, until the Lord Jesus comes in glory to destroy *wickedness and the wicked*, and set up His glorious kingdom. Until that glorious event, believers are to trust and be patient, knowing that, *"If God be for us, who can be against us?"* We know that even though we are in the minority now, we are still on the winning side!

We must study and rightly divide the Word of Truth. Read carefully I Thessalonians 2:15–19; I Corinthians 1:7; I Peter 1:7–13 and 4:13. This phase of the coming of the Lord Jesus is called His *Revelation—*"when He shall be revealed from heaven." When He comes, He will exhibit majesty, glory, power and such splendor as is now unknown and inconceivable. Also, when He comes there will be a "revelation of the sons of God" and a revelation of *the righteous judgment of God* which will be poured out upon the wicked (Rom. 1:18; 2:5,6).

In the remaining verses of our present chapter, we are not to confuse the Revelation with the Rapture:

The Rapture will be secret and unannounced; Jesus will descend in the air above us, and the Church will be caught up out of the world (I Thess. 4:13–18; I Cor. 15:51–55). When Jesus comes in the Rapture He will come to make up His jewels (Mal. 3:17).

The Revelation is the time when He will come with His mighty angels, every eye shall see Him, and all the kindreds of the earth shall wail because of Him. At that time, His feet will stand on the mount of Olives. The Jews will ask Him where He received the scars in His hands. Jude 14,15 describes this as the time when He comes with tens of thousands of His saints, and He will come to execute judgment.

In the last part of verse 7 Paul is speaking of the

226

Revelation when he says Jesus will be *"revealed from heaven"*—that is, He will *descend out of* the glory of His Father with the holy angels (Mark 8:38). Concerning the angels, David said, "The Lord hath prepared His throne in the heavens; and His kingdom ruleth over all. Bless the Lord, YE HIS ANGELS, that excel in strength, that do His commandments, hearkening unto the voice of His word" (Psalm 103:19,20). The angels will play a very important role in the last great judgment when Jesus comes in the Revelation:

Verse 8: "In flaming fire taking vengeance on them that know not God, and that obey not the Gospel of our Lord Jesus Christ."

Fire as used in the Scriptures denotes divine anger and majesty. *Flame* is fire in motion, leaping and blazing—denoting the fast-moving judgment of Almighty God. According to II Peter 3:10, this world will one day melt with fervent heat, the world and its works will be burned up—and contrary to the teaching of the liberals and modernists, this will be *literal fire*—not symbolic.

Writing to the believers in Corinth, Paul warned that every man's work shall be tried by fire (I Cor. 3:13—15). If our stewardship is gold, silver and precious stones, it will stand the divine *fire-test*; but if our stewardship is selfish and in the flesh (wood, hay, stubble), it will be consumed and we will suffer loss. In Jeremiah 23:29 we are told that God's Word is like fire. Truly, *God is a God of love* (I John 4:8), but He is also *a consuming fire* (Heb. 12:29); and when Jesus comes in the Revelation to judge the wicked, He will come in a gigantic flame of fire, *"taking vengeance on them that know not God and that obey not the Gospel of our Lord Jesus Christ."*

When Jesus comes to judge the wicked, He will mete out FULL JUSTICE to each and every unbeliever—nothing more, nothing less. He will not judge in passion, but in righteousness. Deuteronomy 32:35 tells us, "To (the Lord) belongeth vengeance and recompense." We find the same statement in Romans 12:19: "Vengeance is mine; I will repay, saith the Lord." Hebrews 10:30 says, "Vengeance belongeth unto me, I will recompense, saith the Lord." The believers who have been wronged, persecuted and mistreated by unbelievers will not be permitted to avenge themselves. Jesus, the righteous One, will pay off in full to every wicked person. ". . . The Father . . . hath committed all judgment unto the Son" (John 5:22). Jesus will judge the quick and the dead at His appearing (II Tim. 4:1).

Two classes are distinguished in verse 8:

(1) *"Them that know not God."* Paul is speaking here of the heathenism in his own day—primarily Gentile idolatry. He declared that these people were ignorant willfully, practicing ungodliness, idolatry and wickedness—not because they had never had the opportunity to KNOW God, but because *when they KNEW God they refused to glorify Him AS God* (I Thess. 4:5; Rom. 1:18–32). The literal Greek in Romans 1:28 reads, *"They did not think God worth having in their knowledge."* Therefore, the paganism in Paul's day deserved the vengeance of God upon it.

All peoples of earth at one time or another have had an opportunity to know God. *Adam* (the father of all) and *Eve* (the mother of all) knew God; Noah and his family knew God—and God has never left Himself without a witness on this earth (Acts 14:17; John 1:6–8). Therefore, every man will be judged according to the light to which he was exposed and the opportunity that could have been his. His light and opportunities will be weighed in God's righteous scales, and God will judge that individual accordingly.

Here Paul is thinking primarily of the Gentile per-secutors of the believers in Thessalonica. They refused to receive the knowledge of God, they hated God—and they *proved* that hatred *by hating the children of God.* Read John 15:24 and I John 3:13.

(2) The second group pointed out are *those who obey not the Gospel.* That group includes all who were ex-posed to the Gospel—all who have been or will be ex-posed to the Gospel from this day until the consummation of all things . . . Jews and Gentiles, rich and poor, bond and free—who have heard the truth but *refused to obey that truth.* They refused to be obedient to the faith or to submit their hearts and lives to God. They will be judged and rewarded according to the light they had and the opportunities they refused to grasp. They that "obey not the Gospel" refuse to believe on Jesus as Lord. (Note I Corinthians 12:3 and Philippians 2:10.) Those who heard about Jesus and rejected Him became Paul's worst enemies and his most severe and determined per-secutors. The Lord Jesus Christ warned when He was on earth, "He that believeth not shall be damned (con-demned)" (Mark 16:16). Paul is saying the same thing in our present passage.

John tells us, ". . . He that believeth not is con-demned already, because he hath not believed in the name of the only begotten Son of God. And this is the condemnation, that light is come into the world, and men loved darkness rather than light, because their deeds were evil" (John 3:18,19). Better had we never *heard* the Gospel of the marvelous grace of God, than to hear the Gospel and *refuse to obey it.* One of the most solemn verses in all Scripture is found in John's Gospel: "He that rejecteth me, and receiveth not my words, hath one that judgeth him: *the word that I have spoken, the same shall judge him in the last day*" (John 12:48).

We will never know this side of eternity the importance of the Word of God: The Word of God *brings the good news of salvation.* The Word of God is *the seed* that produces the power to bring about the new birth. The Gospel is *the power of God unto salvation.* The Gospel *brings faith through which we receive the grace of God* that saves us; and we will be *judged by the Word* in that last day, for our stewardship.

Verse 9: "Who shall be punished with everlasting destruction from the presence of the Lord, and from the glory of His power."

In these penetrating, cutting words Paul describes the horrible judgment that awaits godless men who reject the Gospel of the marvelous grace of God and refuse to believe on the Son of God's love as Saviour. The statement applies to ALL who know not God and to ALL who obey not the Gospel; but Paul was thinking primarily of the ungodly opposers and persecutors of the believers in Thessalonica, who were doing everything in their demented power to crush and destroy the infant church there. Such sin corresponds in some degree to the sin Jesus denounced in Matthew 12:31,32 and Mark 3:28,29 as the sin against the Holy Spirit. These persecutors certainly in measure attributed the work of the Thessalonian believers to the devil, and they were attempting to wipe it out. Therefore, certain judgment and eternal damnation hung heavily over their heads, and in the great judgment day *they will be judged* and "punished with everlasting destruction from the presence of the Lord and from the glory of His power."

Destruction here refers to the destiny of the unbeliever. The Greek word signifies "perdition, ruin, utter loss, and without blessedness"—the exact opposite of salvation. Eternal destruction is the exact opposite of eternal life. If salvation gives life unending—everlasting and eternal through the ages of ages—then the wicked shall be *destroyed* forever and ever through the ages of ages. There is no reason whatsoever for any person to interpret *destruction* in the Greek to mean annihilation or extinction. The meaning of *destruction* is *to be lost forever* . . . lost to God and God's goodness, lost to peace and rest that only God can give.

The Greek word here for "*everlasting*" has no limit of range. The meaning removes all limits of time, and it is the exact opposite of *temporary* (see II Corinthians 4:18). The word "everlasting" or "eternal" is found seventy-two times in the books of the New Testament; forty-four of the seventy-two times the phrase has to do with eternal life, the remaining twenty-eight times with eternal destruction. Therefore, if there is no *eternal destruction*, there can be no *eternal life*. If the wicked *cease to be* after the final judgment, then the *righteous* will also cease to be, because the same word is used as applying to both *eternal life and eternal destruction*!

Speaking of the wicked, Jesus said, "And these shall go away into everlasting punishment; but the righteous into life eternal" (Matt. 25:46). There is no need to warp and twist the Word of God to fit a denomination, cult, dogma or man-made doctrine, when the Word is so clear. In one single verse Jesus declares that *the wicked will be PUNISHED eternally* and that *the righteous will LIVE eternally*. Yet there are those who put the righteous in Paradise forever and burn up the wicked, annihilating the spirit and soul, thus making them cease to exist!

How anyone can be so willingly ignorant and cruel is beyond my understanding. Regardless of what teachers, preachers or anyone else has to say about everlasting destruction, those who refuse to believe it on this side of the grave will certainly be convinced of it on the other side!

Verse 9 closes with *"from the presence of the Lord, and from the glory of His power"*—or, in the original Greek: *". . . from the face of the Lord and from the glory of His might."* This statement is similar to Isaiah 2:10–21, where Isaiah describes the judgment of Jehovah in the last great day: "Enter into the rock, and hide thee in the dust, for fear of the Lord, and for the glory of His majesty. . . . And they shall go into the holes of the rocks, and into the caves of the earth, for fear of the Lord, and for the glory of His majesty, when He ariseth to shake terribly the earth. . . . To go into the clefts of the rocks, and into the tops of the ragged rocks, for fear of the Lord, and for the glory of His majesty, when he ariseth to shake terribly the earth" (Isa. 2:10,19,21).

Almost the same words are used in Revelation 6:15,16, where John describes the gigantic prayer meeting that will be attended by kings, rich men, chief captains and mighty men, bondmen, free men, all classes and creeds praying one prayer: That the rocks and the mountains fall on them and hide them "from the face of Him that sitteth on the throne, AND FROM THE WRATH OF THE LAMB!" What a day that will be!!

At the sight of the Lord Jesus Christ, the Righteous Judge—His Almightiness robed in flaming fire and followed by His host of shining angels—these wretched unbelievers will be terror-stricken beyond words. They will scream for the rocks and the mountains to fall on them and hide them from the face of the Lord! David said, "The face of the Lord is against them that do evil, to cut off the remembrance of them from the earth" (Psalm 34:16). ". . . In thine anger cast down the people, O God" (Psalm 56:7b). *"God is angry with the wicked every day"* (Psalm 7:11).

Verse 10: "When He shall come to be glorified in

His saints, and to be admired in all them that believe (because our testimony among you was believed) in that day."

In the original Greek this verse reads, *"He hath come to be glorified in His holy ones and wondered at in all those who believed."*

At the coming of Jesus, "the glory of His might" brings utter destruction to the wicked (verse 9). However, there is another glory that is much dearer to Jesus— the "glory of His grace" (Eph. 1:4-6)—which will be exhibited in its full splendor "in His holy ones" when Jesus puts His bride on display in the heavenlies to show the exceeding riches of God's grace in us who believe and who make up the New Testament Church, the bride of Christ. ". . . And hath raised us up together, and made us sit together in heavenly places in Christ Jesus: That in the ages to come He might shew the exceeding riches of His grace in His kindness toward us through Christ Jesus" (Eph. 2:6,7).

When Jesus displays His bride in the Pearly White City as set forth in Revelation 21, then all God's new creation will behold the exceeding riches of God's grace in the bride in the Pearly White City. In the Lord's intercessory prayer in John 17, Jesus said, "I am glorified in them." Jesus Himself is the holy One of God—He is the firstborn among many brethren; and believers will be raised when He comes in the Rapture to make up His jewels and to catch the Church up into the clouds in the air to meet Him. Then when He comes with His saints to execute judgment He will display His bride, showing the exceeding riches of God's grace in us! All creation will marvel and glorify God because of the exceeding riches of God's grace provided through the sacrificial death of the Son of His love on the cruel cross. All heaven and earth will sing unto the Lamb: ". . . Unto

Him that loved us, and washed us from our sins in His own blood, and hath made us kings and priests unto God and His Father; to Him be glory and dominion for ever and ever. Amen'' (Rev. 1:5,6).

The parenthetical portion of verse 10—(*"because our testimony among you was believed"*)—means simply that the believers in Thessalonica were a part of the New Testament Church because they had received the testimony of the Apostle Paul, addressed to them by the Holy Spirit through Paul as minister. The fact of their unshakeable faith proved that they were genuinely born again and part of the bride who will share in the glory in that great day when Jesus will be glorified in His saints, admired in all them that believe and praised by all creation.

Verse 10 closes with ". . . *in that day*," simply meaning *the day when Jesus will declare final victory* over the wicked and over sin—the day when the knowledge of the Lord will cover the earth as the waters now cover the sea. In that day the bride will be displayed in the Pearly White City in the heavenlies, and God Himself shall wipe all tears from the eyes of His people. There will be no more weeping, no more crying, no more heartaches in that day of all days, when God will commit all things unto His Son, the Lord Jesus Christ. In that day *He will reign supremely*, and we (the bride) will be glorified together with Him and will reign with Him. In that day there will be peace on earth, good will toward men; there will be a Paradise in which there will be no sin, because Satan will be forever sealed in the lake of fire along with those whom he led astray, to be tormented day and night in fire and brimstone forever and ever.

Verse 11: "Wherefore also we pray always for you, that our God would count you worthy of this calling, and fulfil all the good pleasure of His goodness, and the work of faith with power."

Compare this verse with I Thessalonians 1:2 and 3:10. Paul wanted the believers at Thessalonica to keep in mind always that it was God who called them; it was God who loved them and provided grace to save them "to His own kingdom and glory"; and God was now calling them to sanctification and full surrender, in order that they be "preserved blameless unto the coming of our Lord Jesus Christ." Read I Thessalonians 2:12; 4:3-8; and 5:23,24.

In our present verse, a third aspect of God's calling is set forth, which combines and completes the other two. The believers at Thessalonica, *in Christ*, are called to *crown their Saviour with glory* by the fruit and effect of their faith. Verses 10 and 12 definitely indicate that Paul had this in mind. He wanted them to exhibit such honor in their daily living, and live lives of such true devotion and sacrifice as would be worthy of the Lord Jesus, who had sacrificed that they might be saved. He wanted them to live this kind of life in order to make others think more highly of the Lord Jesus, and by so living add splendor to His heavenly crown. To be able to do this is a privilege of which we may well pray that "God may count us worthy."

John, the beloved disciple, reveals this same truth in writing to the church in Sardis: "Thou hast a few names even in Sardis which have not defiled their garments; AND THEY SHALL WALK WITH ME IN WHITE: FOR THEY ARE WORTHY" (Rev. 3:4). Read also I Thessalonians 2:12, 3:13, and Luke 20:35.

The last part of verse 11: ". . . *And fulfil all the good pleasure of His goodness, and the work of faith with power.*" This simply means that Paul wanted the believers to live in such a way that God could mightily accomplish in them all the goodness humanly possible as divine strength was provided, and that they would accomplish all the good that faith could effect through them. In Romans 14:23 Paul said, *"Whatsoever is not of faith is sin."* James said, *"To him that knoweth to do good, and doeth it not, to him it is sin"* (James 4:17).

Paul wanted the Thessalonians to live lives through which God could mightily accomplish much goodness and all spiritual works possible through the greatest degree of faith they could exercise. The goodness and faith mentioned here must be in the believers; and, of course, the only way we can be good or have faith is *in God.* Jesus said, "There is none good save one, and that is God."

To the believers in Rome, Paul said, "And I myself also am persuaded of you, my brethren, that ye also are full of goodness, filled with all knowledge, able also to admonish one another" (Rom. 15:14).

"GOODNESS" is the fruit of light; *God is light*, and in Him is no darkness at all. Jesus said, "I am the light of the world." In Ephesians 5:8,9 Paul said, "For ye were sometimes darkness, but now are ye light in the Lord: walk as children of light: (for the fruit of the Spirit is in all goodness and righteousness and truth)." Love is the fruit of the Holy Spirit (Gal. 5:22).

Paul knew that it is utterly impossible for believers to bring forth fruit unless they are yielded to God *in the Lord Jesus.* Jesus said, "I am the true vine, and my Father is the husbandman. . . . Abide in me, and I in you. As the branch cannot bear fruit of itself, except it abide in the vine; no more can ye, except ye abide in me. I am the vine, ye are the branches: He that abideth in me, and I in Him, the same bringeth forth much fruit: for without me ye can do nothing" (John 15:1–5). It is not by might nor by power nor through our ability, education or training—but because of and through complete surrender to Christ that we bring forth goodness and the work of faith that God desires of every child of His. Paul walked in the steps of Jesus, and he admonished his converts to follow him as he followed Jesus.

Verse 12: "That the name of our Lord Jesus Christ may be glorified in you, and ye in Him, according to the grace of our God and the Lord Jesus Christ."

Let me again remind you that Jesus did not enjoy the cross; "He *endured the cross, despising the shame*," because of the joy that was set before Him . . . joy on the other side of Calvary—and part of that joy was His returning to the seat beside the Father (Heb. 1:1–3). When Jesus purged our sins, He returned and sat down at the right hand of God the Father, and He is there now to make intercession for us (I Tim. 2:5); but the ultimate joy was the Church—without spot or wrinkle or any such thing—on display in the heavenlies, showing forth the exceeding riches of God's grace. The uppermost desire in the heart of Paul was that Christ might be magnified in everything he did, and he held the same desire for his converts. In Philippians 1:20 he said, "According to my earnest expectation and my hope, that in nothing I shall be ashamed, but that with all boldness, as always, so now also *Christ shall be magnified in my body, whether it be by life, or by death.*"

Notice again the opening words of verse 12: "That the name of our Lord Jesus Christ may be glorified in you." There is a day coming when the name of Jesus Christ will be glorified and honored to the highest by all: "Wherefore God also hath highly exalted Him, and given Him a name which is above every name: That at the name of Jesus every knee should bow, of things in heaven, and things in earth, and things under the earth; and that every tongue should confess that Jesus is Lord, TO THE GLORY OF GOD THE FATHER" (Phil. 2:9-11).

". . . *And ye in Him.*" This future glorification will be mutual—that is, between Jesus, the Head of the Church, and the members who make up the bride. It will be an honor to the Head to have such members "without spot or wrinkle or any such thing"; and it will be a distinct glory and honor to the members to BE members of the Head—"the firstborn among many brethren" (Rom. 8:29). This will be love perfected. Each will see its own joy and pride and honor in the other. The Head of the Church will glory in the spotless bride, and the Church will glory in the bridegroom, the Lord Jesus.

In II Corinthians 1:14 Paul expresses it thus: "AS ALSO YE HAVE ACKNOWLEDGED US IN PART, THAT WE ARE YOUR REJOICING, EVEN AS YE ALSO ARE OUR'S IN THE DAY OF THE LORD JESUS." Study carefully Romans 8:17-23, 28-30; Colossians 3:1-4; Philippians 3:20,21 and II Timothy 2:10-13.

Verse 12 closes with the HOW of this glorification: ". . . *According to the grace of our God and the Lord Jesus Christ.*" God is the spring (the fountain) of grace; the Lord Jesus Christ is the channel; and *grace is the means* of all spiritual blessings and glory.

Often we read of the grace of God, and of Christ *as grace*—but seldom do we read, "the grace of God AND the Lord Jesus Christ," naming Father and Son as bestowers of this marvelous grace. The grace that we possess is the grace of our God, making Him ours *personally*. God is our salvation; He is our refuge. *We are kept by the power of God.* Paul seldom uses the expression "our God." It occurs twice here—in verses 11 and 12—and twice in I Thessalonians, chapters 2:2 and 3:9. Paul uses it only one more time: I Corinthians 6:11. However, he often uses the term, "God our Father" or "our God and Father."

We should never forget to "joy in God," because God is the source of saving grace. Jesus brought grace down to men, but it was God the Father who so loved us that He turned His head while the Son of His love paid the sin-debt on the cruel cross. The Greek word used here by the Apostle Paul and translated "grace" means "THE UNMERITED FAVOR OF GOD TOWARD MAN-KIND." This unmerited favor (revealed in Jesus Christ, the only begotten Son of God) stands in contrast to human sin and the rightful divine sentence passed upon man *apart* from grace. But the Apostle Paul tells us that *where sin multiplied, grace superabounded* (Rom. 5:20). The grace of God brings salvation; and God's grace was embodied in and revealed through the sinless life, the sacrificial death, the burial and resurrection of the Lord Jesus *"according to the Scriptures"* (I Cor. 15:1–4). Study John 1:17; Titus 2:11; 3:5; Galatians 2:21 and Ephesians 2:8,9.

God's grace is God's redeeming love to sinners. God's grace is not only opposed to sin, which it conquers and destroys—but it is also opposed to human merit, which it sets aside. Grace and human merit are as far apart as are grace and sin. Everything that we receive from God our Father—all of God's benefits that become ours—*are ours because of Christ*. God saves and forgives us "FOR CHRIST'S SAKE" (Eph. 4:32). We are not saved by works of righteousness which we have done (Titus 3:5), neither of works, lest any man should boast (Eph. 2:9). *We are saved, redeemed, forgiven, totally apart from human merit!*

Grace is not only an act of God whereby unmerited favor is bestowed upon us (Rom. 1:5; Eph. 3:8), but some-

239

times in the Scriptures grace denotes A STATE OF GRACE in the believers—that is, the *grace of God operates* in the believer, as declared in Paul's letter to the believers at Rome:

"Therefore being justified by faith, we have peace with God through our Lord Jesus Christ: by whom also WE HAVE ACCESS BY FAITH INTO THIS GRACE WHEREIN WE STAND, and rejoice in hope of the glory of God" (Rom. 5:1,2).

In II Timothy 2:1 Paul says, "Thou therefore, my son, be strong IN THE GRACE THAT IS IN CHRIST JESUS." "But grow in grace, AND IN THE KNOWLEDGE OF OUR LORD AND SAVIOUR JESUS CHRIST. To Him be glory both now and for ever. Amen" (II Pet. 3:18).

Therefore, grace is not only the divine source of salvation; it is also the method of God in the believer's life and service. Believers are not under the law, but under grace (Rom. 6:14). Therefore the believer, BY GRACE, is brought into the highest conceivable position as having to do with God (Eph. 1:6). And when the believer is saved by grace, that believer is then in a position of *standing* in the grace of God. Thereby God continues to work through grace in believers, imparting divine strength and spiritual growth, causing them to grow from babes in Christ up to sons who cry, "Abba, Father" (I Pet. 2:1,2 and Rom. 8:15)—and then still further in the spiritual aspect to become good soldiers, full grown in spiritual stature, *that we might be all that God would have us be to His glory as we sojourn on this earth.*

The grace of God saved us—but the grace of God never ceases to operate in our lives.

1. Now we beseech you, brethren, by the coming of our Lord Jesus Christ, and by our gathering together unto him,

2. That ye be not soon shaken in mind, or be troubled, neither by spirit, nor by word, nor by letter as from us, as that the day of Christ is at hand.

3. Let no man deceive you by any means: for that day shall not come, except there come a falling away first, and that man of sin be revealed, the son of perdition;

4. Who opposeth and exalteth himself above all that is called God, or that is worshipped; so that he as God sitteth in the temple of God, shewing himself that he is God.

5. Remember ye not, that, when I was yet with you, I told you these things?

6. And now ye know what withholdeth that he might be revealed in his time.

7. For the mystery of iniquity doth already work: only he who now letteth will let, until he be taken out of the way.

8. And then shall that Wicked be revealed, whom the Lord shall consume with the spirit of his mouth, and shall destroy with the brightness of his coming:

9. Even him, whose coming is after the working of Satan with all power and signs and lying wonders,

10. And with all deceivableness of unrighteousness in them that perish; because they received not the love of the truth, that they might be saved.

11. And for this cause God shall send them strong delusion, that they should believe a lie:

12. That they all might be damned who believed not the truth, but had pleasure in unrighteousness.

13. But we are bound to give thanks alway to God for you, brethren beloved of the Lord, because God hath from the beginning chosen you to salvation through sanctification of the Spirit and belief of the truth:

14. Whereunto he called you by our gospel, to the obtaining of the glory of our Lord Jesus Christ.

15. Therefore, brethren, stand fast, and hold the traditions which ye have been taught, whether by word, or our epistle.

16. Now our Lord Jesus Christ himself, and God, even our Father, which hath loved us, and hath given us everlasting consolation and good hope through grace,

17. Comfort your hearts, and stablish you in every good word and work.

THE DAY OF THE LORD – THE ANTICHRIST

The specific object and purpose of this second letter is clearly stated in this chapter. The believers at Thessalonica were too eager concerning the Rapture of the Church and the coming of the Lord Jesus in the first resurrection. In verses 1 and 2 Paul begs them to be cautious, because false teachers—perhaps even forging Paul's name to a letter (verse 2)—had announced in the assembly that the Day of the Lord had *already come*. The church in Thessalonica was therefore in danger of falling victim to deception and error (verse 3), and Paul immediately sets them straight concerning the things that must precede the Day of the Lord, referred to in Jeremiah as "the time of Jacob's trouble," a time of horrible suffering such as this world has never known.

In chapter 2, verses 3 through 12, Paul declares that before the Day of the Lord there will be a supreme manifestation of wickedness and evil (the Apostasy), and also the unveiling of the Man of Sin—a human monstrosity who will be none other than Satan in flesh. Until the falling away and the revealing of Antichrist, the horrible Day of the Lord cannot and will not come.

This, however, has nothing to do with the Rapture (the catching away of the saints and the resurrection of those who sleep in Jesus)—which will not be preceded by signs, as such; the signs point to the *Revelation*, which will occur approximately seven years *after the Rapture*. If the signs of the Revelation are with us—and they ARE—then how near the Rapture of the Church must be!

Paul assured the Thessalonian believers that the *spirit* of Antichrist was already with them, but that the

Man of Sin himself had not been revealed, but WOULD BE revealed before the terrible Day of the Lord.

Verse 1: "Now we beseech you, brethren, by the coming of our Lord Jesus Christ, and by our gathering together unto Him."

The Greek reads, "But we beseech you, brethren, *on behalf of the coming of our Lord Jesus Christ.*" "*On behalf of*" means "*in the interest of*" . . . not "with *reference* to," but "IN THE INTEREST OF the coming of our Lord Jesus Christ." Certainly the coming of the Lord Jesus was the hope held out to the Thessalonians (chapter 1:7–10); but they were not to listen to any unreasonable teaching concerning the second coming of Jesus—which was to them "the blessed hope."

The second advent of Christ will be in two phases: (1) The Rapture, (2) The Revelation. Confusion prevailed in the minds of the Thessalonians concerning the difference between these two. Paul therefore closes verse 1 with the words, "*. . . by our gathering together unto Him,*" this being the Rapture described in I Thessalonians 4: 13–18 and also in the first part of chapter 5.

As I have stated several times previously, someone had erroneously taught that the church at Thessalonica was *already in the tribulation*; and they knew that if this were true, Paul had taught error. So Paul points out that Jesus IS coming—and WHEN He comes, the living saints will be gathered up into the clouds in the air to meet Him, along with the resurrected bodies of the saints who sleep in Him.

Verse 2: "That ye be not soon shaken in mind, or be troubled, neither by spirit, nor by word, nor by letter as from us, as that the day of Christ is at hand."

Greek scholars tell us that this verse reads literally,

"To the end that you be not quickly shaken from your mind—we beseech you not to lose your balance of mind under any sudden shock—not to be shaken out of your wits."

What Paul is saying here is simply, "Do not let these sensational announcements disturb you, but PROVE ALL THINGS: and when you prove these sensational announcements by comparing them with the teaching I delivered unto you, you will see how baseless and untrue they really are! Do not let these spectacular teachers shake you out of your wits: do not let the sudden shock of these announcements cause you to become unbalanced in your thinking, but by the Word of God *prove* everything they say—and if the Word disproves it, *reject it!*"

The phrase *"or be troubled"* is better translated *"nor be kept in alarm,"* which would eventually overthrow one's mental equilibrium. If the Thessalonians were continually upset and alarmed about these announcements, the agitation and nervousness thus brought about would cause them to become unbalanced in mind, and they could not think straight about the Word of God. We must think right about GOD before we can think right about *His Word*; and we must think right about the *Word of God* before we can receive the blessings the Word holds for us. So if the devil can upset our minds, he has practically won the victory so far as our enjoyment of our spiritual birthright is concerned.

Jesus used this same word in Matthew 24:6 when He said to His disciples, ". . . Ye shall hear of wars and rumours of wars: *see that ye be not troubled*: for all these things must come to pass, but the end is not yet." Paul gives the Thessalonian believers good, sound Bible teaching to help them keep their equilibrium and mental composure, thus enabling them to be effective soul winners.

The verses that follow assure us that attempts *had been made* to disturb the church concerning the Day of the Lord—the coming of the Great Tribulation and the Man of Sin. Some had no doubt been startled the moment they heard these things, while others at first pushed them aside; but then the rumors came thick and fast, and Paul knew that Satan would continue his attempt, through such rumors, to rob the Christians of their power in witnessing to those in the communities all around them.

". . . *Neither by spirit, nor by word, nor by letter as from us.*" During the first days of the New Testament Church, certain believers had the gift of prophecy, and in fact *did* prophesy through the Spirit (I Thess. 5:19–21). In other epistles Paul refers to those who had the gift of prophecy; but he also said, ". . . Whether there be prophecies, they shall fail . . . for we know in part, and we prophesy in part. But when that which is perfect is come, that which is in part shall be done away" (I Cor. 13:8–10).

Now, "that which is perfect IS come"—the perfect law of liberty—the Word of God; and all we need to know about things eternal—anything pertaining to salvation— we find in God's holy Word. In our day, that which is perfect has already come, and God is not adding any new epistles or prophecies today.

In Paul's day, however, when there were those who had the genuine gift of prophecy, believers were admonished to "*try the spirits*" and be sure they were following the Spirit of God and not the spirit of error. That is the reason Paul is saying here, "Be not shaken in mind. Do not be troubled—either by spirit, by word or by letter (supposedly from *us*). Let none of this trouble you."

In Galatians 1:8 Paul said, ". . . Though we, or an angel from heaven, preach any other gospel unto you

245

than that which we have preached unto you, let him be accursed." (That means, *"Let him drop into hell fire!"*)

The statement *"as from us"* refers to Paul, Silas and Timothy. What Paul is saying is, "If anyone reads a statement, declaring it to be from us or upon our authority, do not let it trouble you. We still believe what we preached to you when we were with you, and we have not written anything contrary to that belief."

I personally believe that someone HAD written an epistle of error and forged Paul's name to it, with the one intention to upset this evangelistic, missionary church that was turning the country upside down for Jesus; and Paul sent this solemn warning that the believers should pay no attention to anything they heard contrary to what he preached and taught when he was with them.

Verse 2 closes with the words, ". . . *As that the day of Christ is at hand.*" Greek authorities assure us that this last statement is faulty insofar as the Greek language is concerned. It should read, ". . . *Supposing that the Day of the Lord is upon us.*" "The Day of Christ" is definitely not intended here, but "the Day of the Lord." Jesus warned His disciples, "If any man shall say unto you, Lo, here is Christ, or there; *believe it not*" (Matt. 24:23; Luke 21:8). When Jesus comes in the Revelation, there will be no need for anyone to shout, "Here He is" or "There He is," for "AS THE LIGHTNING COMETH OUT OF THE EAST, AND SHINETH EVEN UNTO THE WEST; SO SHALL ALSO THE COMING OF THE SON OF MAN BE" (Matt. 24:27).

The Day of the Lord is described in detail in the Old Testament: "For the Day of the Lord of hosts shall be upon every one that is proud and lofty, and upon every one that is lifted up; and he shall be brought low . . . and the loftiness of man shall be bowed down, and the haughtiness of men shall be made low: and the Lord alone shall be exalted in that day. And the idols He shall utterly abolish (the Antichrist and his system). And they shall go into the holes of the rocks, and into the caves of the earth, for fear of the Lord, and for the glory of His majesty, when He ariseth to shake terribly the earth. In that day a man shall cast his idols of silver, and his idols of gold, which they made each one for himself to worship, to the moles and to the bats; to go into the clefts of the rocks, and into the tops of the ragged rocks, for fear of the Lord, and for the glory of His majesty, when He ariseth to shake terribly the earth'' (Isaiah 2:12,17–21).

"Therefore the Lord, the God of hosts, the Lord, saith thus: Wailing shall be in all streets; and they shall say in all the highways, Alas! alas! and they shall call the husbandman to mourning, and such as are skilful of lamentation to wailing. And in all vineyards shall be wailing: for I will pass through thee, saith the Lord. Woe unto you that desire the day of the Lord! to what end is it for you? the day of the Lord is darkness, and not light. As if a man did flee from a lion, and a bear met him; or went into the house, and leaned his hand on the wall, and a serpent bit him. Shall not the day of the Lord be darkness, and not light? even very dark, and no brightness in it?'' (Amos 5:16–20).

The Day of the Lord will be a day of weeping, mourning and wailing; a day of darkness—not light. It will be as though a man is running from a lion, only to come face to face with a bear! It will be a day of utter darkness, with no brightness in it. That certainly does not sound like "comfort one another with these words" (I Thess. 4:18); nor does it sound like the words Paul used in Titus 2:13: "LOOKING FOR THAT BLESSED HOPE, AND THE GLORIOUS APPEARING OF THE GREAT GOD AND OUR SAVIOUR JESUS CHRIST."

The time Paul is speaking of in our present study is *the Day of the Lord of hosts*—NOT the Rapture of the Church, the glorious day to which all believers look forward and pray, "Even so, come, Lord Jesus!" It is very unfortunate that this verse in II Thessalonians is mistranslated in our King James Bible. The Word "Christ" should be "Lord," and in this case the mistranslation changes the entire meaning of the event Paul is describing.

Verse 3: "Let no man deceive you by any means: for that day shall not come, except there come a falling away first, and that man of sin be revealed, the son of perdition."

"Let no man deceive you . . . ." The Greek word here is commonly rendered "beguile," and signifies "wicked deception." "Let no man *beguile* you." This word in the Greek is the same as the Hebrew word in Genesis 3:13, where the Scriptures tell us that the serpent *beguiled Eve*. Our English word very much akin to this is "deceit." Read Romans 7:11 and 16:18; I Timothy 2:14; II Corinthians 11:3.

The statement *"by any means"* simply points to the fact that there are a variety of ways in which the devil beguiles or deceives. It may be done through a wicked spirit, through a wicked person or through the lying tongue of a false prophet. Paul warns the believers in Thessalonica not to allow the enemy "in ANY wise" to beguile them concerning the Day of the Lord, as if it were already upon them.

Paul declares, *"That day shall not come, except there come a falling away first, and that man of sin be revealed."* The words here, ". . . except there come a falling away," should read, "except THE APOSTASY come." "THE" is a definite article, pointing to a specific apostasy that MUST come preceding the unveiling of the Man of Sin. And when THE apostasy comes and the Man of Sin is revealed, then the peoples on earth may rest assured that they are in the Great Tribulation and that the Day of the Lord is upon them. But Paul is pointing out that the believers in Thessalonica assuredly are not in the midst of the Day of the Lord and that the Tribulation time is NOT upon them, as they had been told by the teachers of error.

Greek authorities tell us that in the original language the word here translated "apostasy" denotes political or military revolt—"a defection." The Greek word here is the same as the Hebrew word in Jeremiah 29:32, and it means "rebellion against the Lord"—revolt consisting of sacrificing to other gods (idols).

This is the same language used by Peter when he warns against apostate teachers who deny redemption by the blood: "But there were false prophets also among the people, even as there shall be false teachers among you, who privily shall bring in damnable heresies, even denying the Lord that bought them and bring upon themselves swift destruction. And many shall follow their pernicious ways; by reason of whom the way of truth shall be evil spoken of. And through covetousness shall they with feigned words make merchandise of you: whose judgment now of a long time lingereth not, and their damnation slumbereth not" (II Pet. 2:1–3).

In the New Testament, Jesus was the first to give warning about the spirit of Antichrist that would lead to the appearing of the Man of Sin: His disciples asked, "Tell us, when shall these things be? and what shall be the sign of thy coming, and of the end of the world?" (Matt. 24:3). He replied, "And then shall many be offended, and shall betray one another, and shall hate one another. And many false prophets shall rise, and shall deceive many. And because iniquity shall abound, the love of many shall wax cold. But he that shall endure unto the end, the same shall be saved" (Matt. 24:10–13).

The spirit of Antichrist was already in operation in Paul's day; but the Man of Sin will not be revealed until the Apostasy—the great turning to idols from the true God, just before the great and terrible Day of the Lord. The Day of the Lord is not the Rapture of the Church, but the Revelation of Jesus, "in flaming fire taking vengeance on them that know not God."

Read what Paul says in Romans 16:17–20, Acts 20:29,30, Ephesians 4:14, I Timothy 6:1 and I Corinthians 16:22. Hear his scorching words: "If any man love not the Lord, let him be Anathema!" The liberalism and modernism of our day is definitely the spirit of Antichrist, and the spirit that exists today in the National Council and World Council of Churches will eventually lead into THE APOSTASY and the time when Antichrist will be unveiled and made known. Any person who reads current events in the field of religion knows that the verbal inspiration of the Bible is being attacked today as never before. Jesus Christ has been demoted to the level of all great religious leaders, and there is a movement now under way to unite all religions under one giant world-head. Students of prophecy see the handwriting on the wall and know that religion is weighed in God's great balance and found wanting. Surely it cannot be long until Jesus will catch out the true Church—and *spew out* the Laodiceans, from among whom will come the world-church and the Antichrist. But: *That day shall not come . . . except the Apostasy come and that Man of Sin be revealed, the Son of Perdition!*

Please notice again that it is THE Man of Sin—a specific personage. It is not *a* man of sin nor *a* spirit of wickedness and lawlessness; but THE Man of Sin, pointing out that before the great and terrible Day of the Lord there will be revealed a man who is known in Scripture as "the Man of Sin."

As the end of the day of grace approaches, lawlessness will become more prevalent in every way, but especially from the standpoint of pure religion—*Christianity*. Today, as never before in the history of the Church, Jesus is being attacked by church leaders. He is being stripped of His deity and of His virgin birth; He is being lowered to the level of great religious leaders and the founders of various religions and cults. All of this will lead to mass idolatry; and when the world is educated to the point where the masses will fall down and worship an image, the Rapture will occur and the Church will be caught up. Immediately after the Rapture the Antichrist will make his appearance and offer peace and prosperity to the world—the Utopia the Post-Millennialists have *talked* about but have never *brought* about.

The Antichrist will bring peace . . . a false peace. He will work miracles; He will ride out on a white horse (the symbol of peace), and there WILL BE peace for three and one-half years. Then, in the middle of the Tribulation period, he will break every promise he has made; he will break the covenant with Israel; he will put a stop to temple worship; he will sit in the temple and announce that he is God, and at the point of a sword he will force all peoples to bow down and worship him AS God. Those who *refuse* to worship him will be killed.

The stage is being so rapidly set for this gigantic event that it is almost beyond comprehension; but believers have the blessed hope that we will not be here when this Man of Sin is revealed . . . we will be with Jesus at the marriage supper in the sky!

There have been many forerunners of Antichrist: I personally believe Nimrod was one of them. I also believe

Pharaoh and Herod were forerunners and types of Antichrist. This Man of Sin has been on this earth before; he is now "in his own place" awaiting the time of his final appearance to play his role in the consummation of all things, when God once and forever puts down evil and the devil.

There is a marvelous outline of this age in the Book of Acts, beginning at Pentecost and running on through to the building of the temple in Jerusalem: "And after they had held their peace, James answered, saying, Men and brethren, hearken unto me: Simeon hath declared how God at the first did visit the Gentiles, to take out of them a people for His name. And to this agree the words of the prophets; as it is written, After this I will return, and will build again the tabernacle of David, which is fallen down; and I will build again the ruins thereof, and I will set it up: That the residue of men might seek after the Lord, and all the Gentiles, upon whom my name is called, saith the Lord, who doeth all these things. Known unto God are all His works from the beginning of the world" (Acts 15:13–18).

First, God will take out a Gentile people—the Gentile bride, the Church. When the bride is complete, Jesus will return for His own. All the prophets agree to this. Then the tabernacle of David, which is fallen down, will be built again, and the residue of men will go to that tabernacle.

"KNOWN UNTO GOD ARE ALL HIS WORKS FROM THE BEGINNING OF THE WORLD!" (Acts 15:18). Our sovereign, righteous God has a blueprint, and He will *follow* that blueprint to its completion. The Man of Sin (the devil in flesh) will play a very important role in the consummation of all things just before the eternity of eternities is ushered in—the eternity when for the righteous there will be no more tears, sorrow, sin, heartache or devil . . . the eternal ages of perfect bliss where all things will have been made new.

Who IS this Man of Sin? We can find the answer in the Word of God, exclusive of what we have heard or what men have said:

In the prayer of intercession prayed by Jesus in John 17, He said, "While I was with them in the world, I kept them in thy name: those that thou gavest me I have kept, and none of them is lost, but the SON OF PERDITION; that the Scripture might be fulfilled" (John 17:12).

Jesus lost only ONE of the twelve while here on earth, and the one He lost is clearly pointed out as *"the Son of Perdition."* Not only is he pointed out, but the *reason* that one was lost is also clearly given: "THAT THE SCRIPTURE MIGHT BE FULFILLED!" Remember— "Known unto God are all His works from the beginning of the world." We must let the Scripture tell us of whom Jesus spoke when He said, "I have kept all except ONE." *Who is that one?*

John 6:70: "Jesus answered them, Have not I chosen you twelve, and one of you is a DEVIL?" Renowned Greek authorities tell us that there should be no article before "devil"; the "a" should not be there. What Jesus actually said to the twelve is, *"One of you is DEVIL."* Not *A* devil, but actually the *one and only* devil. There are multiplied millions of demons and evil spirits, but there is only *ONE devil*—and Jesus had that devil among the chosen twelve.

There is no need to ask, "Did Jesus Christ actually *choose a devil* among His disciple band?"—for in the verse just quoted *Jesus Himself tells us* that He chose a devil. We know, of course, that He is talking about Judas Iscariot, because out of the twelve He lost only Judas. Very definitely Judas was the devil in flesh, and anyone who will rightly divide the Scriptures instead of trying to prove some denominational doctrine can plainly see this fact.

You may search the Scripture from Matthew to Revelation, verse by verse, word by word, and you will find no other place where Jesus called any man a devil. He referred to people as displaying the *spirit* of the devil (as do all sinners)—but Jesus never made that statement about any person other than Judas Iscariot. He classified people as goats, sheep, sons of God or sons of the devil—but never as a *devil*.

John 13 records the account of Jesus washing the disciples' feet. He said, "He that is washed needeth not save to wash his feet, but is clean every whit: and ye are clean, but not all. FOR HE KNEW WHO SHOULD BETRAY HIM; therefore said He, Ye are not all clean" (John 13:10,11).

From the moment He chose the twelve, Jesus knew that Judas was not clean. He was a devil when he was chosen, and he *remained* a devil throughout the public ministry of Jesus. He took his own physical life and returned to his specific place, as we will see later in our study.

John 13:11 clearly tells us that Jesus *knew* who would betray Him. Matthew adds more detail: "And as they did eat, He said, Verily I say unto you, that one of you shall betray me. And they were exceeding sorrowful, and began every one of them to say unto Him, Lord, is it I? And He answered and said, He that dippeth his hand with me in the dish, the same shall betray me. The Son of man goeth as it is written of Him: *but woe unto that man by whom the Son of man is betrayed!* IT HAD BEEN GOOD FOR THAT MAN IF HE HAD NOT BEEN BORN. Then Judas, which betrayed Him, answered

254

and said, Master, is it I? He said unto him, THOU HAST SAID" (Matt. 26:21–25).

Scripture clearly teaches that it was foreordained of God that Jesus should come into the world and pay the sin-debt. Every minute detail of the divine plan was mapped out, blueprinted and agreed upon by Father, Son and Holy Ghost. The fact that Jesus would be betrayed by one of the twelve—one whom He had chosen—was in the blueprint.

Jesus chose twelve, and one of them was devil. Since Jesus is truth and Satan is a liar; since Jesus is righteousness and Satan is unrighteousness; since Jesus was one hundred percent true to the Father, we can expect the counterfeit Christ to be exactly His opposite. Judas was the devil; and he betrayed the Lord Jesus, who is the Truth, the Door, the Way, the Life—yea, SALVATION!

After the Day of Pentecost the disciples met and cast lots to select one to take the place of Judas. They prayed, ". . . Thou, Lord, which knowest the hearts of all men, shew whether of these two thou hast chosen, that he may take part OF THIS MINISTRY AND APOSTLESHIP, FROM WHICH JUDAS BY TRANSGRESSION FELL, THAT HE MIGHT GO TO HIS OWN PLACE" (Acts 1:24,25).

Two things I would like to point out in this passage:

1. *Judas fell—but not from grace.* He fell from the *ministry*—from *apostleship*. We know that any man or woman can be a minister or an apostle and not necessarily be born again! Judas Iscariot was never saved . . . he was never a child of God; he was never covered by the blood. Jesus chose him, as clearly and unmistakably stated in John 17:12, "THAT THE SCRIPTURE MIGHT BE FULFILLED." Judas was lost; he *fell from apostleship* because it was in God's plan, "that the

Scriptures might be fulfilled."

Why God had this plan is none of my business, and if you are wise you will accept it in the same spirit. It is not *our* business; it is *God's* business. Why Judas was the devil in flesh is God's business; why he was *lost* is God's business. He was never a born again believer as were Peter, James, John, Matthew, Luke, Paul and others.

Judas fell "by transgression" from the ministry and from his apostleship—and his *transgression* was the betrayal of Jesus. He sold the Lord to the high priests—the religious leaders who were God's enemies—for thirty pieces of silver (the price of a slave)! He fell from his office, he betrayed the Lord Jesus; but what is so significant about Acts 1:25 is the last statement in the verse: ". . . THAT HE (Judas) MIGHT GO *TO HIS OWN PLACE.*"

2. *Judas returned to his abode*—the Bible says, "his own place." Therefore we know that Judas Iscariot (so-called in the disciple band) has a special cell. He had been there before; he left that special place, took a body, and was on the spot when Jesus chose the twelve disciples. Judas took his place in the disciple band to fulfill his mission in the plan and program of God; he played the role God ordained in the beginning, and then returned to his own place! Such a statement is not made about any person who ever existed—except Judas Iscariot.

Certainly HELL is not his place; hell is the place of the abode of wicked spirits and sinners, but it cannot be said to belong specifically to Judas Iscariot. I am sure the prison where he is now confined is IN hell—but hell does not belong exclusively to Judas . . . he has a *special place.* I personally believe that the spirit of Judas has been embodied on this earth before—in Nimrod,

256

Pharaoh and others; but when he comes in the role of Antichrist that will be his last appearance on earth.

Just one thing more about Judas before we leave him: Six days before the Passover, Jesus visited Bethany (where Lazarus was raised from the dead), and they made a supper for Him. Martha served; Lazarus was also present and sat at the table with Jesus. At this supper, Mary took a pound of costly ointment with which she anointed the feet of Jesus, and wiped His feet with her hair. The sweet odor of the ointment filled the room, and one of the disciples—JUDAS ISCARIOT . . . "WHICH SHOULD BETRAY HIM"—asked Jesus a question which, on the surface, seemed very timely, wise and commendable. He asked, *"Why was not this ointment sold for three hundred pence, and given to the poor?"* (Three hundred pence would add up to more than fifty dollars in our money today.) Yes, that seemed an excellent question: Why DID Jesus allow more than fifty dollars worth of perfume to be poured out upon Him at one time? Why NOT take the fifty dollars and give it to poor people?

But Jesus knew the heart of Judas: "This (Judas) said, not that he cared for the poor; BUT BECAUSE HE WAS A THIEF, and had the bag, and bare what was put therein." Judas cared nothing for the poor; but he was a thief, and he wanted the money put into the bag so he could steal it. Jesus said to him, "Let her alone: against the day of my burying hath she kept this. For the poor always ye have with you; but me ye have not always." (Read John 12:1–8 for the complete account.)

Let me sum up what I have said, so that you can clearly see that the Man of Sin (the Antichrist) will be the spirit of Judas Iscariot in flesh. *The Antichrist will be the devil himself walking on earth as a man!*

Jesus said, "Of those that thou gavest me, I have

lost only one . . . that the Scriptures might be fulfilled.''
(He lost Judas.)

Jesus said, "I have chosen you twelve, and one of
you is devil." (He was speaking of Judas Iscariot.)

When Jesus sat at the last supper He said, "The
Son of man will go, as determined; *but woe unto him who
betrays the Son of man!*" He then gave Judas a sop and
pointed him out as the betrayer. Judas immediately went
out into the night and sold the Lord for thirty pieces of
silver.

The disciples set about to choose one to take the
place of Judas. The Scriptures tell us Judas fell from
the ministry and apostleship, and "went to his own place."
This statement is not made of any other person in all of
the Word of God. Judas had a special cell; he had been
there before; he left that place and came to this earth—
and now he has returned "to his own place" . . . and he
will come again, *embodied in the Antichrist.*

Judas was devil, betrayer, thief—and these statements were made about him by the Lamb of God, who
looks upon and knows the heart. It is very probable that
the disciples detected nothing wrong with Judas up to
the very last moments they were together; but Jesus knew
from the beginning that he had the devil in His disciple
band.

Jesus said to the Jews, "I am come in my Father's
name, and ye receive me not: if another shall come in
his own name, him ye will receive" (John 5:43). Jesus
is speaking here of the false messiah (the counterfeit
Christ, the Man of Sin, the Son of Perdition), who will
come immediately following the Rapture.

Verse 4: "Who opposeth and exalteth himself above
all that is called God, or that is worshipped; so that he
as God sitteth in the temple of God, shewing himself

that he is God."

Let me point out first of all that the event Paul describes here *could not be the Rapture*; the temple in Jerusalem will not be rebuilt before the Rapture. When I visited Jerusalem I learned that the Mosque of Omar stands at the present time on the spot where the temple will be built. Moslems now own the ground. During the war between the Arabs and Jews, the Jews pushed right up to the spot where Solomon's temple stood and where the new temple will be built after the Rapture; but they could not take the area because it is not yet time. When the time is ripe the Jews will overrun the Arabs and take the spot where Abraham was about to offer Isaac and where Solomon's temple was built—*the holy area where God met His people in Old Testament days.*

The Day of the Lord is NOT the Rapture. The day Paul is describing here is not the Rapture; Paul is speaking of the day when the Lord will come with His saints in fury and fiery judgment upon the wicked. When Jesus comes thus, the Antichrist will be at the height of his power and glory. He will exalt himself above all that is called God; he will exalt himself above all that is worshipped. Notice the statement in the last part of the verse: *He will sit in the temple announcing to the world that he is God*!

This Man of Sin will make great speeches on television. A few short months ago, television across the Atlantic was an impossibility except by film; but today *Telstar* makes it possible for a person to speak in London (or any place across the sea where television facilities are available) and be seen here in the United States. It has been said on good authority that Jerusalem is now in the process of building the most powerful television station on earth—and, of course, this move is definitely in the plan of God, because the Antichrist will make his

259

appearance on television, that the whole world may see him. He will pull fire down from heaven in the sight of men (Rev. 13), and he will deceive the peoples of earth with his miracles. He will show himself to the whole world and will declare that he is God Almighty!

Since the apostasy will be at its height at that time, the whole world (saving those who believe the preaching of the 144,000) will become idolaters. They will fall down and worship the Antichrist and the image that will be set up to this Man of Sin. Antichrist will announce that he is God and will set himself up above all that is *called* God. Notice Paul's words in I Corinthians 8:5: "For though there be that are *called gods*, whether in heaven or in earth, (as there be gods many, and lords many.)"

When this occurs, the Man of Sin will lead a revolt against all religion; he will abolish religion in every existing form, making himself the one and only one to be worshipped by mankind—and those who *refuse* to worship him will be killed! Many will hide and will live in the mountains and in the clefts of the rocks. But all such who are found will be annihilated if they refuse to worship Antichrist and receive his mark. Read Revelation 13.

The opening words of verse 4, "*Who opposeth*," in the Greek read, "the adversary." (Notice I Thessalonians 2:18.) Satan is the adversary of all things godly; and this personage, as I have already pointed out, IS Satan in flesh—God's arch enemy, the adversary of God and of mankind.

Ever since the day God cast Lucifer out of heaven (Ezek. 28; Isa. 14; Luke 10:18), Satan has been working and scheming to overthrow God and take His position. In the body of Antichrist, Satan will make his last great stab at Jehovah God and God's people; but in the end, fire will come down from God out of heaven and devour the armies of the devil, and the devil himself will be put into the lake of fire by the Lord Jesus Christ. Read Revelation 19:20; 20:7—10.

Daniel saw this Man of Sin and describes him: "And in *the latter time* of their kingdom, when the transgressors are come to the full, A KING OF FIERCE COUNTENANCE, and understanding dark sentences, shall stand up. And HIS POWER SHALL BE MIGHTY, but not by his own power: and he shall destroy wonderfully, and shall prosper, and practise, and shall destroy the mighty and the holy people. And through his policy also he shall cause craft to prosper in his hand; and he shall magnify himself in his heart, and by peace shall destroy many: he shall also stand up against the PRINCE OF PRINCES; but he shall be broken without hand. And the vision of the evening and the morning which was told is true: wherefore shut thou up the vision; for it shall be for many days. AND I DANIEL FAINTED, AND WAS SICK CERTAIN DAYS; afterward I rose up, and did the king's business; and I was astonished at the vision, but none understood it" (Dan. 8:23—27).

"And the king shall do according to his will; and he shall exalt himself, and magnify himself above every god, and shall speak marvellous things against the God of gods, and shall prosper till the indignation be accomplished: for that that is determined shall be done. Neither shall he regard the God of his fathers, nor the desire of women, nor regard any god: *for he shall magnify himself above all*" (Dan. 11:36,37).

Daniel could face kings, rulers, lions, the fiery furnace—and face them undisturbed; but when in a vision he saw the Antichrist, *he fainted—and was sick "certain days."* This Man of Sin must certainly be a demon mon-

261

strosity! I am so happy that I will not be here when he makes his appearance and rules in blood! If you are born again, you will not be here, either—but if you are NOT born again, you could be here to experience the fulfillment of this prophecy.

Verse 5: "Remember ye not, that, when I was yet with you, I told you these things?"

In these words we feel that Paul, although gentle in reproof, was nevertheless reproving the believers in Thessalonica. In essence he is saying, "You should not have been so easily alarmed. You should not have so easily become unsettled." He reminds them that he had instructed them as clearly as he could and made it as clear as possible that they should not be shaken by false doctrine, which he knew was sure to be introduced by his enemies.

In Acts 17 we read of the founding of the church in Thessalonica. As Paul "reasoned with them out of the Scriptures . . . some of them believed, and consorted with Paul and Silas." Some of the Jews, however, were moved with envy, and they assaulted the house of Jason where the church was organized, and "drew Jason and certain brethren unto the rulers of the city, crying, These that have turned the world upside down are come hither also; whom Jason hath received: and these all do contrary to the decrees of Caesar, saying that there is another king, one Jesus. And they troubled the people and the rulers of the city, when they heard these things. And when they had taken security of Jason, and of the other, they let them go. And the brethren immediately sent away Paul and Silas by night unto Berea . . ." (Acts 17:1–10).

Paul now *reminds* the church in Thessalonica that when he was with them, he had warned them of these things that would come to pass, and had fully instructed them. Often in my meetings I make the statement that I have never been able to understand why the TRUTH does not seem to make a deep impression upon the minds of people. Church people are seemingly ready to listen to false doctrine and false teachers; but TRUTH must be repeated again and again and again before it finds a lodging place in the heart, there to convince the believer that it IS truth and can be depended upon to the end!

Verse 6: "And now ye know what withholdeth that he might be revealed in his time."

Paul undoubtedly believed that when the Thessalonian Christians called to memory the things he had previously told them concerning the Rapture of the Church and the resurrection of their loved ones who had fallen asleep in Jesus; when they remembered his instruction about the judgment that was sure to come upon the ungodly; when they were reminded of the things which he had told them would *certainly precede* the terrible Day of the Lord, then they would understand what was going on all around them.

In everyday language Paul would have said, "Now that you have recalled what I told you when I was with you, about the final struggle which will take place between the powers of God and the powers of evil just before the coming of the Lord Jesus, you also know what *withholdeth*; you remember what I told you about a Power that *restraineth*—and that this Wicked One will be revealed at the appointed time."

The Greek word for "letteth" in verse 7 is masculine, denoting a *person*; here in verse 6 the word for "withholdeth" is neuter—indicating a principal or power. Paul had told the believers at Thessalonica that the Holy Ghost was with them . . . not only *present with* them, but actually *dwelling within them.* The Holy Ghost leads believers and restrains the forces of the underworld. When the Church is taken out of the world, the Holy Ghost will go out with the Church; and the world will then be at the mercy of the devil. There will be no restraining power, because all believers will be taken away, and the Holy Ghost will also be gone. Evil will flood the earth!

Shortly after the Rapture, however, God will seal 144,000 missionaries to spread THE GOSPEL OF THE KINGDOM—and teeming millions who have never heard the Gospel of grace will hear the announcement that the kingdom is coming, that it will be set up on earth and Jesus will sit on the throne of David in Jerusalem. The knowledge of the Lord will then cover the earth as the waters now cover the sea. All who receive this message and accept the coming King will be saved—a great multitude that no man can number (Rev. 7:9–17).

Verse 6 closes with the statement, ". . . *that he might be revealed in his time.*" The Greek reading is more exact: "To the end that he may be revealed in his own season." The unnamed person here is the dreaded personality whose form can be seen through this portion of our present epistle. As we proceed with our study we will see that this monstrosity grows in prominence, in diabolical wickedness and in power.

God does not carry on His work in a haphazard, hit-or-miss fashion. "Known unto Him are all His works from the beginning . . . ." He has a plan, and the order of things laid down in our present passage belongs to God's purpose and program. This Lawless One will be suppressed by the Holy Spirit until the appointed moment when he is to be unveiled; he cannot step into power until "his season" is fully ripe.

In Genesis 3:15 God promised the Seed of the woman. In Galatians 4:4,5 that promise came to fruition: "When the fulness of the time was come, God sent forth His Son, made of a woman, made under the law, to redeem them that were under the law . . . ." Many centuries elapsed between the promise and the birth of Jesus—but everything worked according to God's purpose and program. So will it be in the case of the counterfeit Christ. In Genesis 3:15 the devil was clearly told that there would be enmity between his seed and the Seed of the woman— deadly enmity between the son of Satan and the Son of God. Satan was to bruise the heel of the Seed of the woman, but the Seed of the woman will crush the head of the serpent. God's blueprint and program will be carried out to the letter.

When Jesus was here on earth He said to His enemies, "This is your hour, and the power of darkness" (Luke 22:53). When they arrested Him and led Him away to be whipped, crowned with thorns, spat upon and nailed to a cross, it seemed that He had gone down in utter defeat. But three days later, when Rome's best guards went to the authorities with the cry that His body was missing from the tomb . . . *that was another story!*

When Judas came to Gethsemane, bringing with him the enemies of Jesus with lanterns, sticks and clubs, Jesus did not attempt to hide or run. He simply stepped forward and asked, "Whom seek ye?" They replied, "Jesus of Nazareth," and Jesus answered, *"I AM HE!"* When Jesus spoke those three words, His enemies "WENT BACKWARD AND FELL TO THE GROUND." (Greek authorities tell us that the personal pronoun "He" should not be there. The Greek reads simply, "I AM!"—and this is the same "I AM" who spoke to Moses in Exodus 3:14.) One moment the Lord seemed powerless; the next moment His words had the power of an atomic bomb! It seems today that believers are on the losing side—but the opposite is true. We are on the WINNING side, because

265

"if God be FOR us, who CAN be against us?" (Rom. 8:31).

Verse 7: "For the mystery of iniquity doth already work: only He who now letteth will let, until He be taken out of the way."

"*The mystery of iniquity*" (the spirit of lawlessness) is already in operation. Ever since Adam fell, iniquity has been at work in the earth; but this mystery of iniquity is the *spirit* of Antichrist—not the personality. The devil is responsible for the mystery of iniquity already in operation in Paul's day; but we are not to confuse *that spirit* with the *Man of Sin* who will personally operate here on this earth after the Rapture. John tells us that antichrists will come, and even in his day there were already many antichrists (I John 2:18). The *spirit of Antichrist* has been operating ever since Jesus went back to heaven.

The devil is anti-God. His ministers deny the virgin birth, the blood atonement and the deity of Christ. They are little antichrists; they are disciples of the devil; they are against God's Christ—and John says we may know that we are living in the last days *because* of these antichrists. But these are not to be confused with the *one Man of Sin* to be unveiled after the Church is taken out of the world.

The mystery referred to here denotes something that by its nature is above man's knowledge, and can be understood only insofar as God reveals it to us. The mystery—the thing that will finally head up the Man of Sin, who is yet to be revealed—was already in operation in Paul's day. The only reason the Man of Sin has not already taken over the reins of the governments of earth is because "He (the Holy Spirit) that now letteth *will let*, until He be taken out of the way." Paul is referring here to the Holy Ghost—the restraining power of God on

266

earth today; and as long as the Holy Ghost remains in this earth, the counterfeit Christ cannot and will not be unveiled. I do not believe in Biblical speculation, but I do not hesitate to say that it is altogether possible that Antichrist is alive on earth today.

Jesus was conceived of the Holy Ghost and born of a virgin. I believe the Antichrist (exactly opposite) will be conceived of the devil and born of a harlot! This is my belief—but *you* do not have to accept it, for it has nothing whatsoever to do with salvation. I believe the devil will counterfeit in detail every phase of the first coming of Jesus. I believe Satan will come in a body after the same fashion in which GOD came to earth in a body (II Cor. 5:19). God was in the man Christ Jesus, reconciling sinners unto Himself; the devil will be in the body of Antichrist, making his last powerful drive to damn every soul he possibly can, because he knows his days are numbered. It does not seem feasible to me that Antichrist will come as a full-grown man. I believe he will be born a babe, exactly as Jesus was born a babe. Christ was born of a virgin; ANTIchrist will be born of a harlot. But as long as the Church remains on earth, the Holy Ghost IN the Church (in the heart of each and every believer) *restrains the unveiling and revelation of Antichrist.*

In the true sense of the word, Jesus is on earth today in His Church. We know that the Man Christ Jesus sits at the right hand of God the Father (I Tim. 2:5; Heb. 1:1—3); but He also dwells in the heart of every believer, in the person of the Holy Spirit (Col. 1:27). Romans 8:1 says, "There is therefore now no condemnation to them which are *in Christ Jesus.*" Christ is in us; we are in Christ—and this earth is not big enough for the Church of the living God with Jesus as head AND the Antichrist (Satan in flesh) with his vast army of idolaters! When the Church is taken out, Satan in the person of Antichrist will take over the reins of government and religion on earth—but NOT UNTIL the Church is safely seated at the marriage supper in the sky with the Lord Jesus.

Dear believer, never let any preacher, evangelist or Bible teacher tell you that the Church will enter or go through any part of the Great Tribulation period. Before that terrible time of suffering begins, we will be caught up to meet Jesus in the clouds in the air. Believers "are not appointed unto wrath" (I Thess. 5:9). "Because thou hast kept the word of my patience, I also will keep thee from the hour of temptation (the Great Tribulation and reign of the Antichrist), which shall come upon all the world, to try them that dwell upon the earth" (Rev. 3:10). Not one believer will be called upon to enter or go through any part of the Great Tribulation.

Verse 8: "And then shall that Wicked be revealed, whom the Lord shall consume with the spirit of His mouth, and shall destroy with the brightness of His coming."

That is, "When He who now letteth (the Holy Ghost who hinders the work of Satan) is taken out, then shall be revealed the Lawless One." Three times with persistent emphasis the Holy Ghost uses the word "revealed"— verses 3, 6 and 8. This would indicate that when this event occurs, some unearthly monstrosity will be unveiled that will hold earth's gazers spellbound! Paul is not here referring to some influence or spirit—but to an overpowering, unearthly, diabolical monstrosity in a body. This one is none other than the Antichrist, the Lawless One, the Man of Sin, the King of Fierce Countenance; in other words, *the devil in flesh.* "This Wicked" will not be revealed until after the Holy Ghost (who now hinders the revealing) is taken out with the Church.

Verse 8 closes with, ". . . *Whom the Lord shall consume with the spirit of His mouth, and shall destroy with the brightness of His coming."* Jesus needs no armies, jet planes nor guided missiles. All He need do is speak the word: ". . . He shall smite the earth with the rod of His mouth, and with the breath of His lips shall He slay the wicked" (Isa. 11:4). The Psalmist puts it in these words: "The heathen raged, the kingdoms were moved: HE UTTERED HIS VOICE, THE EARTH MELTED" (Psalm 46:6).

In chapter 1:7,8 of our present study we learned that Jesus will come in flaming fire, taking vengeance on them that know not God, and they shall be destroyed with everlasting destruction. On that terrible blazing Day of the Lord, when Jesus comes to execute righteous judgment upon all, there will be kings, great men, captains, bondmen, rich men, who will pray for the rocks and the mountains to fall on them and hide them from His face (Rev. 6:16). The rocks and the mountains will not answer their prayer, and the Christ (whose face terrorizes the enemies of God) will need only to speak a word and the diabolical, titanic Antichrist will be slain!

The Greek for the statement "with the brightness of His coming" signifies superhuman, divine appearance. The blazing brightness of the face of Jesus will be sufficient to destroy the Antichrist and wipe out all of his followers. When the enemies of Jesus see His face it will paralyze them in such fashion that they will become maniacs, screaming and begging for the great boulders of the mountains to roll down upon them and hide them from the face of the Christ!

In verse 8, "Wicked" is capitalized, denoting a person. Here the Antichrist is called "that Wicked." Bible scholars and language authorities agree that Paul is speaking of a personality who will be unveiled during Daniel's seventieth week of prophecy, the time of Jacob's trouble, referred to in the New Testament as the Great

Tribulation. This terrible time will be poured out primarily upon Israel, but it will affect every square inch of the whole world. Today it seems that the devil is loved and idolized by the masses of mankind who revel in lust and sin. The average person does not want very much of God in his schedule—and sad to say, this is also true of many church members. Since the world craves the devil, one day Jesus will take His children OUT of the world and turn mankind over to the devil.

Verse 9: "Even him, whose coming is after the working of Satan with all power and signs and lying wonders."

We have two comings here—one in verse 8 (Jesus) and one in verse 9 (Antichrist). In verse 8, Jesus is coming in brightness. (This is the Revelation at the end of the reign of Antichrist, when Jesus comes with the angels as mentioned in Jude 14 and 15—and when "every eye shall see Him"—Rev. 1:7.) Shekinah glory will fill the sky, and the brightness will testify that a *divine Personality* is appearing. However, the *Man of Sin*, Antichrist (powerful because he is Satan in flesh), also comes—at the beginning of the Tribulation—working miracles through the power of the devil; and he, too, causes great signs and wonders.

The literal Greek in the first part of verse 8 and in the first part of verse 9 reads, "Then shall be revealed the Lawless One, the Wicked, whose coming is according to the working of Satan." All one need do to be convinced that Satan is a powerful being who CAN work miracles is to study the experience of Moses in the land of Pharaoh. *Never minimize the power of Satan!* Michael, the mighty archangel, would not rebuke him, but said, "The *Lord* rebuke thee!" If Michael would not rebuke Satan, then far be it from me to minimize his power or limit his accomplishments. He is a powerful creature; and when Antichrist makes his appearance on television,

270

sitting in the temple in Jerusalem with the whole world gazing upon him, the first thing he will do is described in Revelation 13:13–15:

"And he (Antichrist) doeth great wonders, so that HE MAKETH FIRE COME DOWN FROM HEAVEN ON EARTH IN THE SIGHT OF MEN, and deceiveth them that dwell on the earth by the means of THOSE MIRACLES WHICH HE HAD POWER TO DO in the sight of the beast; saying to them that dwell on the earth, that they should make an image to the beast, which had the wound by a sword, and did live. And he had power to give life unto the image of the beast, that the image of the beast should both speak, and cause that as many as would not worship the image of the beast should be killed."

This mighty personage will pull forked fire down from heaven. He will do many unbelievable miracles. He will build a gigantic image and will make that cold stone image speak! And of course, through these miracles he will deceive the people; and they will fall at his feet and worship him as God. As far as he is allowed to go, he will counterfeit everything the Lord Jesus has done. He is the counterfeit Christ, and he is presenting himself primarily to the Jews, who crucified their Christ when He came in His Father's name. Jesus, speaking of the personality we are discussing, told the Jews clearly that another would *come in his own name*, and they would receive him.

Jesus said, "I am the Truth. . . . Sanctify them through thy truth: thy word is truth" (John 14:6; 17:17). Jesus is truth. "Anti" is *opposite* or *opposed*; therefore, the Antichrist will be THE LIE. The signs and wonders he will perform will be literally executed in power, signs and wonders of *falsehood*, and these manifestations will duplicate the miracles of Jesus and the apostles as nearly as possible. Let me illustrate:

271

Peter, preaching on the day of Pentecost, reminded the men of Israel of "Jesus of Nazareth, a man approved of God among you BY MIRACLES AND WONDERS AND SIGNS, which God did by Him in the midst of you, as ye yourselves also know" (Acts 2:22). Paul told the Romans that God had honored his ministry and convinced the Gentiles that he was sent of God, "THROUGH MIGHTY SIGNS AND WONDERS, BY THE POWER OF THE SPIRIT OF GOD" (Rom. 15:19). To the Corinthians, Paul said, "Truly THE SIGNS OF AN APOSTLE were wrought among you in all patience, IN SIGNS, AND WONDERS, AND MIGHTY DEEDS" (II Cor. 12:12).

Later, he warned the Hebrews, "Therefore we ought to give the more earnest heed to the things which we have heard, lest at any time we should let them slip. For if the word spoken by angels was stedfast, and every transgression and disobedience received a just recompence of reward; *how shall WE escape, if we neglect so great salvation*; which at the first began to be spoken by the Lord, and was confirmed unto us by them that heard Him; God also bearing them witness, both with SIGNS AND WONDERS, AND WITH DIVERS MIRACLES, AND GIFTS OF THE HOLY GHOST, according to His own will?" (Heb. 2:1–4).

God put His stamp of approval upon Jesus and the apostles through miracles and signs and wonders. The Jews rejected Jesus, killed the prophets and martyred the apostles. Jesus sat and wept over the holy city: "O Jerusalem, Jerusalem, which killest the prophets, and stonest them that are sent unto thee; how often would I have gathered thy children together, as a hen doth gather her brood under her wings, *and ye would not*!" (Luke 13:34).

The *false* messiah will come on the scene, he will pull fire down from heaven, he will do mighty miracles, he will make an image talk. Israel and teeming millions will fall at his feet and declare that he is God, only to be brutally butchered, murdered and tormented when he has made merchandise of their souls!

Verse 10: "And with all deceivableness of unrighteousness in them that perish; because they received not the love of the truth, that they might be saved."

Because of the miracles, signs and lying wonders performed by the Man of Sin, the millions who follow this Son of Perdition must also share his ruin! Those who follow the Antichrist will travel in the exact opposite direction from those who are being saved and added to the Church daily (Acts 2:47; I Cor. 1:18; II Cor. 2:15).

The spirit of Antichrist was already operating in the days of Paul; and therefore he admonished believers, "Prove all things . . . hold fast that which is good" (I Thess. 5:21). In I John 4:1–6 we are solemnly warned to beware of the spirit of Antichrist. Therefore I say to my beloved brothers and sisters in the Lord, be careful *what* you believe and *whom you believe and follow* today!

Notice carefully the last part of verse 10: ". . . *because they received not the love of the truth, that they might be saved.*" The first thing I would like to point out here is that the people of whom Paul was speaking were exposed to the truth—the Word of God: "Ye shall know the truth, and the truth shall make you free" (John 17:17). Jesus said to Thomas, "I AM THE TRUTH" (John 14:6).

The people mentioned here in verse 10 will not be heathen who never heard of Jesus or the Word of God. These people will be *exposed* to the preaching of the truth; but they will refuse the truth—and when truth is rejected, the light that could have come into the heart and life becomes darkness. The more Gospel an unbeliever hears and rejects, the harder his heart becomes.

273

The more light is rejected, the darker grows the intelligence. Because these people received not the love of the truth, their hearts became hard and calloused, and they had no desire to KNOW the truth. They loved wickedness and ungodliness, and they had no place in their hearts and lives for truth and righteousness. Jesus said, ". . . Every one that doeth evil hateth the light, neither cometh to the light, lest his deeds should be reproved" (John 3:20).

Paul, writing to the Corinthians, said, ". . . If our Gospel be hid, it is hid to them that are lost: in whom the god of this world (age) hath blinded the minds of them which believe not, lest the light of the glorious Gospel of Christ, who is the image of God, should shine unto them" (II Cor. 4:3,4).

The Gospel is the power of God unto salvation (Rom. 1:16), but the Gospel rejected hardens the heart and causes an individual to become so calloused in heart and mind that he does not want the salvation Jesus purchased with His own precious blood. The same sun that melts the ice also bakes clay and makes brick. If received, the Gospel softens the heart; by like token, it hardens the heart if rejected. Paul speaks of those "having their conscience seared with a hot iron" (I Tim. 4:2). The most dangerous thing any individual can do is hear the plan of salvation, realize his need of a Saviour—*and then reject the call of the Holy Spirit.*

The people of whom Paul is speaking in our present passage are those who will be left when the Church is raptured. They will be primarily of the Laodiceans—lukewarm, rich, increased with goods, having need of nothing. That is the spirit of this age. Many modern churches have need of nothing; they do not need God . . . they have a pastor who interprets the Word to fit the minds and lives of members who love the world. Such

274

are blind guides leading the blind, with the result that all will fall into the ditch! (Matt. 15:14).

Still further proof that Paul is speaking of people who have heard the Gospel is contained in the closing phrase of this verse: *". . . that they might be saved."* This must of necessity refer to people who have heard the name of Jesus and the Word of God—because it is utterly impossible to become a Christian APART from hearing the Word (John 3:3,5; 5:24; Eph. 2:8,9; Rom. 10:17; I Peter 1:23; Acts 4:12). Jesus said, "I am the Way, the Truth, and the Life: no man cometh unto the Father, but by me."

These people heard the truth and rejected that truth. They could have been saved, but they rejected the light—instead of accepting the death, burial and resurrection of Jesus, confessing Him as Lord and believing in their hearts that God raised Him from the dead, thereby receiving salvation. They rejected the power of the Gospel, they rejected the incorruptible seed, they did not love the truth. *What will be the result of such rejection?*

Verse 11: "AND FOR THIS CAUSE GOD SHALL SEND THEM STRONG DELUSION, THAT THEY SHOULD BELIEVE A LIE!"

Because they heard and rejected the Gospel; because they had opportunity to be saved but refused that opportunity, God will send them "strong delusion" and they will no longer be able to believe the truth! Their minds will be disillusioned, blacked out, deadened; they will reach the place Ephraim reached when God said, "Ephraim is joined to idols: *let him alone*"!

They will be like the people of whom Paul speaks in Romans 1:19–32, who knew God, but refused to glorify Him AS God. They were not thankful; they were vain in their imaginations; they professed to be wise, but changed the glory of the incorruptible God into an image; and because they did these things, "GOD GAVE THEM UP." These people changed the truth of God into a lie. (Remember—they "loved not the truth.") They worshipped and served the creature rather than the Creator; and because of this, God gave them up. They did not like to retain God in their knowledge . . . they *knew about* God, but they would not THINK on God. And because they did not like to keep God in their thinking and in their planning, God gave them over to a reprobate mind. Study these verses in Romans; I have quoted them only in part. They show us that God does give people up.

When one is exposed to the truth and rejects that truth again and again, there is grave danger that God will give that one up and send strong delusion, blacking out the mind; then that person cannot love truth, but rather will follow error, loving sin and lust. I think this explains the condition in which we live today, with such hideous, unbelievable crimes committed by man against his fellowman. Surely such atrocities are committed by those who are past reason and who are not capable of a decent thought!

"Delusion" is *deceit accepted*; it is the acceptance of falsehood FOR truth. Please notice that it is GOD who sends this delusion, with the result that "they should believe THE LIE." (In the Greek language it is not "*a* lie," as in the authorized King James Version; but the Greek says, "THE lie"—and, of course, this refers to Antichrist. Jesus is *The Truth*; Antichrist is *The Lie*.)

"*GOD shall send them strong delusion.*" It is not the devil, but Jehovah God, who sends the delusion. Satan is never represented in the Word of God as an independent power nor as rival deity of evil. Satan is allowed great power and much activity in this world; he is the prince of the power of the air; he is the god of

276

this age—but he is always under divine control. The devil is mighty—but GOD is ALMIGHTY, and the devil cannot move without God's permission. Study the first two chapters of Job, and also I Corinthians 5:5 and 10:13.

It is a solemn fact that when one continuously rejects the truth, persistent rejection of truth will destroy the *sense* of truth, and the result will be fatal error. One cannot be exposed to truth, reject that truth, and remain the same. One who believes that Jehovah God is the moral ruler of this universe, knows that the natural laws of this universe are the expression of God's will and that He controls the earth, the solar systems and all that therein is. Therefore, since this Satanic delusion is the moral consequence of willful rejection of the truth, it is clear that God is at work here. God makes Satan His instrument in punishing those who follow lies instead of truth. Because these peoples refuse to love truth, and thereby automatically love UNTRUTH, God sends them lies for their portion.

Earlier in this study I made the statement that it seems the masses of mankind today love evil, lust, ungodliness, sin, debauchery and the devil. They have no time for God, righteousness, truth, honor and purity. Since the masses crave the devil and hell, God will remove His people, turn the devil loose, and allow the people to have what they crave—*for a season*. But before the end of the day of the Man of Sin, the people who loved his lies will be begging God to kill them—but they will not be able to die (Rev. 9:6). Read also Ezekiel 14:9 and I Kings, chapter 22. Revelation 16:7 declares: ". . . Even so, Lord God Almighty, true and righteous are thy judgments."

The next great event in store for this old world is the Rapture of the Church, and immediately following that will be the appearance of the Antichrist. God will

277

send strong delusion upon those who have heard and rejected the truth; and at the appointed time He will send His Son in flaming fire, taking vengeance on them that know not God and those who obeyed The Lie, refusing to love the truth of God.

I am keenly aware of the Bible truth that a great multitude will be saved during the Tribulation period— a great multitude made up of all tribes, tongues, kindreds and peoples of the earth; but these who will be saved are those who have never heard the Gospel of truth. These will be the people who never heard of salvation by grace through faith in the blood of Jesus. There are multiplied millions on earth today who have never heard John 3:16. They know nothing of God's love-gift to this world.

Revelation 7 describes the 144,000 missionaries who will preach the Gospel of the Kingdom, and as a result of their message a great multitude that no man can number will be saved out of great tribulation. But you may rest assured, beloved, if you have heard the Gospel of the truth and refused to accept it, if the Rapture takes place and you are left on earth, *you will not be saved AFTER the Rapture!* God will send you strong delusion, and it will be impossible for you to believe the truth. You will believe The Lie—the Antichrist—and you will be damned. That is God's precious, holy Word.

Verse 12: "That they all might be damned who believed not the truth, but had pleasure in unrighteousness."

"They" refers back to the people who are to be sent strong delusion—those who believe THE LIE—and they ALL will be damned. Not one will escape. Why? Because *"they believed not the Truth."*

In John 3:18 we have one of the greatest verses in the Bible: "He that believeth on (the Son of God) is not condemned: but he that believeth not is condemned already, because he hath not believed in the name of the only begotten Son of God.''

First: *Believers* are not condemned.

Second: *Unbelievers* ARE condemned.

Third: *The reason* they are condemned is that they believe not the Son of God—the Truth. The truth is that Jesus sets men free (John 8:32 and 36). The damning sin of all ages is the sin of unbelief—the sin of rejecting the truth of the Lord Jesus Christ.

Verse 12 closes: ''. . . *But had pleasure in unrighteousness.*'' The reason these had pleasure in unrighteousness is because they believed not the truth. When man believes the truth of God, the truth believed sets him free from love of and pleasure in unrighteousness (Titus 2:11–15). All we need is found in grace; grace is Jesus, and Jesus is truth (John 1:14 and 14:6).

In closing this section, let me emphasize the undeniable Bible fact that all who have heard the Gospel— all who have been exposed to the truth—*before the Rapture*, will NOT be saved AFTER the Rapture. They will be· sent strong delusion, they will believe The Lie, and *they ALL will be damned*! There will be a great multitude saved during the Tribulation, but that multitude will be made up of those who have never before heard the Gospel of Truth.

Verse 13: ''But we are bound to give thanks alway to God for you, brethren beloved of the Lord, because God hath from the beginning chosen you to salvation through sanctification of the Spirit and belief of the truth.''

How refreshing to pass from the horrible description of the Man of Sin and those who will be damned because of him, to the faithful believers whom Paul loved as a mother loves her child or as a nurse loves the children for whom she cares. Paul gives thanks to God, who so loved the Thessalonians that He provided salvation for them. He urges the believers to be stedfast, and prays that God's love may be their comfort in and through the terrible tribulation they are enduring. He assures them that God's faithfulness shall be theirs, and that he has confidence in them that they will be stedfast and defend the faith once for all delivered to the saints. He prays once more that God will guide in every avenue of their daily living until Jesus comes: "And the Lord direct your hearts into the love of God, and into the patient waiting for Christ" (chapter 3:5).

Knowing that the terrible Day of the Lord will come upon the wicked and that the Man of Sin will appear, Paul is bound to give thanks to God for true believers, *"brethren beloved of the Lord."* He wants to assure them that even though they are passing through persecution, misery, heartaches and hardships, they possess a refuge in the love of Christ. I am sure Paul had this in mind, as applied to every believer under all circumstances, when he penned Romans 8:35–39:

"Who shall separate us from the love of Christ? shall tribulation, or distress, or persecution, or famine, or nakedness, or peril, or sword? As it is written, For thy sake we are killed all the day long; we are accounted as sheep for the slaughter. Nay, in all these things we are more than conquerors through Him that loved us. For I am persuaded, that neither death, nor life, nor angels, nor principalities, nor powers, nor things present, nor things to come, nor height, nor depth, nor any other creature, shall be able to separate us from the love of God, which is in Christ Jesus our Lord."

How refreshing to know that "IN ALL THESE THINGS WE ARE MORE THAN CONQUERORS THROUGH HIM

THAT LOVED US." Thank God for the blessed assurance that He who has begun a good work in us will perform it unto the end. He is able to keep that which we have committed unto Him against that day, He will never leave us nor forsake us, and we may boldly say, "God is our helper!"

The true Church has a divine Protector; and to that Protector Paul commits his brethren, so dear to his heart. It is possible Paul was thinking of the blessing pronounced upon Benjamin in Deuteronomy 33:12: ". . . The beloved of the Lord shall dwell in safety by Him; and the Lord shall cover him all the day long, and he shall dwell between His shoulders."

"Chosen unto salvation." Paul sets this forth in contrast to the "Son of Perdition" (verse 3) and "them that perish" (verse 10). He draws marked contrast between the sons of God and the sons of the devil . . . those who held belief in truth and sanctification of spirit, and those who had pleasure in unrighteousness and believed The Lie. *"From the beginning"* points to the time when the Gospel first visited the Thessalonians. The Thessalonian believers were sons of God because "from the beginning" they embraced the truth and turned to God from idols. Then they immediately began to serve and to wait for the coming of Jesus. But those who believed The Lie had no pleasure in the truth. They were EXPOSED to the truth, but they loved a lie instead, thereby becoming the dupes of Antichrist.

Verse 13 closes with the statement, *"Salvation through sanctification of the Spirit and belief of the truth."* Some Bible scholars point out that this is the HOLY Spirit; but the Greek language definitely indicates that it is the sanctification of man's spirit—*the inner man.* The close connection of this phrase with "belief of truth" would incline us to read the two phrases alike—"truth" being the object of "faith," and "spirit" of "sanctification."

In other words, Paul is saying, "YOUR SPIRIT is the primary object of the sanctification that I am praying you will experience fully." Please read again I Thessalonians 5:23, which we fully discussed in the previous chapters of this book. In this verse, Paul prayed for the sanctification of *spirit*, *soul* and *body*; and since the spirit of man is that part of him that knows, reasons and thinks, it is absolutely imperative that the spirit be sanctified before any man can think right concerning the truth of God.

Paul prayed for the sanctification of the spirit of the Thessalonians. The people in the end-time who believe The Lie will have no pleasure in the truth and no love for it—simply because, in the words of Paul, "they did not like to retain God in their knowledge." They pushed the truth aside and crowded it out of their minds for so long, that God will give them over to a deluded mind—a mind that cannot grasp the truth. Paul knows that to be a successful, fruitbearing Christian, the spirit must be sanctified. Therefore the sanctification of spirit, as mentioned here, has to do with the *inward state of the believer*.

The believers in Thessalonica *became* believers by accepting the truth. Paul warns that they must surrender their *spirit* to the truth and believe ALL of the truth, if they are to be what they should be for Jesus and if they are to enjoy their spiritual birthright. Those who believe the truth will share in the glorious resurrection, Rapture and reign of the Lord Jesus; those who believe The Lie will be sent strong delusion and will be damned. Paul wants this fact to be thoroughly understood, deeply grounded in the minds and hearts of the believers at Thessalonica, as well as in your heart and mine.

The trustful acceptance of the truth (John 8:32)—truth

revealed and brought to man in Christ (John 1:14)—brings with its acceptance the consecration of our spirit to God. It is in such faith and consecration that our salvation lies. The root of perdition and damnation is to believe The Lie—the devil. There should be no question whatsoever about the truth of God's Word. Jesus prayed concerning His disciples, "Sanctify them through thy truth: THY WORD IS TRUTH" (John 17:17). When we accept the truth revealed in Christ, that faith brings salvation!

Verse 14: "Whereunto He called you by our Gospel, to the obtaining of the glory of our Lord Jesus Christ."

The Greek reads, "To which end" . . . that is, including the whole salvation described in verse 13. *"God called you by our Gospel,* through the good news we brought to you when we came to Thessalonica with the message of the death, burial and resurrection of the Lord Jesus according to the Scriptures." Read I Thessalonians 1:5; 2:12,13; 4:7; 5:24.

God's call came to the Thessalonians through the good news of the Gospel preached by Paul, Silas and Timothy. Through these messengers they learned God's good will toward them and His loving choice of each one who believed the truth and accepted the message of grace.

Verse 14 closes: ". . . *To the obtaining of the glory of our Lord Jesus Christ."* The Greek wording makes it clearer: "To which end God sent you the Gospel message through us, that you might have Christ's glory at last for your own—that you might win the glory of our Lord Jesus Christ." According to Paul, the glory of Christ and the glory of His saints is mutual. The glory which the exalted, matchless, perfect Lord Jesus Christ received, the believers in Thessalonica were called to share; and the same is true of each and every believer on the Lord Jesus Christ—each a part of the New Testament Church. This is the ultimate goal of salvation; Paul called it "the prize of the high calling" (Phil. 3:14).

In John's Gospel we read, "Now is the Son of man glorified, and God is glorified in Him" (John 13:31). Jesus prayed, "And now, O Father, glorify thou me with thine own self with the glory which I had with thee before the world was" (John 17:5). Later in the same prayer Jesus declares, "And the glory which thou gavest me I have given them (the disciples); that they may be one, even as we are one" (John 17:22). Christ's glory is unending, ever advancing; and as His glory unfolds in the lives of consecrated, Spirit-filled believers, others see the good works and glorify Jesus because of the upright and righteous living of Christians before the world. This will continue until it is at last consummated in "the Revelation of the Lord Jesus Christ from heaven" (II Thess. 1:7–12, 2:8; Titus 2:13; Matt. 24:30). Then—and ONLY then—the glory of His saints will be complete. We will be "WITH HIM IN GLORY" (Col. 3:4; Phil. 3: 20,21). In that glorious moment, "WE SHALL BE LIKE HIM; FOR WE SHALL SEE HIM AS HE IS!" (I John 3:2).

Verse 15: "Therefore, brethren, stand fast, and hold the traditions which ye have been taught, whether by word, or our epistle."

"THEREFORE" . . . that is, "Because of all that has been said concerning the return of the Lord in glory for the saints, and in judgment upon the wicked," *we should occupy at all times*. No man knows the day or the hour of His return, but *we DO know that He is coming*! And inasmuch as God, through the death of Jesus and the good news of the Gospel, has made all believers heirs of His glorious kingdom, we should "STAND FAST," looking up at all times, keeping our eyes upon Jesus rather than upon the wicked things that are going on around us. We know that evil men and seducers will wax worse and worse, deceiving and being deceived, until that day when the true Church will be caught out to meet the Lord Jesus in the air; and that fierce day of the Lord will then come upon the wicked. Read I Corinthians 15:51—58 and Colossians 1:23.

"*. . . And hold the traditions which ye have been taught, whether by word, or our epistle.*" The Greek for our English word "hold" is a very emphatic word meaning "*stand firm and hold fast.*" The traditions to which Paul refers here have nothing to do with traditions of men nor traditions as set forth by the church of Rome. What Paul is actually saying is, "I want you to believe the doctrine that I have spoken and the truth that I am writing. Hold fast to ALL of it, because I speak and write by revelation of God."

Notice verse 2 in our present chapter and verses 14 through 17 in chapter 3. We must remember that Paul is just beginning to communicate with the churches by letter. He is assuring the Thessalonians that his written word is *God's Word* and must be accepted with the same authority as his spoken word. He assured the believers that he spoke by revelation from God, not the words of man; and he warned them against any who would beguile them and draw the church away from the revealed truth he had given them.

Writing to the believers at Corinth Paul said, "I praise you, brethren, that ye remember me in all things, and keep the ordinances, as I delivered them to you" (I Cor. 11:2). Paul's traditions included doctrine and commands concerning practical Christian life and morals. II Thessalonians 3:4: "And we have confidence in the Lord touching you, that ye both do and will do the things which we command you." I Thessalonians 4:2: "For ye know what commandments we gave you by the Lord Jesus."

To Timothy Paul said, "O Timothy, keep that which is committed to thy trust, avoiding profane and vain babblings, and oppositions of science falsely so called" (I Tim. 6:20). "Hold fast the form of sound words, which thou hast heard of me, in faith and love which is in Christ Jesus. That good thing which was committed unto thee keep by the Holy Ghost which dwelleth in us" (II Tim. 1:13,14). Study carefully I Timothy 1:5–18.

Verses 16 and 17: "Now our Lord Jesus Christ Himself, and God, even our Father, which hath loved us, and hath given us everlasting consolation and good hope through grace, comfort your hearts, and stablish you in every good word and work."

Paul uses similar words in I Thessalonians 3:11; the only difference is that in our present verse he names our Lord Jesus Christ first, and then God, "even our Father." This is no accident. The Holy Spirit names the Lord Jesus Christ first to set forth His deity. In essence, Paul is saying, "Where are those teachers who deny the divinity of the Christ who saved you, delivered you from idols, and caused you to turn to the true God, to serve Him and wait for His Son from heaven?" Paul commits the believers unto the Lord Jesus Christ and God our Father, for keeping and stability.

The Thessalonian believers had already experienced joy and comfort in their troubled hearts (I Thess. 1:6 and II Thess. 1:4). In II Corinthians 1:4–6 Paul acknowledges the gladness and comfort God has given HIM in his hour of sorrow and persecution. Just to know that God the Father loves us and God the Son cares for us, is infinitely rich and rewarding—comfort beyond the description of words! In Jesus we have consolation. (The Greek word means *"heartening encouragement"* and goes deeper than our English words of "consolation or comfort."

I pointed out earlier in the study that in Romans 5:11 Paul said, "We . . . joy in God through our Lord Jesus Christ." We should never forget that God the Father loved us and gave His only begotten Son that we might have the gift of salvation. Jesus prayed, "Not my will, but thine be done." So we thank *God* for His love, and we thank *the Lord Jesus* for His sacrifice on the cross. It is the good pleasure of God to give His children every good thing. Read Matthew 7:11; Luke 12:32; John 3:16; I John 3:1 and Romans 5:8.

The believers at Thessalonica were beloved of God (I Thess. 1:4). They were also "BELOVED OF THE LORD" (II Thess. 2:13). Since they are beloved of God and "beloved of the Lord," Paul assures them that God the Father and God the Son are ONE in love and ONE in comfort and spiritual encouragement.

The consolation Jesus gives is everlasting; the hope we have in Him is a "good hope." Such a hope gives joy unspeakable and full of glory (I Pet. 1:8). We have never seen God; we do not see Him now—but we love Him and rejoice with joy that cannot be expressed in words. Whether it be salvation, comfort, encouragement, joy or hope, these blessings are made possible *only by grace.* Read I Thessalonians 1:1 and II Thessalonians 1:12.

"Comfort your hearts . . . ." (In connection with this, read II Thessalonians 3:5, I Thessalonians 3:13 and Colossians 2:2.) The heart is the seat of life; from the heart proceed the *issues* of life. The heart is the seat of emotion; it is in the heart that doubts and fears arise— doubts and fears that can be conquered only through divine comfort. Such consolation and encouragement can come only from our God and our Christ.

". . . And stablish you in every good word and work." The literal reading is "establish *them*," *"your hearts"*

287

being understood from the last clause. In I Thessalonians 3:2 Paul said, "And sent Timotheus, our brother, and minister of God, and our fellowlabourer in the Gospel of Christ, to establish you, and to comfort you concerning your faith."

Paul knew that the Thessalonian believers were busy — they were alert unto good works and they worked untiringly. What Paul is saying in the closing portion of verse 17 is, "May God, our heavenly Father, give you courage and confidence of heart in all the good that you may say or do." Read I Thessalonians 1:3 and 4:10.

Paul wanted the Thessalonian Christians to do all the good they could—but he also wanted them to work and witness with a cheerful, joyous heart. Read I Thessalonians 5:16—18. Of the believers in Thessalonica Paul said, "For ye are our glory and joy!" (I Thess. 2:20).

1. Finally, brethren, pray for us, that the word of the Lord may have free course, and be glorified, even as it is with you:

2. And that we may be delivered from unreasonable and wicked men: for all men have not faith.

3. But the Lord is faithful, who shall stablish you, and keep you from evil.

4. And we have confidence in the Lord touching you, that ye both do and will do the things which we command you.

5. And the Lord direct your hearts into the love of God, and into the patient waiting for Christ.

6. Now we command you, brethren, in the name of our Lord Jesus Christ, that ye withdraw yourselves from every brother that walketh disorderly, and not after the tradition which he received of us.

7. For yourselves know how ye ought to follow us: for we behaved not ourselves disorderly among you;

8. Neither did we eat any man's bread for nought; but wrought with labour and travail night and day, that we might not be chargeable to any of you:

9. Not because we have not power, but to make ourselves an ensample unto you to follow us.

10. For even when we were with you, this we commanded you, that if any would not work, neither should he eat.

11. For we hear that there are some which walk among you disorderly, working not at all, but are busybodies.

12. Now them that are such we command and exhort by our Lord Jesus Christ, that with quietness they work, and eat their own bread.

13. But ye, brethren, be not weary in well doing.

14. And if any man obey not our word by this epistle, note that man, and have no company with him, that he may be ashamed.

15. Yet count him not as an enemy, but admonish him as a brother.

16. Now the Lord of peace himself give you peace always by all means. The Lord be with you all.

17. The salutation of Paul with mine own hand, which is the token in every epistle: so I write.

18. The grace of our Lord Jesus Christ be with you all. Amen.

Verse 1: "Finally, brethren, pray for us, that the

word of the Lord may have free course, and be glorified, even as it is with you."

"FINALLY!" The main topic of this epistle has been dealt with; and having corrected error, Paul now wants to make a personal request—and the subject of that request is very brief:

"Brethren, PRAY FOR US!" Many times in Paul's epistles he requests prayer of the brethren on his behalf. Christians are admonished to pray one for another, and certainly Paul needed the prayers of his fellow-believers. In this verse he makes a very specific prayer request: "*. . . That the Word of the Lord may have free course, and be glorified, even as it is with you.*"

In I Thessalonians 1:7,8 we learned that through the believers at Thessalonica the Word of the Lord had spread to all the neighboring villages throughout that region. "*In every place your faith is known.*" Paul is now asking the believers to pray that the same thing might be true in Corinth, Achaia, Macedonia, and wherever the good news of the Gospel goes forth. Paul knew that the enemy who had fought the Thessalonians would also be fighting desperately in these new mission fields; and he wanted the spiritually-minded children of God in Thessalonica to pray for the work of the missionaries, that the work would be just as successful in other churches as it had been in Thessalonica. Read I Thessalonians 3:7,8.

It was Paul who said, "I am not ashamed of the Gospel of Christ: for it is the power of God unto salvation to every one that believeth" (Rom. 1:16); "By grace are ye saved through faith; and that not of yourselves: it is the gift of God" (Eph. 2:8); "Faith cometh by hearing, and hearing by the Word of God" (Rom. 10:17); and "Whosoever shall call upon the name of the Lord shall be saved. How then shall they call on Him in whom they have not believed? and how shall they believe in Him of whom they have not heard? and how shall they hear without a preacher? And how shall they preach, except they be sent?'' (Rom. 10:13—15a).

Paul knew that the hope of the sinner depended totally upon hearing the message of the sacrificial death, the burial and resurrection of Jesus; and he knew that Satan, through teachers of error and wicked and perverse men, would do all in his diabolical power to hinder that message, lest it bring salvation to people in other areas as it had to the Thessalonian idolaters. For that reason he makes a very special request that the believers in Thessalonica pray that the Word of God ''may have free course, and be glorified'' in other communities as it had been in Thessalonica.

Verse 2: ''And that we may be delivered from unreasonable and wicked men: for all men have not faith.''

Paul could have been thinking of the wicked, fanatical Jews in the city of Corinth, who stood in the way of the Gospel there (Acts 18:5—17). When Gallio's judgment removed this hindering cause, the Gospel had free course and Christianity spread rapidly in Corinth. Four years later, Paul wrote from the city of Ephesus, ''A great and effectual door is opened unto me, and there are many adversaries'' (I Cor. 16:9). I suppose no man apart from Jesus Christ had more deadly enemies than did the Apostle Paul. II Corinthians 11:23—33 describes some of the perils he endured.

Paul continues, *"For all men have not faith."* In other words, ''Not all men share our faith; many men are our enemies and hate us with deadly hatred *because* of our faith. Many of our enemies would love to see me dead; so pray that God will deliver me from these perverse and evil men."

Paul was known as "the man who turned the world upside down." Everywhere he went, one of two things happened quickly—*revival*, or *riot*! He was hated with vehement hatred; and had not God protected him, he would have been martyred long before the day when he finally DID seal his testimony with his blood.

Verse 3: "But the Lord is faithful, who shall stablish you, and keep you from evil."

Throughout First and Second Thessalonians Paul shows the Lord to be the Ruler and Defender of His children. In II Timothy 4:17 he says, "Notwithstanding the Lord stood with me, and strengthened me; that by me the preaching might be fully known, and that all the Gentiles might hear: and I was delivered out of the mouth of the lion."

Paul assures the Christians at Thessalonica that the Lord in whom they have put their trust is faithful and cannot break His promise. If believers fail, it is not the Lord's fault—it is our own. He has promised to supply our every need; He has promised never to leave us nor forsake us; He has promised to sustain us by His power and keep us through His grace.

Verse 3 closes: ". . . *Who shall stablish you and keep you from evil*." The Greek here reads, "Who *will* establish you and guard you from the evil one." The Greek word for "stablish" denotes the "settled, steady confidence" the believers at Thessalonica NEEDED. This was a young church, assailed by various and sundry kinds of persecution.

Behind the "unreasonable and wicked men" of verse 2, Paul saw another even greater enemy: he saw "THE EVIL ONE." Paul believed in a personal devil. He did not believe Satan to be just an evil influence, but a personality. In the model prayer given in Matthew 6:13 Jesus mentions the evil one, and again in Matthew 13:19 and in John 17:15. He is also mentioned in I John 2:13,14 and 5:18. This evil one (the devil) has always been the enemy of God's people and the hinderer of their work. In Ephesians 6:16 it is this wicked one against whose fiery darts we are to protect ourselves by putting on the whole armor of God, in order that we will be able to stand in the hour of severe temptation and trial. The Christian life is a continuous battle with Satan, the evil one. Read I Thessalonians 2:18, 3:5 and II Thessalonians 2:9.

In the closing words of verse 3 Paul promises the believers of Thessalonica that the Lord who will establish them will also keep them (or, as the Greek reads, "The Lord will guard you") against the evil one—the devil. Jesus prayed in John 17:12, "While I was with them in the world, I kept them in thy name: those that thou gavest me I have kept, and none of them is lost, but the son of perdition; that the Scripture might be fulfilled!"

Paul is here stating that the safety of the believers in Thessalonica is insured by the Lord's fidelity, although it requires their own obedience unto the Lord—and Paul had unshakable faith that they WOULD BE obedient. A faithful Lord watching over faithful believers will win an assured victory over Satan, regardless of his schemes or power.

Verse 4: "And we have confidence in the Lord touching you, that ye both do and will do the things which we command you."

In this verse Paul is saying, *"In the Lord* we have confidence in you. We believe that you are in Christ, and Christ in you. We have confidence that you will fully trust, obey and follow the steps of Jesus, and He will therefore establish you; He will keep and protect you all the way, even to the end." Paul had the same confidence toward the believers at Thessalonica that he had when he said, "*I know whom I have believed*, and am persuaded that He is able to keep that which I have committed unto Him against that day" (II Tim. 1:12). Paul's faith in the Thessalonians was not in the flesh, but "*in the LORD we have confidence in you.* I do not believe that any one of you will put a question mark around anything that you read in this letter nor any command that I make in the Lord. I delivered unto you the Gospel that transformed your life. You heard that Gospel, you turned to the true God from idols, and you have been faithful in service and in witnessing, thus proving your faith to be genuine. And now, *in the Lord* I know you will follow the instructions I am sending you." Read I Thessalonians 1:3; 3:6–10; 4:1,9,10; 5:11; II Thessalonians 1:3,5; 2:13.

Verse 5: "And the Lord direct your hearts into the love of God, and into the patient waiting for Christ."

Paul is counting on the Thessalonians to hear his admonition and follow his commands; but he reminds them that *the Lord* is the Shepherd who leads the sheep, and they are to follow the leading and direction of the Holy Spirit. The Greek word for "direct" signifies "a fixed direction, a steady purpose, a sure position." The instruction Paul is giving in the last part of this verse is that the Thessalonians are to accept the endurance of Christ as their model. Study carefully I Peter 2:19–24; 3:17,18; 4:1,2 and Hebrews 12:2,3. Paul speaks often of believers looking to Jesus as their model in suffering, for if we suffer with Him we will also reign with Him (read II Corinthians 1:5 and Philippians 3:10); but *we must suffer with patience.* Jesus willingly suffered:

"It pleased the Lord to bruise Him," and we should follow His example.

The believers in Thessalonica were awaiting and eagerly looking for the return of Jesus (I Thess. 1:10); but in waiting, they must not become weary in well doing. They must *patiently* wait for Jesus; they must not become unsettled, nor say, "The Lord delayeth His coming." They must be willing to suffer if needs be, even as Jesus, our example, suffered. To the Romans Paul said, "For even Christ pleased not Himself; but, as it is written, The reproaches of them that reproached thee fell on me" (Rom. 15:3). Therefore we should be patient as Christ was patient. He endured the cross and the contradiction of sinners.

Christ is the *great ideal* of every true believer. Christ is the only begotten Son of God's love, the most precious jewel in heaven. According to the Lord Jesus, to love God is the great and first commandment (Matt. 22:36—38). To love God with all one's heart is the very soul and essence of Christianity (Rom. 8:28; I Cor. 13:1—3). If we love God as we should, we will willingly suffer for Him and for His cause and patiently wait for His Son from heaven. Paul wants Christ to direct the hearts of the believers at Thessalonica into the fulness of the love of God, and thereby fill their hearts with patience, rather than with anxiety concerning the glorious appearing of the great God and Saviour, Jesus Christ.

Verse 6: "Now we command you, brethren, in the name of our Lord Jesus Christ, that ye withdraw yourselves from every brother that walketh disorderly, and not after the tradition which he received of us."

In I Thessalonians, Paul found it necessary to exhort some of the believers to live a quiet life and *attend to their daily duties.* Some members of the church had become idle because they thought the coming of the Lord was imminent and felt that there was no need for diligence in worldly occupations and secular matters. They were under the impression that the end would soon come and there was no need for them to attend to any business except to prepare for His coming. Paul knew that their conduct would bring discredit on the entire church, thereby injuring the testimony of the believers in Thessalonica. The faithful brethren in the church who DID labor and provide the necessities of life were forced to take care of those who did not work. These men were the "unruly" of I Thessalonians 5:14. Their unruliness, which should have been checked by the reproofs of the first epistle, had grown to larger proportions.

The error that had been taught in Thessalonica had made matters worse. These people had misunderstood Paul's teaching on the imminent coming of Christ; they listened to false teachers and became even *more disorderly*. They gave trouble to the officers of the church, whom the Apostle in the first epistle had urged the Thessalonians to loyally support (I Thess. 5:12,13). This had created quite a problem in the church, and Paul sternly rebuked these idlers in I Thessalonians 4:11 and 12.

In verse six of this chapter he gives further admonition and warning to those who continued to be disorderly and refused to work to earn a living. First of all, he advises the leaders in the church to avoid those who persist in being disorderly—but please notice that he still calls them "brethren." In verses 7 through 10 he reminds them again of his personal example and teaching concerning this matter when he was with them; and in verse 12 of this chapter he commands that all who have been disorderly should straighten up and go to work, earning their own livelihood and eating their own bread.

Verse 7: "For yourselves know how ye ought to

follow us: for we behaved not ourselves disorderly among you." (The Greek reads literally, "imitate us.") Read I Thessalonians 1:6; 2:14; and verse 9 of our present chapter.

Paul is saying here, "You should not need me to remind you of how I walked before you. You know of yourselves, without my telling you again." They knew that Paul made tents—hard labor in his day—to earn his way, so that he might not be chargeable to anyone. It is true that later in his ministry he accepted gifts from those to whom he preached, but in these first churches he refused to accept anything from the believers. He labored with his own hands. He reminds them that his conduct was not disorderly among them and that they should imitate him in their daily walk and activities— in secular matters as well as spiritual, as having to do with unbelievers. Especially were those in authority in the church to keep their lives above reproach.

Verse 8: "Neither did we eat any man's bread for nought; but wrought with labour and travail night and day, that we might not be chargeable to any of you."

"Neither did we eat any man's bread for nought" seems to settle the question concerning the disorderly conduct of believers. The chief complaint against the brethren who walked disorderly was that they would not work for their bread . . . they expected the church to support and feed them. The church officers resisted this demand, telling them to return to their occupations and earn their own bread; so they became ugly and disorderly.

Paul had already instructed the believers that they should work for a livelihood (I Thess. 4:11,12). From verse 11 in our present chapter it seems that some of them not only refused to work, but also went about over the city sounding out their grievances against the church.

Seemingly they took sides with the false prophets, and had great pride and joy in attempting to disrupt the unity and fellowship among other believers. This nucleus of lazy believers who refused to work and expected the church to feed them stirred up much trouble; but the vast majority of the Thessalonian Christians were consecrated, dedicated, loving each other with a pure and fervent love. Study Acts 2:44,45 and 4:32—35.

Personally, I think we need an Apostle Paul in the United States of America today. I believe in helping those who are worthy of help—I say feed those who are unfortunate from the standpoint of health or otherwise—and certainly the church should take care of its needy members; but there are thousands today who have able bodies and could work, who nevertheless depend on charity for their support. If the Apostle Paul were alive today, I believe he would set some things in order in this blessed country of ours.

Paul worked hard at manual labor and set an example before those to whom he ministered. People who refuse to work because they are religious may call it grace— but according to Paul, it is not grace, but rather, DIS-GRACE. In Paul's churches, no work, no bread—and that is the way it should be for able-bodied men. The man who is too lazy to work should not be fed. In I Timothy 5:8 Paul declared, ". . . If any provide not for his own, and specially for those of his own house, he hath denied the faith, and is worse than an infidel."

Thank God, Paul had "manly pride"—the *right kind of pride*. He was a Christian gentleman; there was not a lazy bone in his body nor an ounce of lazy flesh on his bones! God give us men who are willing to work and serve, thereby proving to the world that Christianity does not make one a "sissy." Christianity makes a real man of an individual who will wholeheartedly surrender soul, spirit and body to God, to serve Him under the leadership of the Holy Spirit and wait for Jesus. Read II Corinthians 11:9,10 and I Corinthians 9:11–15· 4:12.

The heart of verse 8 in the literal Greek reads thus: "Neither did we eat bread for nought at any man's hand, but in labor and travail, night and day, working." The meaning is simply this: "It was not for nought that we ate our bread, but in labor and travail, working night and day." It was through hard labor that Paul, Silas and Timothy earned their daily bread, and the Thessalonians knew it—they had seen it. Lazy, trifling church members who expected the church to feed them were a disgrace TO the church, and Paul admonished the believers to withdraw from them and have no fellowship with them. If the disorderly ones were born again, they were to be treated as brothers; but they were not to be fed unless they worked.

I fear that some of our leaders in the United States are responsible for making beggars of people who only a few years ago were willing to work untiringly to support themselves and their families. Our leaders have played "Santa Claus" for so long that instead of helping the people they have caused them to become habitual beggars! If a man is physically handicapped and unable to work, certainly real men should be willing to come to his rescue to feed him, clothe him and take care of him; but God have mercy on any able-bodied man who will not work to provide bread for his family. How dare that man lay claim to Christianity!

The verse closes, ". . . *That we might not be chargeable to any of you*." Or simply, "Silas, Timothy and I did not want to be a burden on any of you."

Verse 9: "Not because we have not power, but to make ourselves an ensample unto you to follow us."

The Greek reads, ". . . have not the right." That is, "Not because we have not the moral authority to lay the charge of our upkeep upon the church. We have the moral and spiritual right to expect a livelihood *from* the church; but lest we be accused of ministering for money, we work night and day to support ourselves and provide our OWN livelihood." Study I Thessalonians 2:6, I Corinthians 10:33, II Corinthians 12:14,15 and Acts 20:34,35.

Paul, Silas and Timothy sacrificed their own rights and comforts of life for the benefit of the Thessalonian church, setting the right example before them that they might be a good testimony to unbelievers. Read I Thessalonians 1:5–7 and 2:8,9. Paul's statement in the last part of verse 9, *"to make ourselves an ensample unto you to follow us,"* does not mean that Paul was setting himself and his co-workers up as little gods. Paul and his fellow workers walked in the footsteps of Jesus in every detail of life; they set an example before the Thessalonians, and Paul commanded them to imitate him as he imitated the Lord. This was no "holier-than-thou" attitude. Paul was God's anointed vessel to the Gentiles; and he expected the believers to follow his example, even as he followed his Lord. That is the primary reason he worked to earn his own living instead of accepting support from the church.

Verse 10: "For even when we were with you, this we commanded you, that if any would not work, neither should he eat."

Here Paul confirms in writing what he had preached to them orally. Read I Thessalonians 4:11. Paul did not use soft, compromising words. He simply said, "IF ANY WILL NOT WORK, NEITHER LET HIM EAT!" This was a stern but necessary rule—for to allow things to go on as they were, with some of the members taking advantage of the charity of the consecrated, dedicated servants in the church, would certainly cause the church to lose its testimony.

David said, "I have been young, and now am old; yet have I not seen the righteous forsaken, nor his seed begging bread" (Psalm 37:25). Read that, and re-read it. Then read it again—and HEAR it! "I HAVE NOT SEEN THE RIGHTEOUS FORSAKEN, NOR HIS SEED BEGGING BREAD." A shut-in or a physically handicapped person who cannot work is not a beggar. A beggar is one who is *able* to work, who *could* get a job, but who will NOT work and expects the charitable people in the church, community or state to feed him!

Verse 11: "For we hear that there are some which walk among you disorderly, working not at all, but are busybodies."

Paul is saying here, "The report has come to me that some of those who have refused to work and expect the church to feed them, have a business—and that business is to be busybodies. They will not work, but they spend their time minding everybody's business but their own. They are idle with their hands, but are very busy with their tongues. These mischief-makers are to get quiet, shut their mouths, and go to work." Read I Thessalonians 4:11 and I Timothy 5:13.

Verse 12: "Now them that are such we command and exhort by our Lord Jesus Christ, that with quietness they work, and eat their own bread."

In I Thessalonians 4:10 Paul simply *exhorts*—but concerning these busybodies who will not work he says, "COMMAND and exhort." This puts a note of sternness in the charge. These idle busybodies and meddlers had become a scandal and a burden to the church; and Paul charges them in the name of the Lord Jesus and on the grounds of their relationship to Christ, that they work

301

and be quiet, eat their own bread and not expect their honest brethren to feed them.

Verse 13:   "But ye, brethren, be not weary in well doing."

Paul contrasts "but ye, *brethren*," with the *lazy busybodies* of verses 11 and 12.   The majority of the believers in Thessalonica were living above reproach, and Paul turns from the busybody crowd in the church to the well-doing, working, serving brethren.   Read I Thessalonians 1:3 and 4:1—10; also II Thessalonians 2:17. Paul held most of the Thessalonian believers in the highest admiration and was exceedingly thankful for them.

"Be not weary in well doing" appeals to the believers to "Faint not, and do not fail of courage; do not falter in well doing.   Stablish your hearts, keep your eyes upon Jesus.   Rebuke the busybodies, and be faithful.   Eating, drinking, whatsoever you do, do all to the glory of God." Read Luke 18:1; Galatians 6:9; II Thessalonians 2:17 and I Thessalonians 3:13.   Paul was afraid that the ugly conduct on the part of the minority might dampen the zeal and hurt the activity of those who were evangelizing and spreading the good news of the Gospel to the ends of the earth in that particular day.   So he urged the "brethren" not to become weary or discouraged, nor faint in their hearts—but to press on to the mark of the high calling of God in Christ Jesus.

Verse 14:   "And if any man obey not our word by this epistle, note that man, and have no company with him, that he may be ashamed."

Paul certainly would not be accepted in some of our religious circles today!   The modernists tell us that we are to preach "Love, love, love."   We are to be kind, tender, compassionate—never to speak harsh words, never to rebuke.   But Paul said, "If any man in the church—any of these lazy busybodies—will not work, if he obeys not the word of this epistle, then *note that man and have no company with him!*"

They are not told to look down upon him, abuse him or mistreat him—but simply to ignore him and refrain from fellowshipping with him, *"to the end that he may be ashamed."* That is all the punishment the Holy Spirit decreed for those busybodies. If shame awakened them and they repented, seeing themselves as condemned by general sentiment and the majority of the church members, then of course the door of repentance was left wide open; they could return to the fellowship of the church and would be loved and treated as "brethren."

That is real Christianity. We are to go the second mile—yea, the third mile and even further—to restore a brother or a sister who has faltered and failed; but we are not to compromise with sin and the devil. We are to be stern, firm, and stand for the whole truth. But when a person is ashamed and repents, we are to forgive and forget. Paul made it clear that if the men who would not work paid no attention to the word the Holy Spirit sent the church by the epistle, then mark that man; have no company with him, that he may be ashamed. The same thought continues into the next verse:

Verse 15: "Yet count him not as an enemy, but admonish him as a brother."

Paul made it clear that the true believers were not to treat him unkindly. There were to be no bitter words against him—for certainly such would provoke the man instead of making him ashamed, and would defeat the very purpose of marking him and letting him alone. Paul had a warm heart, and he had love in his heart for these brethren who would not work; but he could not condone their laziness and was forced to do something about it in the Lord. But he did not want to drive them away; he wanted to win them back if he could. His instruction therefore is, "Do not count such a person as an enemy, but admonish him as a brother. Love him—but do not walk with him nor fellowship with him unless he is willing to be ashamed of his conduct. If he repents, *forgive him*."

In I Thessalonians 5:14 Paul said, "Warn (admonish) them that are unruly." Here he puts all cases of disorderly conduct together, and declares that the church is to have no company with such people, in order to shame them. Regardless of what the disorderly conduct may be—whether it be a man who would not work, or some other form of disorder—that man was to be marked by the church, and they were to have no company with him; but they were not to mistreat him nor be bitter toward him.

Verse 16: "Now the Lord of peace Himself give you peace always by all means. The Lord be with you all."

Peace had been disturbed in the church at Thessalonica. Teachers of error, false rumors concerning the Lord's return, the terrible persecution that had come upon them, members of the church who would not work and who walked disorderly, thus sowing discord among the brethren—all these things had disturbed the peace. The devil was fighting zealously because this was a missionary-minded, soul-winning church. But Paul closes his letter with a spiritual tranquilizer: "THE LORD OF PEACE HIMSELF GIVE YOU PEACE!"

Thus Paul points out that there is only One who can give peace, and that One is the Lord of Peace, the Prince of Peace—He who said, "Peace I leave with thee; *my peace* I give unto thee." Isaiah said, "Thou wilt keep him in *perfect peace*, whose mind is stayed on thee (Jesus)." Paul is saying to these troubled Christians, "May the Lord of peace GIVE you peace—always, by all means."

"*Always*" denotes "through all, continually." Paul is saying, "May the Lord of peace give you peace at all times, in all ways, under all circumstances" (Luke 24:53; Heb. 13:15).

Verse 16 closes with "*The Lord be with you all.*" That is, "The Lord be with you—not only in His sovereign grace and peace, but in His personal presence and authority." Read Matthew 28:18–20. Please notice: "The Lord be with you ALL—yes, even with the brother who walks disorderly." The disorderly brother needs the Lord, too; he is to be excluded from fellowship, but not from the Lord. Read I Corinthians 16:24; II Corinthians 13:14, and I Thessalonians 5:27.

Verse 17: "The salutation of Paul with mine own hand, which is the token in every epistle: so I write."

In this verse Paul gives assurance to the Thessalonians that he is the author of the letter—dictated to him by the Holy Spirit, penned down *with his own hand*. There was undoubtedly something singular and noticeable about Paul's handwriting. His penmanship could not be mistaken. Some Bible authorities believe that he wrote large letters (Gal. 6:11). It could be that Paul's thorn in the flesh was an eye disease that caused him to be almost blind and necessitated his writing large characters. It could be that he used other means to emphasize certain parts of his writing. There is no need to speculate—but we DO know there was something unusual about his writing; and he assured the Thessalonians that this second letter was written by him in his own hand, signed by him as a guarantee, and they would recognize this. Read I Corinthians 16:21 and Colossians 4:18.

Verse 18: "The grace of our Lord Jesus Christ be with you all. Amen."

The benediction here is like that of the first Thessalonian epistle, and is repeated in Paul's letter to the Romans (Rom. 16:20). (Notice also Revelation 22:21.)

In verses 16 and 18 of this closing chapter, Paul invokes the blessing of God upon "ALL"; he does not exclude any believer in the church at Thessalonica—not even those whom he had reprimanded for their disorderly conduct.

Christianity *begins* in grace: "By grace are ye saved through faith; and that not of yourselves: it is the gift of God" (Eph. 2:8). Victory over the world, the flesh and the devil is *taught* by grace: "For the grace of God that bringeth salvation hath appeared to all men, teaching us that, denying ungodliness and worldly lusts, we should live soberly, righteously, and godly, in this present world; looking for that blessed hope, and the glorious appearing of the great God and our Saviour Jesus Christ" (Titus 2:11–13).

The grace of God SAVES us; the grace of God TEACHES us; and Paul said, *"I am what I am by the grace of God!"* It was by grace that Jesus tasted death for every man (Heb. 2:9); and when we walk through the portals of glory and stand face to face with our precious Redeemer, it will be "not by works of righteousness which we have done, but according to His mercy He saved us, by the washing of regeneration, and renewing of the Holy Ghost" (Titus 3:5). The Christian life *begins* in grace and *climaxes* in grace.

The Apostle Paul was called and commissioned of God, and *sent by God as a minister to the Gentiles* to make known the mystery of the grace of God—"Christ in you, the hope of glory" (Col. 1:27). Paul was jealous of this message because He knew God gave it to him by revelation. He admonished the Galatians who were plagued and troubled with Judaizers mixing law and grace, "But though WE, or *an angel from heaven*, preach any other

306

gospel unto you than that which we have preached unto you, let him be accursed! As we said before, so say I now again, *If any man preach any other gospel unto you than that ye have received, let him be accursed!*" (Gal. 1:8,9).

This may seem severe, but *Paul preached the grace of God to the Galatians*—pure grace, ALL grace—nothing added, nothing taken away. He said, "If any man on earth, or even an angel in heaven, preach any OTHER gospel, let him—man or angel—drop into hell!!!" Paul was jealous for the message of grace; he knew it was the only message that would save sinners, and he had a deep burden for lost souls. He said, "I became as all men are, that I might save some. . . . I could wish myself accursed from Christ for my brethren."

Paul carried a burden; he toiled, wept, suffered and prayed. He was beaten, stoned, imprisoned, with his feet made fast in the stocks. No *mortal* ever suffered as did the Apostle Paul. *Jesus*? Yes—Jesus was the God-Man, and He suffered as no MAN has ever suffered; but aside from the God-Man, no man ever knew the pain and agony Paul knew in his body *for the sake of the Gospel*. He said, "I bear in my body the marks of the Lord Jesus." Yet sitting in a cold dungeon—hungry, weary, in pain from his floggings and almost blind—he wrote, "(Timothy), I am now ready to be offered, and the time of my departure is at hand. I have fought a good fight, I have finished my course, I have kept the faith: Henceforth there is laid up for me a crown of righteousness, which the Lord, the righteous judge, shall give me at that day . . ." (II Tim. 4:6–8).

Paul preached the Word straight; he cut no corners to please men, and he pulled no punches to stay out of jail. He was a faithful minister. In essence he said to Timothy, "I am in jail now, and I am ready to be offered.

My death is imminent. At any moment they will be coming for me. But to me, TO DIE IS GAIN! So Timothy, I CHARGE THEE THEREFORE BEFORE GOD AND THE LORD JESUS CHRIST, who shall judge the quick and the dead at His appearing and His kingdom; Preach the Word; be instant in season, out of season; reprove, rebuke, exhort with all longsuffering and doctrine. . . . Watch thou in all things, endure afflictions, do the work of an evangelist, make full proof of thy ministry" (II Tim. 4:1–5).

It is evident that although Paul's preaching of the Gospel had cost him his head, if he had had another life to give, he would have given it in the preaching of the same Gospel! On the Damascus road that day, when he said, "Lord, what wilt thou have me to do?" he surrendered soul, spirit, body, time, talents and energy—all that he was, all that he had, all that he ever hoped to be or have. That was the day when Paul *"let go and let God*!"

Oh, that today we had more preachers like Paul—men who are jealous for the pure Gospel; men who refuse to compromise to please religious leaders; men who refuse to fellowship with the enemies of the Gospel; men who preach the unbiased truth, untiringly! Many times such men labor with their own hands to earn bread for their families, but they nevertheless faithfully proclaim the Gospel. The greatest need in the American church today is for men in the pulpit who know God as Paul knew Him, who fear God as Paul feared Him, who honor God as Paul honored Him, and who preach the Gospel of the grace of God as Paul preached it.

To my dear readers I say, in the words of the Apostle Paul, "THE GRACE OF OUR LORD JESUS CHRIST BE WITH YOU ALL. AMEN."